Programming with
Standard ML

Programming with Standard ML

Colin Myers
Chris Clack
Ellen Poon

Prentice Hall
New York   London   Toronto   Sydney   Tokyo   Singapore

First published 1993 by
Prentice Hall International (UK) Ltd
Campus 400, Maylands Avenue
Hemel Hempstead
Hertfordshire, HP2 7EZ
A division of
Simon & Schuster International Group

Typeset in 10/12 pt Baskerville
by Pentacor PLC, High Wycombe, Bucks.

Printed and bound in Great Britain by
Dotesios Ltd, Trowbridge, Wiltshire.

Library of Congress Cataloging-in-Publication Data

Myers, Colin.
    Programming with Standard ML / Colin Myers, Chris Clack, Ellen Poon.
      p. cm.
    Includes bibliographical references and index.
    ISBN 0–13–722075–8 (pb)
    1. ML (Computer program language) I. Clack, Chris. II. Poon, Ellen.
    III. Title.
QA76.73.M6M94 1993
005.13′3—dc20   92–16419 CIP

British Library Cataloguing in Publicaton Data

A catalogue record for this book is available from the British Library

ISBN 0–13–722075–8 (pbk)

1 2 3 4 5 97 96 95 94 93

Contents

Preface

The purpose of this book is to teach structured programming skills using a functional subset of the language Standard ML (also known as SML). It may be used as an introductory textbook for people with little programming experience or as an intermediate textbook for more advanced programmers who wish to learn a functional programming language. Both novices and advanced programmers will learn how to use a functional language to develop sound software design and code management techniques. Additionally, advanced programmers will find that knowledge of a functional language provides a foundation for further studies in the theory and implementation of programming languages and formal specification.

SML is one of the most popular functional languages used in education and industry. It has evolved from an earlier language ML, which was first developed for theorem proving at the Edinburgh Laboratory for Computer Science during the 1970s. It has now grown into a general-purpose programming language with slightly different implementations available from different sites. This textbook uses version 0.66 of *Standard ML of New Jersey*.

This is a practical programming book. Theoretical issues are avoided unless they are essential for a proper understanding of the use of the language. However, some formal definitions are introduced in order to aid the reader when referring to other texts. The boundary between those theoretical matters that are discussed and those that are not is, unavoidably, somewhat arbitrary. For example, Chapter 3 discusses the use of inductive reasoning to help with software design: however, we do not extend this to the use of denotational semantics to reason about a program. Similarly, we provide a gentle introduction to the theory of strong typing, but we do not discuss type inference mechanisms. We do not discuss the lambda calculus, formal program transformation, efficiency or any implementation methods.

The approach we adopt in this book is to show good software engineering principles by discussion of both correct and incorrect design decisions, using realistic examples. There is no Ackermann function and there are no miracles.

Acknowledgements

We are greatly indebted to Mark Hardie, Neil Harris, Dave Pitt, Mike Poon and Mark Priestley, who devoted many hours of their time to reading the earlier drafts and who provided many detailed comments.

We thank Don Clack, Will Richardson and also our undergraduate and postgraduate students for their suggestions and comments regarding the material in this book. We thank Michael Fourman, Hessam Khoshnevisan and David N. Turner for their many helpful suggestions and corrections, and Simon Courtenage for his help in the final stages of proof-reading and implementing corrections to the text.

Finally, many thanks to Robin Milner for allowing us to quote from the definition of Standard ML and Andrew Appel for allowing us to present examples of sessions from Standard ML of New Jersey.

This book was developed during the teaching of functional programming courses to undergraduate and postgraduate classes at the University of Westminster and University College London. At various times Edinburgh University's SML, Sussex University's Poplog ML, Standard ML of New Jersey and the University of Umea's MicroML for personal computers were used; we are extremely grateful to the implementers for their software.

Colin Myers
Chris Clack
Ellen Poon

Introduction

Programming languages may be grouped into several 'families' with similar characteristics. Two of the most important families are the *imperative* languages (also known as 'procedural' languages) and the *functional* languages. The imperative family includes such languages as BASIC, Pascal, C, Fortran, Ada, Modula-2 and COBOL. The functional family includes SML, Miranda,[1] Lispkit,[2] FP and Haskell; a good survey is provided in Hudak (1989).

The basic difference between functional and imperative languages is that functional languages are concerned with *describing a solution to a problem*, whereas imperative languages are concerned with *giving instructions to a computer*. Rather than attempt an explanation in isolation, this introduction *compares* the functional and imperative styles of programming. A number of claims will be made for the functional style and these will be substantiated in the main body of the text.

The reader should notice that this chapter compares *styles* and not *languages*: it is often possible to use a functional style when programming in an imperative language.

Implications of the imperative style of programming

A program written in an imperative language describes in detail a sequence of actions that the computer must execute (these are sometimes called commands – hence the name 'imperative'). This means that the imperative programmer must be familiar with the way the computer works. In general, a programmer must think in terms of the computer hardware – the conceptual model is one of memory locations which contain values which may change during the execution of a program.

The major consequence of this conceptual model is that a programmer is forced to muddle together the three quite separate activities of:

1. Describing the solution to a problem.

2. Organizing that solution into a set of instructions for a computer.

3. Administering low-level storage allocation.

A programmer should only be concerned wih the first of these.

---

1. Miranda is a trademark of Research Software Limited.
2. Lispkit is a pure functional subset of the well-known language LISP which was the first important language with functional features.

To a great extent this complexity derives from one particular feature – the assignment statement (Backus, 1978). The dangers inherent in the assignment statement include ambiguous assignment, forgetting to initialize variables or incorrectly changing loop control variables (possibly causing an infinite loop). The availability of global variables also offers the opportunity of bad programming style since it becomes very difficult to keep track of what value the variable is meant to have at any time and which parts of the program are changing the value of the variable. Assignment to pointers serves to compound these problems.

Consider the following Modula-2 solution to select all the items in an integer array that are less than 10:

```
j := 1;
FOR i := 1 TO LineLength DO
    IF line[i] < 10 THEN
        newline[j] := line[i];
        j := j + 1
    END
END
```

The code has a relatively difficult interpretation; it is not easy to read compared with the simplicity of the natural language specification. Even in this small program extract the major concern has been with the assignment to storage and maintaining indexes; that is, making the solution fit the hardware model.[3] This intellectual overhead is magnified if the problem were to select all the items less than 10 in a dynamic linked list. The emphasis would be even more towards the manipulation of memory rather than the representation of the data structure or the selection of items from it.

In general, the following observations hold:

1. Imperative languages have a limited set of control structures for expressing iteration and for combining sub-calculations, and hence it is often difficult to take advantage of a high-level modular design.

2. Imperative languages have a limited set of built-in data structures. Although it is possible to model other data structures, the process often involves complex manipulation of pointers and a lot of code.

3. Imperative languages have complex semantics, which make it difficult to apply formal reasoning and hence more difficult to arrive at a correct solution.

Benefits of the functional programming style

Functional languages are an example of the *declarative* style of programming, whereby a program gives a description (or 'declaration') of a problem to be solved together

---

3. To keep this example simple, the problem of retaining knowledge of the size of `newline` has been ignored!

with various relationships that hold for it. It is the responsibility of the language implementation (perhaps a compiler or an interpreter) to convert this description into a list of instructions for a computer to run.[4] There are a number of implications of this alternative computational model:

1. A programmer does not have to worry about storage allocation. There is no assignment statement – a functional programmer does not assign values to storage locations, but instead has the ability to give names to the values of expressions; these names may then be used in other expressions or passed as parameters to functions.

2. The fact that in a functional language a name or an expression has a unique value that will never change is known as *referential transparency*. As a consequence of referential transparency, sub-computations always give the same result for the same arguments. This means that the code is safer and may often be re-used in similar contexts, the net result being a higher level of quality assurance and faster programming.

3. Functions and values are treated as mathematical objects which obey well-established mathematical rules and are therefore *well suited to formal reasoning*. This allows the programmer a high level of abstraction and so greater flexibility in defining control structures and data structures.

4. The syntax and semantics of functional languages tend to be simple and so they are relatively easy to learn. Furthermore, the resultant programs tend to be more concise and have fewer mistakes. Brooks (1975) observes that 'productivity seems constant in terms of elementary statements'; if this applies equally to functional programmers then the conciseness of functional programs should lead to greater programmer efficiency.

It is not possible to justify all of these assertions in this brief introduction but, as a sample of the functional style, a typical solution to the problem discussed in the previous section (of selecting items from a sequence of numbers) would be:

```
filter (lessthan 10) number_sequence
```

There is no need to manage storage, no danger of forgetting to initialize or increment variables and no need to worry about where the results are kept. The code is clearly much nearer to the specification – indeed functional programs are sometimes considered as 'executable specifications' (Turner, 1985).

The functional style is also more flexible. For example, changing the Modula-2 code to select all items not equal to "fred" from a sequence of strings requires writing

---

4. Functional languages are based on a mathematical theory known as the 'lambda calculus' (Revesz, 1988). At advanced levels it may be useful for a programmer to understand this theory but, in general, it is not necessary for the novice or intermediate programmer.

a new function – even though the structure of the solution is identical. Changing the functional code is straightforward:[5]

```
filter (notequal "fred") string_sequence
```

Finally, there is the question of efficiency. It is claimed that the higher the level of the programming language (that is, the further away from the hardware model) the less efficient the language is in terms of speed and memory utilization. To a certain extent this may be true;[6] however, two very important points are worth making:

1. The first concern of a programmer is that a program is written on time and is *correct*; performance is generally a secondary concern.

2. Functional languages are not tied to the von Neumann architecture (Backus, 1978). This allows for implementations on other hardware configurations such as multi-processors.

Consider the following:

```
sumofsquares := square (x) + square (y)
```

In an imperative language it is necessary to have an ordering of instructions; typically `square (x)` is executed before `square (y)`. Logically, however, it does not matter whether `square (x)` is executed first or second; actually both `square (x)` and `square (y)` could be calculated simultaneously. The very fact that functional languages are not based on any particular hardware conceptual model enables them to take advantage of parallel and multi-processor hardware (Peyton Jones, 1987; Matthews, 1991). In summary, the programmer is freed from the burden of implementation.[7]

However, the above discussion should not lead the reader to the idea that functional languages are the cure for all programming evils. There is still the need to recognize problems and find sensible solutions. There are also a number of software engineering issues that arise from large-scale programming tasks, though in the main these are beyond the scope of this book.

SML in context

SML, which stands for *Standard Meta-Language*, has developed from a language first designed in the late 1970s to support the Edinburgh Logic for Computable Functions formal proof system (Gordon *et al.*, 1979). A brief outline of its conceptual framework

5. In SML it is first necessary to write the function `filter` – this takes three statements! The reason why the code is so flexible derives directly from the ability to treat functions as parameters to other functions; `filter` takes any function which returns a Boolean value.
6. Although modern implementations of functional languages rival the speed of compiled imperative languages such as Pascal and C.
7. Because of this freedom, functional languages are also well suited to program transformation techniques, which allow programs to be mathematically derived from their specifications, or an inefficient algorithm

and development is available in Milner (1990). SML is now a general purpose programming language and is used for a wide variety of activities including, for example, graphics (Salmon and Slater, 1987) and especially in the areas of proof systems and specification.

SML shares with all other functional languages the notion that functions and data values have 'equal citizenship'; that is, they can be manipulated in the same manner (Landin, 1966). Other SML characteristics of note include polymorphism (which gives flexibility to the strong type system), pattern matching (to provide an elegant selection control structure), partial function application, new type construction and a modules system to enhance complex program organization. These topics are dealt with in depth in the main text.

SML is an example of a *strict* functional language, which means that a function's parameters are normally evaluated before the function body itself. This is in contrast to the alternative *lazy* style of evaluation, whereby a function's parameters are evaluated only if they are needed. It is possible to mimic some aspects of lazy evaluation in SML, as shown in Appendix F; the Bibliography contains references which will provide further discussion of strict and lazy implementations.

How to use this book

This book can be studied in four or five separate blocks. The first two chapters serve to re-orientate the imperative programmer. They provide an introduction to SML syntax and the functional approach to programming. Some of the features shown will be quite familiar to anyone with imperative programming experience; these features include the standard mathematical operators, the clear distinction made between different types of data and the idea of function definition and application. Novel features are dealt with in greater depth; these include the SML conditional form, pattern matching, polymorphism and the use of recursion for program control.

The third and fourth chapters explore in depth the heart of the functional style. They are core to SML (and functional) programming and will probably appear quite new to a programmer only familiar with an imperative programming language. In Chapter 3, the list aggregate type is introduced as the most important SML data structure and various styles of recursive programming using lists are investigated. The chapter ends with the design of a program similar to the UNIX[8] utility *grep*, which is used in subsequent chapters to highlight the expressive power of new features. Chapter 4 introduces the important concept of partial application and demonstrates that functions can be treated as data. It also shows how recursive solutions to programming tasks can be generalized to facilitate control structure abstraction.

Chapter 5 demonstrates a feature of SML that is essential for any production programming: the ability to make blocks of code private to other blocks of code, thereby enabling safer and more re-usable software.

to be automatically converted to an efficient one by the compiler (Darlington *et al.*, 1982). These program transformation techniques guarantee that new errors are not introduced into the code. However, optimization techniques are outside the scope of this book.

8. UNIX is a trademark of AT&T Bell Laboratories

The final two chapters show more advanced programming features. Chapter 6 explores the relationship between data and process by showing SML's powerful facilities for data abstraction and allowing the user to create new types. Chapter 7 introduces the important concept of the module and provides an elegant tool for medium to large-scale program construction.

There are also appendices which cover input and output, imperative aspects of SML, the UNIX–SML interface, and those SML features which are mainly 'syntactic sugaring', together with a summary of the initial SML environment and a short discussion of delayed evaluation in SML.

It is recommended that the main body of the book is studied sequentially, and that the reader should attempt the exercises as they are encountered. The exercises serve both as a review of the student's current knowledge and also as a commentary on the text; sample solutions are given at the end of the book.

1 · *Operators, Values and Types*

This chapter starts by showing some elementary SML programs where only simple expressions involving built-in arithmetic and relational operators are used. Since these simple expressions can only make simple programs, more enhanced features are needed in order to create real-life applications. These include the access to built-in functions, such as those to calculate the sine or square root of a number and, more importantly, the ability to associate names either with immediate data values or with expressions which are evaluated to some data value. Once a name is defined, it can be recalled in all subsequent expressions within a program. This makes programs more readable and makes it easier to create more complex expressions.

In order to promote good programming, SML has a strong type system whereby a function can only be applied to an argument of the expected type. Any attempt to give an argument of a type other than the one it expects will result in a 'type clash' error. In practice, the strong type system is a useful debugging tool.

Good style is further encouraged by the use of comments in order to document the code.

1.1 *An SML session*

Typically the SML system will be entered from the host system by typing the command `sml`. SML responds by displaying an initial message, such as:

```
Standard ML of New Jersey, Version 0.66
```

This message may be surrounded by site and version specific details and may be followed by the SML system prompt, such as `-`.

Exit from SML is implementation dependent; on UNIX systems this is achieved by typing the 'End of File' character (normally *<Control>-D*).

Using the SML system

The SML interactive system issues a prompt and waits for the programmer to type something. The programmer may type either an expression to be evaluated, a definition which gives a name to an expression, or an instruction to the SML system (for example, to ask SML to read from a file). SML will either evaluate the expression, or remember the definition, or obey the instruction; it then issues a fresh prompt and waits for the programmer to type something else.

The simplest use of SML is to type in an expression to be evaluated; in this way, SML acts rather like a desk calculator.

All SML expressions, definitions and instructions must be terminated by a semicolon. The following is an example of an expression with the SML system response:

```
— 3 + 4;
val it = 7 : int
```

SML responds to the expression by displaying the characters `val it =` (which will be explained shortly, in Section 1.2.1) followed by the actual result `7` and the characters `:int` which show that this result is an integer. SML always responds with both the value of the result and its *type*. If the semicolon is forgotten then the system will give a secondary prompt, such as =:

```
— 3 + 4
= ;
val it = 7 : int
```

However, for clarity, this text will not include the secondary prompt when displaying user input over more than one line.

Similarly, it is possible to enter more than one expression on a single line (provided each is terminated by a semicolon) because SML takes no action until a new line is entered. Whilst this feature may be convenient for short interactive sessions, it is considered a poor documentation standard for programs stored in a file (as discussed in Section 1.8).

Standard operators

SML provides built-in functions for the standard arithmetic and relational operations. The rest of this section discusses their general characteristics, more specific detail being provided in subsequent sections.

Examples:

```
— 34 + 56;
val it = 90 : int

— 2.0 * 3.5;
val it = 7.0 : real

— 3 > 4;
val it = false : bool
```

```
— 3 = 3;
val it = true : bool
```

All of the arithmetic operations can be used several times in an expression or in combination with other operators. For example:

```
— 2 + 3 + 5;
val it = 10 : int

— 2 + 3 * 5;
val it = 17 : int

— (2 + 3) * 5;
val it = 25 : int
```

The above behave as expected, with brackets being used to enforce the order of evaluation. However, the relational operators >, >= etc., cannot be linked so readily; for example, the expression (2 < 3 < 4) would give an error, as explained later in this chapter.

Simple function application

SML provides a number of useful functions. The actual functions provided may vary according to the implementation of SML being used; the standard set of functions is given in Appendix D. To use one of these functions it must be applied to an argument. Function application is denoted by giving the name of the function, followed by the argument enclosed in brackets. If the argument is a single value then the brackets may be omitted.

Examples:

```
— sqrt (4.0 + 12.0);
val it = 4.0 : real

— sqrt (25.0);
val it = 5.0 : real

— sqrt 9.0;
val it = 3.0 : real

— (sqrt 9.0) + (sqrt 25.0);
val it = 8.0 : real

— sqrt (sqrt 81.0);
val it = 3.0 : real
```

1.2 *Value definitions*

In SML it is possible to give a name (or *identifier*) to the value of an expression. This is achieved by use of the **val** keyword which has the general format:

> **val** *name* = *expression*

The simplest kind of expression is a basic data value, examples of this being:

```
— val hours = 24;
val hours = 24 :   int

— val message =   "Hello World";
val message =   "Hello World" : string
```

The value associated with the name hours is now 24 and the value associated with the name message is "Hello World". The value given to a name can readily be recalled by entering the name as an expression to be evaluated:

```
— hours;
val it = 24 : int
```

Similarly, the value returned by the expression ((4 * 30) + (7 * 31) + 28) may be given a name as follows:

```
— val days = ((4 * 30) + (7 * 31) + 28);
val days = 365 : int
```

In general, any name may appear on the left-hand side of the equals sign and any expression may appear on the right-hand side. Note that a name is a kind of expression but an expression is not a name, so val days = hours is legal but val (3+4) = hours is illegal. Giving a name to a value is useful because that name can then be used in subsequent expressions; the choice of meaningful names will make a program easier to read.

The following is a simple example of an expression that itself involves names that have been previously defined by **val** definitions:

```
— val hours_in_year = (days * hours);
val hours_in_year = 8760 : int

— val hours_in_leapyear = ((days + 1) * hours);
val hours_in_leapyear = 8784 : int
```

Legal and sensible names

In practice there is a limitation to the choice of names. There are four restrictions:

1. Certain words are reserved for use by the SML system and therefore *cannot* be used:[1]

    **abstype and andalso as case datatype do else end eqtype
    exception fn fun functor handle if in include infix infixr
    let local nonfix of op open orelse raise rec sharing sig
    signature struct structure then type val with withtype while**

2. Certain words already have a meaning in a particular context in the SML system and *should not* be used as names. For example, using 'int' or 'real' as names may lead to confusion (although it would not be illegal).

3. The redefinition of predefined function names should similarly be avoided. Appendix D contains a list of those functions typically provided by an SML system.

4. Only certain combinations of characters form a legal name in SML. For example, a name cannot begin with a digit. The full syntax is given in Appendix D.

1.2.1 *Referential transparency and redefining names*

Referential transparency

The functional programming style is that a name is given to a value rather than to a memory location. In an imperative programming language, the memory location referred to by a name is constant, but the value stored in that location may change: in a functional programming language the value itself is constant and the programmer is not concerned with how or where this value is stored in memory.

The functional style has the important consequence that the values of names do not change and therefore the result of a given expression will be the same wherever it appears in a program. Any program written in this style is said to have the property of *referential transparency*. Programs exhibiting referential transparency have many benefits, including the fact that it is easier to reason about these programs and hence easier to debug them. For example, one part of a program may be tested independently of the rest.

Redefining names

Notwithstanding the above, the fact that SML is an interactive system means that it is sometimes convenient to re-use a name (to save the bother of inventing new names during a session). Thus the following command sequence is legal:

```
— val message = "Hello World";
val message = "Hello World" : string
```

1. Throughout this book, reserved names are shown in **bold**.

```
— val message = "Goodbye Cruel World";
val message = "Goodbye Cruel World" : string
```

If the name `message` is used subsequently it will take the value given by the most recent definition `"Goodbye Cruel World"`. In general, any definition which refers to a name *will not* be affected by future changes to that name's definition:[2]

```
— val message = "Hello World";
val message = "Hello World" : string

— val try_me = message;
val try_me = "Hello World" : string

— val message = "Goodbye Cruel World";
val message = "Goodbye Cruel World" : string

— message;
val it = "Goodbye Cruel World" : string

— try_me;
val it = "Hello World" : string
```

However, this redefinition feature is *dangerous* to use within any real program because it makes it difficult to reason about a program. As an example of the dangers of redefinition, if the above two commands were separated by many other commands it is quite feasible that the programmer would be uncertain as to the current value of `message`.

The value i t

It can now be seen that the system response `val it =` indicates that the built-in name `it` always holds the result of the last evaluated command. It is therefore *very unwise* to use `it` as a **val** name because its value keeps on changing.[3]

```
— val it = 6;
val it = 6 : int

— 5;
val it = 5 : int
```

---

2. This mechanism is known as *static binding*.
3. This also holds for many other SML implementations which have different system responses, the distinction being that the name `it` may be silently redefined.

1.3 *Types*

Types are a way of classifying data values according to their intended use. A data type may be specified either by enumerating the values that data items of that type may have, or by the operations that may be performed upon data items of that type. Conscientious use of a type classification system aids the construction of clear, reliable, well-structured programs.

SML has a number of built-in data types, including the simple types – integers, real numbers, strings and Booleans – together with fixed-length aggregate types which are discussed in this chapter. Chapter 3 introduces the variable-length list aggregate type, whilst the facility to define new data types is presented in Chapter 6.

SML is a *strongly-typed* language. This means that the system uses information about the types of data values to ensure that they are used in the correct way. For example, the predefined function sqrt expects to be applied to an argument that is a real number. In SML, real numbers must contain a decimal point and so the following is detected as an error:

```
— sqrt 4;

Error: operator and operand don't agree (tycon mismatch)
   operator domain: real
   operand:         int
   in expression:   sqrt 4
```

This principle extends to the infix arithmetic operators, in that an error will arise if the wrong type of value is used. For example, in the following session SML expects the function div to be used with two integers and gives an error if used with an integer and a real number:

```
— 2 div 1.0;

Error: operator and operand don't agree (tycon mismatch)
   operator domain: int * int
   operand:         int * real
   in expression:   div (2,1.0)
```

Error messages

The above error message highlights the fact that SML silently turns the expression 2 div 1.0 into the function application div (2,1.0); such functions will be introduced in Section 2.3.2. Furthermore, the message operator domain: int * int shows that the operator div is expected to be used with two integers.

The system response to errors is not defined by SML and may vary between implementations. The above examples are typical responses from Standard ML of New Jersey. Most implementations also give the line number and many give the character position of the error, although in all the error messages in this book the positional information will be omitted for reasons of clarity.

Error messages may highlight two kinds of error – syntax errors and type errors. The type errors may include obscure information for advanced programmers and system implementors as well as information that is useful for relative beginners. The type error messages will become clearer in later chapters.

1.4 Numeric types

SML separates numbers into two types: integers and real numbers. As part of the strong typing approach, SML does not allow these two types to mix.

1.4.1 Integers

Integers are denoted by the type name int. Data values of type int may be manipulated by the operators shown in Table 1.1.

Table 1.1. Operations on integers

+	addition
−	subtraction
*	multiplication
div	division
mod	remainder

For example:

```
— 365 div 7;
val it = 52 : int

— 365 mod 7;
val it = 1 : int

— val days = 365;
val days = 365 : int

— val weeks = days div 7;
val weeks = 52 : int
```

1.4.2 Real numbers

Real numbers are denoted by the type name real. Data values of type real may be manipulated by the operators shown in Table 1.2.

Table 1.2. Operations on real numbers

+	*addition*
−	*subtraction*
∗	*multiplication*
/	*division*

Real numbers are indicated by decimal points (trailing zeros are required) or by using exponential format. The precision cannot be specified by the programmer and is determined by the machine that is being used.

```
— val y = 77.0;
val y = 77.0 : real

— val z = 32E5;
val z = 3200000.0 : real

— 365.0 / 7.0;
val it = 52.1428571428571 : real
```

1.4.3 Negative numbers

Negative numbers are prefixed with the tilde sign ˜. For example:

```
— val x = ˜33;
val x = ˜33 : int
```

If there is no space between the ˜ and the number then this is treated as a single data value. The number may be an integer or a real number.

However, the ˜ character is also a built-in prefix function that takes a single argument and negates the value:

```
— val y = ˜ 33.0;
val y = ˜33.0 : real

— val y = ˜ (˜33.0);
val y = 33.0 : real

— val y = ˜ (˜ (33.0));
val y = 33.0 : real

— val z = ˜ y;
val z = ˜33.0 : real

— val z = ˜y;
val z = ˜33.0 : real
```

The last of the above examples shows that there need not be a space between the ~ and a **val** name. However, because a **val** name is not a constant value, the ~ is still treated as a prefix function.

The difference between ~ as part of a negative number and ~ as a prefix function is important, as illustrated by the following session which uses the built-in function **abs** (**abs** takes an integer, either positive or negative, and returns its absolute, that is, unsigned, value):

```
— val x = abs ~33;
val x = 33 : int

— val z = abs ~x;
Error: overloaded variable "abs" not defined at
type: int —> int
```

The first definition succeeds because ~33 is interpreted as a single constant value and therefore **abs** is applied (correctly) to a negative integer. By contrast, in the second definition ~ is interpreted as a prefix function – this is treated separately from the x and appears as the first object after the function name **abs** and therefore SML believes that ~ is the argument for **abs** (which obviously gives an error). The intended meaning can be enforced by bracketing the ~x, thus forcing SML to interpret the whole sub-expression as the argument to the function **abs**:

```
— val z = abs (~x);
val z = 33 : int
```

A similar error arises if a space occurs between the ~ and the constant to be negated. Here is one incorrect example followed by two correct examples:

```
— val z = abs ~ 33;
Error: overloaded variable "abs" not defined at
type: int —> int

— val z = abs (~ 33);
val z = 33 : int

— val z = abs ~33;
val z = 33 : int
```

1.4.4 Type conversion

Real numbers may be explicitly converted into integers by using the built-in function floor, which returns the largest integer that is smaller than its argument:

```
— floor 77.0;
val it = 77 : int
```

Conversely, the built-in function real converts from an integer to a real number:

```
— real 77;
val it = 77.0 : real
```

1.5 Non-numeric types

1.5.1 Strings

Character strings are denoted by the type name string. Data values of type string may be operated on by the functions given in Table 1.3.

Table 1.3.   Operations on strings

^	string concatenation
size	length of a string

SML, unlike many other programming languages, makes *no distinction* between characters and strings: an SML character is just a string of size 1.

Examples:

```
— val achar = "a";
val achar = "a" : string

— val testing = "Hello 1 2 3 4";
val testing = "Hello 1 2 3 4" : string

— val shout = "aaa" ^ "rgh" ^ "!!!!";
val shout = "aaargh!!!!" : string

— size achar;
val it = 1 : int
```

Concatenation treats the empty string in the same way as addition treats the constant value zero, as illustrated below:

```
— "" ^ "";
val it = "" : string

— "1" ^ "";
val it = "1" : string

— "" ^ "anything";
val it = "anything" : string
```

Special characters

SML follows the UNIX philosophy of implementing 'special characters' by a two-character sequence (the first character of which is a backslash). The special characters include the new-line character (\n), the tab character (\t), backslash itself (\\) and double-quote (\"). Thus, the string "\"Buy us a drink\"" when produced as output from a program will appear as the characters "Buy us a drink".[4] Notice that the two-character sequence is considered to be a single character, hence:

```
— size "\"Buy us a drink\"";
val it = 16 : int
```

It is also possible to use the ASCII decimal codes for characters e.g. \065 for the character A (in this format, a three-digit sequence is used after the backslash character).

Type conversion

SML assumes an underlying character set of 256 characters, numbered from 0 to 255, where the first 128 characters correspond to the ASCII character set. The built-in function ord returns the ASCII number of the first character in its string argument, whilst chr decodes its integer argument to produce a single character string. For example:

```
— ord "A";
val it = 65 : int

— chr 65;
val it = "A" : string

— ord "AA";
val it = 65 : int
```

However, an attempt to apply ord to the empty string will result in an error:

```
— ord "";
uncaught exception Ord
```

Furthermore, an attempt to apply chr to a value not in the range 0 to 255 will also result in an error:

```
— chr 256;
uncaught exception Chr
```

Many SML implementations provide a special built-in function makestring[5] which converts either an integer or a real number into a string representation of that number:

---

4. To facilitate debugging, Standard ML of New Jersey does not perform this conversion when writing to the screen during an interactive session.
5. Note that makestring is not part of the initial SML environment, as defined in Milner *et al.* (1990). It has been included in this text for convenience. In SML, it is actually impossible to write makestring because it is overloaded (see Section 1.7) and user-defined functions may not be overloaded (although Standard ML of New Jersey has some non-standard extensions in this area). Of course, individual *makeint* and *makereal* functions may be defined.

```
— makestring 123;
val it = "123" : string

— makestring 12.3;
val it = "12.3" : string
```

In addition, a string may be explicitly converted into a list of single character strings using the `explode` function, and vice versa by `implode`. These functions and the list aggregate type are discussed more fully in Chapter 3.

1.5.2. *Boolean values*

Boolean values are truth values that are denoted by the type name `bool`. Data values of type `bool` are represented by one of the two constant values `true` and `false`. Data values of type `bool` may be operated on by the keywords shown in Table 1.4.

Table 1.4.   Operations on Booleans

not	logical negation
andalso	logical conjunction
orelse	logical disjunction
if .. then .. else	conditional selection

They may also be produced as a result of the *relational* operators (`>`, `>=`, `<`, `<=`) and the *equality* operators (`=`, `<>`).

The following presents some simple examples of their use. Especial notice should be taken of the fact that the sign `=` is used both as a way of giving a name to a value and to check if two values are equal.

```
— 3 = 4;
val it = false : bool

— 7.8 < 9.2;
val it = true : bool

— val x = 3;
val x = 3 : int

— x <= 7;
val it = true : bool

— not true;
val it = false : bool

— (2 < 3) = not (not true);
val it = true : bool
```

Notice that the relational operators cannot be combined to form more extended expressions such as (1 < 2 < 3) because (1 < 2) evaluates to the Boolean value true which cannot legally be compared to the integer value 3.

Type conversion

The function makestring will also convert a Boolean value to a string. For example:

```
— makestring (1 < 2);
val it = "true" : string
```

Lexicographic ordering

As can be seen the relational operators will work with integers and real numbers. Many SML implementations also allow two strings to be compared,[6] the results being based on normal (ASCII) lexicographic ordering:

```
— "A" < "a";
val it = true : bool

— "A" < "A1";
val it = true : bool

— "B" < "A1";
val it = false : bool
```

As expected, different types cannot be compared, hence it is meaningless to attempt to compare an integer with a string:

```
— "A" < 66;

Error: operator and operand don't agree (tycon mismatch)
    operator domain: string * string
    operand:         string * int
    in expression:     < ("A",66)
```

1.5.3. Conditional evaluation

SML provides logical operators for both conjunction (logical and) and disjunction (logical or). There is also a construct for conditional evaluation based upon the truth value of a given sub-expression. These operators for conditional evaluation are sometimes known as 'lazy' operators because they only evaluate as many of their operands as is necessary.

6. Note that this feature is not part of the initial SML environment, as defined in Milner *et al.* (1990). If it is not provided, it may be explicitly defined by the programmer using explode, implode and the techniques described in Chapter 3.

Conjunction and disjunction

The keywords **andalso** and **orelse** are special operators which first evaluate their left operand and only evaluate their right operand if necessary to determine their overall truth value.[7] The special operator **andalso** evaluates to `true` when both of its operands evaluate to `true` otherwise it evaluates to `false`. Similarly, the special operator **orelse** evaluates to `false` when both of its operands evaluate to `false` otherwise it evaluates to `true`.

Example session:

```
— val x = 0;
val x = 0 : int

— val y = 42;
val y = 42 : int

— (y = 42) andalso (x = 0) andalso (y = x);
val it = false : bool

— (y = 42) andalso ((x = 0) andalso (y = x));
val it = false : bool

— val z = (x = 0) orelse ((y div x) > 23);
val z = true : bool
```

The last of these examples shows that the left to right evaluation of the operands is quite useful when it is not desirable to attempt an evaluation of the second argument. In this case a divide by zero error has been avoided.[8]

The conditional expression – if .. then .. else

The SML conditional expression highlights an important difference between functional and imperative programming styles. In SML the conditional evaluates to a value[9] rather than being used as a control statement. Thus SML syntax is:

if *condition*
then *return a value x of a given type*
else *return a value y of the same type*

7. In this respect they are similar to the LISP conditional 'cond' and the C operators '&&' and '‖' but dissimilar to the Pascal 'and' and 'or' functions (which evaluate each sub-expression in a compound Boolean expression before deciding the overall truth value).
8. Notice that this useful left to right evaluation means that **orelse** and **andalso** are not the precise equivalent of logical disjunction and conjunction.
9. In a similar manner to the C language ternary operator.

whereas typical imperative style is:

> **if**   *condition*
> **then**   *do something*
> (**else do nothing*)

or:

> **if**   *condition*
> **then**   *do something*
> **else**   *do some other thing*

The consequence of omitting the **else** part in an imperative conditional is that no action takes place: the consequence of omission in SML is that a syntax error occurs! In SML, both alternatives must return a value and both must evaluate to the same type.

    Example session:

```
— val t = true;
val t = true : bool

— val days = 365;
val days = 365 : int

— if days = 365 then "year" else "not a normal year";
val it = "year" : string

— if t then days else 7;
val it = 365 : int

— if days > 366 then "too many days"
else if days < 365 then "too few days"
else "valid year";
val it = "valid year" : string
```

The following emphasizes that **if .. then .. else** returns a value rather than switches program control:

```
— val days_in_Feb = if (days = 365) then 28 else 29;
val days_in_Feb = 28 : int
```

Examples of common mistakes and the resulting error messages are given below:

```
— 1 + (if true then 28);
Error: syntax error found at RPAREN
```

```
— if true then 365 else "my error message";
Error: rules don't agree (tycon mismatch)
  expected: bool —> int
  found:    bool —> string
  rule:     false => "my error message"
```

The first of these is an error because **if .. then .. else** needs both the **then** and the **else** parts to be present, whereas the second is an error because the two alternative expressions have two different types.

Conditional evaluation

The SML **if .. then .. else** operator works in a similar manner to the two special Boolean operators **andalso** and **orelse** since it only evaluates one of its second and third parameters, according to the truth value of its first parameter. If this were not the case the final expression in the following sample session would give rise to a divide by zero error:

```
— val x = 4;
val x = 4 : int

— val y = 0;
val y = 0 : int

— if y <> 0
then x div y
else 0;
val it = 0 : int
```

1.6 Tuples

This section introduces the *tuple* which combines values to create an *aggregate type*. As an example, it is possible to give a name to the combination of an integer, string and integer that represent a given date:

```
— val date = (13, "March", 1066);
val date = (13,"March",1066) : int * string * int
```

The system response indicates that the expression (13,"March",1066) has been treated as a single value with the aggregate type int * string * int. The * symbol in the type expression is not the arithmetic multiplication operator but indicates that the aggregate type is the *Cartesian product* (or *cross product*) of the three component types.

Domains and Cartesian products

In order to understand the type information in error messages (and to create new types as will be shown in Chapter 6) it is useful to understand the concept of *type domains*. The following is an informal introduction to this topic. The reader is referred to Gordon (1979) and Thompson (1991) for more details.

The collection of values that a type can have is known as its *domain*. For example, the domain of type `bool` is the collection of built-in values `true` and `false`. Similarly, the collection of values of the type `int` is the theoretically infinite range of whole numbers from *minus infinity* to *plus infinity*.[10] The type `bool * bool` contains the Cartesian product operator `*`. This indicates that the domain contains all possible combinations which combine one value from the first domain (for type `bool`) with one value from the second domain (for type `bool`). Therefore the domain for the type `bool * bool` is fully represented by the four tuples:

> (*false, false*)
> (*true, false*)
> (*false, true*)
> (*true, true*)

Similarly, the infinite domain `int * string * bool` contains all the tuples (`i,s,b`) where `i` is any value drawn from the integer domain, `s` is any value drawn from the string domain and `b` is any value drawn from the Boolean domain.

1.6.1 Tuple equality

Any base type has at least two operations defined upon its elements; that of equality (`=`) and inequality (`<>`). Thus any two tuples of the same type (whose elements are base types) may be tested for equality, as is shown in the following session:

```
— date = (13, "March", 1066);
val it = true : bool

— (3,4) = (4,3);
val it = false : bool

— val x = ~3;
val x = ~3 : int

— (3, "a", true) = (abs x, "a", (3 > 2));
val it = true : bool
```

As might be expected, tuples with different types cannot be compared:

---

10. Of course, in practice, there is a machine-dependent restriction on this range.

```
— date = (13.0, "March", 1066);
Error: operator and operand don't agree (tycon mismatch)
  operator domain:
  (int * string * int) * (int * string * int)
  operand:
  (int * string * int) * (real * string * int)
  in expression:   =(date,(13.0,"March",1066))

— (3,4,5) = (3,4);
Error: operator and operand don't agree (tycon mismatch)
  operator domain: (int * int * int) * (int * int * int)
  operand:         (int * int * int) * (int*int)
  in expression:   =((3,4,5),(3,4))
```

1.6.2. *Tuple composite format*

The *composite format* of a tuple can be used on the left-hand side of a **val** expression, thereby providing a convenient shorthand for multiple definitions:

```
— val (day, month, year) = (13, "March", 1066);
val day = 13 : int
val month = "March" : string
val year = 1066 : int
```

The names day, month and year can now be used as single **val** names:

```
— if (day = 13) then "unlucky" else "lucky";
val it = "unlucky" : string
```

This shorthand notation is in fact a simple example of the powerful mechanism known as *pattern matching*, which will be discussed in Section 2.5. This general mechanism extends to complex patterns:

```
— val ((day, month, year), wine, price)
      = ((13, "May", 1966), "Margaux", 60);
val day = 13 : int
val month = "May" : string
val year = 1966 : int
val wine = "Margaux" : string
val price = 60 : int
```

1.7 *Properties of operators*

This section explains the key concepts of *precedence, associativity, commutativity* and *overloading*. The first three properties determine the order in which applications of operators (and functions) are evaluated,[11] whereas overloading refers to the fact that some operators may manipulate values of different types. An understanding of the properties of operators may significantly aid debugging and may aid the design of better functions, as will be seen in Chapter 4.

1.7.1 *Precedence*

In an expression such as (3 + 4 * 5) there is an inherent ambiguity as to which sub-expression (3 + 4) or (4 * 5) to evaluate first. This ambiguity is resolved by a set of simple rules for arithmetic operators; in the above example it is clear that the expression really means (3 + (4 * 5)) because the rule is that multiplication should be done before addition. This is known as a rule of *precedence*; multiplication has a higher precedence than addition and therefore the sub-expression with the multiplication operator should be evaluated first. If it is necessary to override the precedence rules then brackets are used to indicate priority. For example.

        ((3 + 4) * (5 + 6))

All SML operators are given a precedence level and a table of precedence levels is given in Appendix D. However, it is important to remember that function application has a very high precedence, so that

        (sqrt 3.0 + 4.0)

is interpreted as:

        ((sqrt 3.0) + 4.0)

In general, the use of brackets is encouraged for reasons of safety and good documentation.

1.7.2 *Order of association*

Some operators (for example, * and /) have the same level of precedence; this means that there is still ambiguity in the meaning of some expressions. For example, the expression (4.0 / 5.0 * 6.0) is ambiguous – it might mean either ((4.0 / 5.0) * 6.0) or (4.0 / (5.0 * 6.0)). Furthermore, repeated use of the same operator leads to similar ambiguity, as with the expression (4.0 / 5.0 / 6.0). This ambiguity may be resolved by determining the *order of association*. In SML, all operators (except for : :, as will be seen in Chapter 3) associate to the *left*; that is, (4.0 / 5.0 * 6.0) is interpreted as ((4.0 / 5.0) * 6.0) and

---

11. Appendix B shows how it is possible for the programmer to alter the precedence and associativity of operators and functions.

(4.0 / 5.0 / 6.0 / 7.0) is interpreted as (((4.0 / 5.0) /6.0) / 7.0). This left-associating behaviour also extends to function application so that (sqrt abs 1) is interpreted as ((sqrt abs) 1) and gives an error – the programmer should therefore take particular care to correctly bracket function applications.

To summarise:

1. Precedence is always considered first; the rules for association are only applied when ambiguity cannot be resolved through precedence.

2. The rules governing the order of association only apply to operators at the same level of precedence; this may be two or more different operators, or perhaps two or more occurrences of the same operator (such as (5 — 6 — 7)).

3. Brackets are used for priority, to override the order of association. For example, although it is now clear that the expression (4.0 / 5.0 * 6.0) means ((4.0 / 5.0) * 6.0), it is possible to bracket the multiplication, to ensure that it happens first: (4.0 / (5.0 * 6.0)).

Associativity

For some operators, it makes no difference whether they associate to the right or to the left. These are called *associative* operators, for example multiplication:

```
- ((4.0 * 5.0) * 6.0) = (4.0 * (5.0 * 6.0));
val it = true : bool
```

However, some operators are *not* associative:

```
- ((4.0 / 5.0) / 6.0) = (4.0 / (5.0 / 6.0));
val it = false : bool
```

This property of *associativity* only refers to repeated use of the same operator in an expression; notice that an operator can only be associative if its result type is the same as its argument type(s).

Commutativity

Some operators are *commutative*; that is, it makes no difference in what order their parameters appear. For example,

```
- (4 * 5) = (5 * 4);
val it = true : bool
```

However, some operators are *not* commutative:

```
- (4 - 5) = (5 - 4);
val it = false : bool
```

Sometimes the non-commutativity of an operator is due to it being lazy:

```
- true orelse ((3 div 0) = 3);
val it = true : bool

- ((3 div 0) = 3) orelse true;
uncaught exception Div
```

The recognition of non-associative and non-commutative operators often aids debugging. The associativity and commutativity of operators is given in Appendix D.

1.7.3 Operator overloading

The idea of an *overloaded* operator such as + or * is that the same symbol may be used for two operations or functions that are internally dissimilar but semantically similar. For example, the internal representation of integers and real numbers on most computers is very different, and thus the implementation of multiplication is also quite different; it would perhaps be logical to have two operators, *int** and *real** to mirror this. However, the behaviour of the two operations appears to the programmer as identical and SML supports this semantic congruence by using the single operator symbol * for both integer and real number multiplication. By contrast, integer division (**div**) and floating point division (/) are semantically quite different to the programmer (integer division ignores the remainder, whereas floating point division does not) and they consequently have different names.

The operators *, +, −, <, <=, >, >= are all *overloaded* in that they will either take two real numbers or two integers (in many implementations the relational operators are further overloaded to take two strings). When an overloaded operator is used, the leftmost argument is inspected first, in order to decide whether real or integer arithmetic is intended.

1.8 Programs and comments

Incorporating existing programs – use [12]

Interactive use of SML is unwieldy for the production of all but the smallest programs. The problem is that there is no interactive way to edit the function definitions and expressions that have already been typed (without entering them again in full). The solution to this problem is the use command, which allows

---

12. Note that use is not part of the initial SML environment, as defined in Milner *et al.* (1990). It is, however, available in many implementations and has been included in this text because it provides a convenient facility.

code to be read in from a file. A program can therefore be developed by using a standard editor on a file; in a subsequent SML session, the system can be instructed to read all the definitions from that file. This is achieved by typing use, followed by a string naming the file to be incorporated into the SML environment. For example, given a file called 'spending_money.ml', typing use "spending_money.ml" will cause the system to read the file from the current directory, echo the types of the definitions and return the special value () of type unit (see Chapter 2). All the definitions contained in the file are now available in the current SML session.[13]

Note that when developing definitions in a file it is *not* necessary to terminate either expressions or definitions with a semicolon. Furthermore, there will of course be no system prompt and no immediate feedback regarding errors.

If the source file contains syntax errors then SML may stop attempting to compile at the first syntax error found, though generally definitions that have already been parsed will be incorporated into the current environment.

Program documentation

To enhance readability all programs in a file should be documented; to this end SML allows comments to be embedded within a program. The commented text must be enclosed by an opening left-bracket asterisk (* and closing asterisk right-bracket *). For example:

```
(* Program "spending_money.sml".
Calculates the amount of holiday spending money.
Only deals with three different currencies.
*)

(* amount of money available *)
val amount_of_sterling = 200.0

(* different exchange rates *)
val UK_to_US = 1.70
val UK_to_DM = 2.93
val UK_to_FR = 10.94

(* amount of spending money in different currencies *)
val US_spending_money = amount_of_sterling * UK_to_US
val DM_spending_money = amount_of_sterling * UK_to_DM
val FR_spending_money = amount_of_sterling * UK_to_FR

(* (* Comments may also be nested. *) *)
```

13. Some versions of SML allow more than one file to be read. In these versions use expects a string list of the form ["file","file2"]. It is best to check the site manual to see which version is applicable.

System responses

For the rest of this book system responses will be ignored where they are self-evident. Examples will be displayed as if written in a file and entered by means of the function use. The system prompt will thus be dropped as will the user-entered semicolon.

1.9 Summary

It is possible to treat the SML command interpreter as a simple desk calculator which evaluates expressions entered by the programmer. However, for the purposes of real programming, four additional features have been introduced:

1. The provision of built-in functions; user-defined functions will be introduced in the next chapter.

2. The classification of data values into different types; the ability to create new types is discussed in Chapter 6.

3. The ability to give names to expressions and thereby use their values in other expressions; Chapter 5 shows how a programmer can specify where a name can and cannot be used.

4. The ability to combine built-in types to form tuples; another important aggregate type is introduced in Chapter 3.

It is worth emphasizing that the classification of data values ensures that they are used correctly and therefore that many common programming errors are detected early in the software development process.

2 · Functions

SML functions may either be built in (for example `sqrt`) or they may be defined by the programmer. This chapter explains how to define new functions and then use these functions by applying them to values. Functions can be defined in terms of built-in functions (and operators) and/or other user-defined functions. The result of a function application may either be saved (by giving it a **val** name) or it may be used immediately in a bigger expression (for example as an argument to another function).

Tuples may be used to package more than one argument to a function. Functions that only operate on the structure of the tuple and not on its components belong to the class of *polymorphic* functions. An example is a function to select the first component of a tuple regardless of the values of its components.

Two powerful tools, *pattern matching* and *recursion*, are introduced in this chapter. Pattern matching allows programmers to give alternative definitions for functions for different values of input data. This forces consideration of all inputs to functions and thus eliminates many potential errors at the design stage. Recursion is used to provide iteration and is an essential mechanism for flow control in programs.

Functions are important because they provide a basic component from which to build modular programs. This facilitates the technique of *top-down design* for problem solving; that is, a problem may be broken down into smaller problems which can easily be translated into SML functions. Programs structured in this way are easier to read and easier to maintain.

This chapter ends with a slightly larger example which shows the use of top-down design to solve a problem.

2.1 Simple functions

This section introduces the simplest form of function definition and discusses how functions may be applied to arguments (or 'parameters')[1] and how SML evaluates such function applications.

2.1.1 Function definition

The simplest function definitions have the following format:

> **fun** *function_name parameter_name* = *function_body*

1. In the rest of this book the words 'argument' and 'parameter' will be used interchangeably.

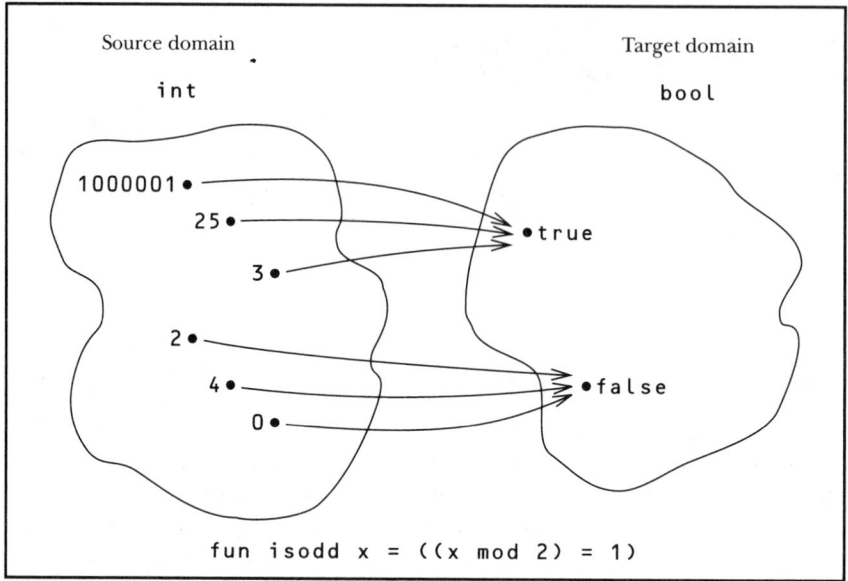

Figure 2.1. Function source domain and target domain

The keyword **fun** introduces the function definition; *function_name* and *parameter_name* may each be any legal identifier. The *parameter_name* is known as the *formal parameter* to the function: it obtains an actual value when the function is applied. This name is local to the function body and bears no relationship to any other value, function or formal parameter of the same name in the rest of the program. The function body may contain any valid expression, including constants, **val** names and applications of built-in functions and user-defined functions.

In the following example twice is the function name, x is the parameter name and x * 2 is the function body:

```
— fun twice x = x * 2;
val twice = fn : int —> int
```

The arrow in the system response indicates that the name twice is a function. The type preceding the arrow is known as the *source type* of the function and states the expected type of the argument to which the function will be applied. The type following the arrow is known as the *target type* and states the type of the value returned by the function. This is illustrated in Figure 2.1.

In general, a function *translates* (or 'maps') a value from a source type (or 'argument type') to another value from a target type (or 'result type'). Though many values from the source type can have the same target value, normally each value from the source type will have just one target result.[2] The source and target types need not be the same. Both of these points are illustrated in the next example which checks if a single character string is upper case:

```
— fun isupper c
    = (c >= "A") andalso (c <= "Z");
val isupper = fn : string —> bool
```

The following example makes use of the built-in functions ord and chr to convert a lower-case alphabetic into its upper-case equivalent, all other characters being left unaltered. The calculation relies upon three facts:

1. Subtracting the ASCII code for lower-case "a" from the ASCII code for a lower-case alphabetic character will give a number within the range 0 to 25.

2. Adding the ASCII code for upper-case "A" to a number within the range 0 to 25 will give the ASCII code for an upper-case alphabetic character.

3. It is assumed that the argument c will be a single-character string.

```
— fun toupper c
    = if (c >= "a") andalso (c <= "z")
        then  chr ((ord c) — (ord "a") + (ord "A"))
        else  c;
val toupper = fn : string —> string
```

2.1.2 Function application

The function twice can be applied to an actual value, in exactly the same manner as system-defined functions:

```
— twice 3;
val it = 6 : int
```

Here, the formal parameter x has obtained the actual value 3.

The integer value returned by the above application may also be used as the actual parameter for another function application. There is no restriction to the number of the times this principle may be employed as long as the types match. However, it is important to remember that function application associates to the left; for example, the application

```
abs twice 3
```

2. The use of reference variables may bypass this rule (see Appendix C). There are, however, some functions that do not have meaningful translations for every value in the source type. Ways of dealing with these functions are considered in Section 2.9.

is interpreted by SML to mean

```
((abs twice) 3)
```

which is clearly an error because abs expects an integer as an argument rather than the name of another function. It is therefore essential to use brackets to give the intended meaning, as shown in the following sample session:

```
— abs (twice ~3);
val it = 6 : int

— twice (twice 3);
val it = 12 : int

— val x = ~8;
val x = ~8 : int

— floor (sqrt (real (abs (twice x))));
val it = 4 : int
```

An application of a previously user-defined function, such as twice, may also appear inside a function body:

```
— fun quad x = twice (twice x);
val quad = fn : int —> int

— quad 5;
val it = 20 : int

— fun is_uppercase c = (c = (toupper c));
val is_uppercase = fn : string —> bool
```

Exercise 2.1
Provide a function to check if a character is alphanumeric, that is, lower case, upper case or numeric.

2.1.3 *Function evaluation*

The example below presents a model of how the application of the function toupper to an argument may be evaluated by an SML system. The example is interesting in that the argument is itself an expression involving an application of a function (the built-in function chr). Note that the double 'equality sign' is used to indicate the result of an evaluation step and has no special meaning in SML; this device is used in the rest of the book to indicate a 'hand evaluation' of an expression.

```
toupper (chr (70 + 10))

== toupper (chr 80)

== toupper "P"

== if ("P" >= "a") andalso ("P" <= "z")
   then   chr ((ord "P") - (ord "a") + (ord "A"))
   else   "P";

== if false
   then   chr ((ord "P") - (ord "a") + (ord "A"))
   else   "P";

== "P"
```

The above example illustrates several important points about function evaluation, about the operator **if .. then .. else** and about evaluation in general:

1. In order to evaluate the function body, effectively a new copy of the function body is created with each occurrence of the formal parameter replaced by a copy of the actual parameter.

2. Using a purely functional subset of SML, it is impossible for any function application to affect the value of its actual parameters.[3]

3. The argument to a function is always evaluated *before* the function body is evaluated (this is sometimes known as 'call-by-value'). This principle also applies to the built-in operators, *except for* the special forms **if .. then .. else, andalso** and **orelse** which delay or ignore the evaluation of some of their arguments (as discussed in Chapter 1).

4. In general, the evaluation of function applications (and indeed evaluation of any expression) may be viewed as a sequence of substitutions and simplifications until a stage is reached where the expression can no longer be simplified.

It should be noted that in the above discussion there has been no mention of *how* the evaluation mechanism is implemented. Indeed, functional languages offer the considerable advantage that programmers need not pay any attention to the underlying implementation.

---

3. Reference variables are an obvious example of a non-functional feature of SML which destroys this property (see Appendix C).

2.2 *Functions as values*

Perhaps surprisingly, a **val** name may also be given to a function. The name then has the same properties as the function:

```
— val tw = twice;
val tw = fn : int —> int

— tw 4;
val it = 8 : int
```

This shows that functions are not only 'black boxes' that translate values to other values, but are values in themselves. They may also be passed as parameters to other functions, as will be shown in Chapter 4.

Thus, entering a function's name without any parameters is the equivalent of entering a value. However, because the function has no constant value the system responds by indicating the function's source and target types:

```
— twice;
val it = fn : int —> int
```

This principle explains the error message for the following incorrect attempt to apply twice:

```
— twice twice 3;

Error: operator and operand don't agree (tycon mismatch)
    operator domain: int
    operand:         int —> int
    in expression: twice twice
```

The error arises because the argument to **twice** is a function **twice**. The above error message highlights the fact that **twice** is a value itself, of type **int —> int**.

The major difference between a function and other values is that two functions may not be tested for equality – even if they have precisely the same code, or always result in the same value. For example, the expression **tw = twice** will give rise to an error.

Redefining functions

It is important to remember that SML allows values and hence functions to be redefined during an interactive session. The consequences are just as undesirable for function redefinitions as for **val** name redefinitions. If **twice** were redefined to return a real number then **tw** would still refer to the prior (integer) definition, despite the fact that a programmer may expect it to refer to the new definition of **twice**.

```
- fun twice x = x * 2;
val twice = fn : int -> int

- val tw = twice;
val tw = fn : int -> int

- fun twice x = x * 2.0;
val twice = fn : real -> real

- tw;
val it = fn : int -> int
```

2.3   Function parameters and results

Normally, functions translate from a single argument into a single result. However, it is often necessary to translate from more than one input argument or even to have functions that do not require any input value to produce a result. This section shows how SML caters for these types of function and also for functions that produce an aggregate result.

2.3.1   Functions without parameters

Sometimes functions do not need any parameters. As such, they have no obvious source type – which unfortunately violates the constraint that all functions are translations from a source type to a target type. For consistency, 'parameterless' functions are given the special parameter (), which is the only value of the special type called unit. This is illustrated in the following example and Figure 2.2.

```
- fun message () = "Buy us several drinks";
val message = fn : unit -> string

- message ();
val it = "Buy us several drinks" : string
```

2.3.2   Functions with more than one parameter

As with 'parameterless' functions, the notion of a function having more than one parameter at first sight also seems to violate the constraint that all functions are translations from a source type to a target type (and so a function to evaluate the greater of two values would be impossible). SML has two ways of coping with this apparent problem – currying and tuples. The currying approach is introduced in Chapter 4, whilst the tuple approach is presented below.

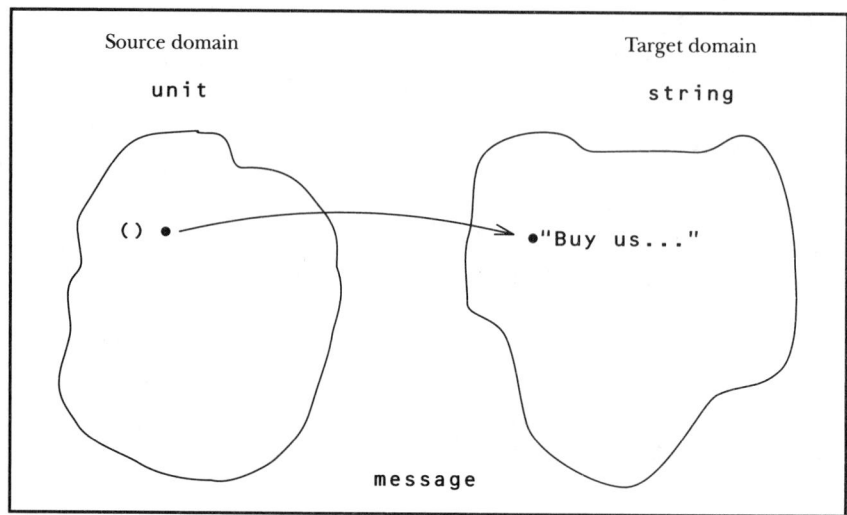

Figure 2.2. Source and target domains for message

Employing tuples to represent the formal parameter of functions with more than one argument is a natural consequence of the fact that a tuple will have a value drawn from an aggregate type (as discussed in Chapter 1). The formal parameter can either use a single name to represent the entire tuple or the tuple composite form to give names to each of the tuple's values.

The following example shows a simple function that checks the entire parameter and uses single name tuple format:

```
- fun ismybirthday date = (date = (1, "April", 1900));
val ismybirthday = fn : int * string * int -> bool
```

The system response makes explicit the fact that the formal parameter date has an aggregate type with three components.

In the next example, which adds a morning or afternoon indicator to a message, it is necessary to extract the individual elements of the tuple and so the composite form is used; the corresponding domains are shown in Figure 2.3.

```
- fun timestamp (time, message)
      = message ^ (if time < 12
                   then " a.m."
                   else " p.m.");
val timestamp = fn : int * string -> string

- timestamp (8, "important meeting today");
val it = "important meeting today a.m." : string
```

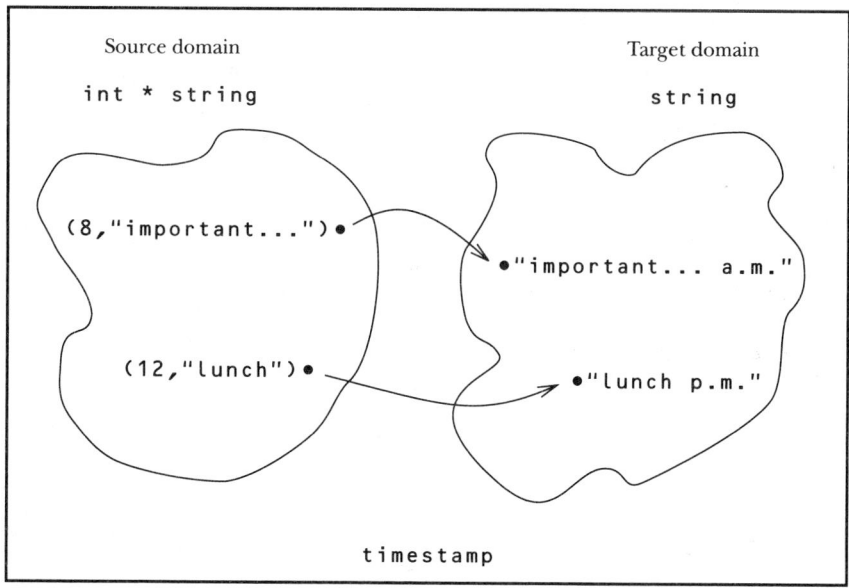

Figure 2.3. Source and target domains for timestamp

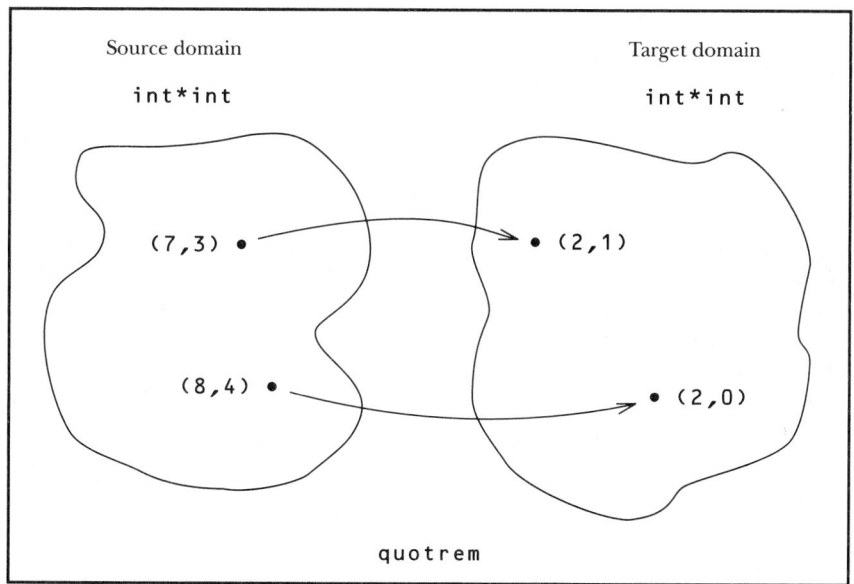

Figure 2.4. Source and target domains for quotrem

2.3.3 *Functions with more than one result*

It is possible for a function to return more than one result because a tuple may also be the target type of a function. This is demonstrated in the following function `quotrem` (and Figure 2.4) whose result holds both the quotient and remainder of dividing the source tuple's first component by its second component:

```
— fun quotrem (x, y)
      = ((x div y), (x mod y));
val quotrem = fn : int * int —> int * int

— quotrem (7, 3);
val it = (2,1) : int * int
```

2.4 *Polymorphic functions*

It can be useful to define functions that provide general operations on tuples regardless of their component types. For example, the functions `fst` and `snd` respectively extract the first item and second item from a pair:

```
— fun fst (x,y) = x;
val fst = fn : 'a * 'b —> 'a

— fun snd (x,y) = y;
val snd = fn : 'a * 'b —> 'b
```

The type of `fst` is different to previously defined functions in that it takes a pair of values of *any* two types and returns a value of the first type. It does not operate on the elements in the pair but on the shape or construction of the pair itself; therefore `fst` does not care about the type of x nor about the type of y. This is indicated by the system response which gives the general purpose type names `'a` and `'b`, which are known as *polytypes*. It should be noted that the actual values of the tuple could be of different types, which is indicated by the two different polytype names. However, because `'a` and `'b` can stand for *any* type the actual components could also be of the same type:

```
— fst (3,4);
val it = 3 : int

— fst (3, ("a", true));
val it = 3 : int;
```

```
— snd (3,("a",true));
val it = ("a",true) : string * bool
```

The above are examples of *polymorphic* functions. In general, a function is said to be polymorphic in the parts of its input which it does not evaluate.[4] Thus, in the above example fst is polymorphic in both x and y whereas in the following example g is only polymorphic in x:

```
— fun g (x,y) = ((if (y>0) then ~y else y),x);
val g = fn: 'a * int —> int * 'a
```

Polymorphic functions need not take a tuple argument. For example, both of the following functions are polymorphic in their argument x:

```
— fun id x = x;
val id = fn: 'a —> 'a
```

```
— fun three x = 3;
val three = fn: 'a —> int
```

Exercise 2.2
What happens in the following application and why?

```
fst (3, 4 div 0)
```

Exercise 2.3
Define a function dup which takes a single element of any type and returns a tuple with the element duplicated.

2.4.1 *Restricted polymorphic functions*

There is a family of functions that are similar to polymorphic functions in that they do not operate on a tuple's elements; they do not use any operations that require knowledge of their types – *except that it must make sense to compare them for equality*. These functions involve the use of the operators = and/or <> and are known as *restricted polymorphic* functions. An example of such a function is all_equal which evaluates to true if all three of its tuple's elements are equal:

---

4. There is, in theory, no restriction on the number of polytypes in the tuple parameter to a function.

```
— fun all_equal (x,y,z)
    = (x = y) andalso (y = z);
val all_equal = fn : ''a * ''a * ''a —>bool
```

A new type `''a` appears in the system response. This indicates that the function will work for any type that can be compared for equality. Note that it will not work for any application where `x`, `y` or `z` are function names, because functions can neither be compared for equality nor for relational ordering.[5]

The concepts of polymorphism, overloading and restricted polymorphism are very similar. The differences are as follows:

1. A polymorphic function does not evaluate its polytype arguments and therefore their types need not be specified in the function definition.

2. An overloaded function (or operator) is defined to work on a small number of specified types; it evaluates its arguments and therefore the types of these arguments must be known.

3. A restricted polymorphic function (or operator) is one that does not evaluate its polytype arguments but may use them in equality tests; the actual parameters used at application time must therefore have types which permit equality testing. These types are called **eqtype**s.

Unlike the operators `=` and `<>`, the other comparison operators (`>`, `<` etc.) are *overloaded*; they are not restricted polymorphic and therefore the following definition fails:

```
— fun wrong_ordered (x, y, z)
    = (x < y) andalso (y < z);
Error: overloaded variable "<" cannot be resolved
```

This failure occurs because SML does not know the types of `x`, `y` and `z`. Section 2.6 shows how to indicate to SML the type of parameters to such overloaded operators.

Exercise 2.4
Evaluate the application `(all_equal (1, 1, 1.0))`.

2.5 *Pattern matching*

One of the more powerful features of SML is *pattern matching*, which allows the format of one value to be compared with a template format (known as a 'pattern'). For

---

5. However, passing functions as parameters to other functions is both legal and very useful, as will be discussed in Chapter 4.

example, the appearance of a tuple composite form as the formal parameter to a function is an instance of pattern matching. Pattern matching is used both in **val** definitions and in function definitions; the former has already been introduced in Section 1.6.2. In this section the principle of pattern matching is extended to enable alternative definitions for a function depending on the format of the actual parameter.

This facility has several advantages:

1. As an alternative to the use of some unwieldy conditional expressions.

2. As a design aid to help the programmer to consider all possible inputs to a function.

3. As an aid to the deconstruction of aggregate types such as tuples, lists and user-defined types (the last two will be introduced in Chapters 3 and 6 respectively).

In most cases it will be seen that the use of pattern matching reduces the risk of programming errors and enhances program readability.

2.5.1 *Alternative patterns*

Pattern matching template

The general template for achieving pattern matching in functions is:

```
fun  function_name  pattern_1  =  function_body_1
|    function_name  pattern_2  =  function_body_2
            .                           .
            .                           .
            .                           .
|    function_name  pattern_N  =  function_body_N
```

The vertical bar | indicates alternative definitions for the function. When the function is applied to an argument, SML sequentially scans the definitions, from the topmost definition, until the actual parameter matches one of the patterns. The associated function body is then evaluated. At its simplest a function will have only one pattern. Since a formal parameter is an instance of a pattern (as is a constant value) all the function definitions so far presented are also examples of this form.

Eliminating explicit conditionals

SML allows choices to be made by using the **if .. then .. else** construct or by using pattern matching. The following two versions of the built-in function `not` (which inverts the truth value of its parameter) are equivalent.

Conditional version:

```
— fun not x
      = if x = true
        then false
        else true;

val not = fn : bool —> bool
```

Pattern matching version:

```
— fun not true = false
  |   not false = true;

val not = fn : bool —> bool
```

The benefits of pattern matching become clearer when more than two possibilities are to be considered. The pattern matching approach is generally concise and readable, whilst the conditional approach often requires a nested **if .. then .. else** and is consequently less easy to read and to modify. The next example translates a string representing a day of the week to an associated activity.

Conditional version:

```
fun SolomonGrundy day
      = if day = "Monday"
        then "Born"
        else if day = "Sunday"
             then "Buried"
             else "Did something else"
```

Pattern matching version:

```
fun SolomonGrundy "Monday" = "Born"
  |   SolomonGrundy "Sunday" = "Buried"
  |   SolomonGrundy  anyday  = "Did something else"
```

In this example, the anyday pattern will match any other input and will therefore act as a default case. Notice that this default must be the bottommost definition (see Section 2.5.3).

Exercise 2.5
Modify both versions of the function SolomonGrundy so that Thursday and Friday may be treated with special significance.

2.5.2 *Legal patterns*

Patterns may consist of constants (e.g. integers or the Boolean values `true` and `false`), tuples and formal parameter names. Patterns containing arithmetic, relational or logical expressions are not allowed. Thus, the following are both wrong:

```
fun wrong (x = y) = "silly"

fun also_wrong ("a" ^ anystring) = "starts with a"
```

No duplicates

A less obvious constraint is demonstrated by the following, intuitive but unsuccessful, attempt at defining the function `equal`. This definition is appealing in that it avoids any conditional testing and only uses pattern matching:

```
fun wrong_equal (x,x) = true
|   wrong_equal (x,y) = false
```

Unfortunately the definition will fail on the first line, as the formal parameter `x` appears twice, giving rise to the error message:

```
Error: duplicate variable in pattern(s): x
```

A formal parameter pattern may contain duplicated constant values but not duplicated names. Hence the following is legal:

```
fun both_zero (0,0) = true
|   both_zero (x,y) = false
```

Non exhaustive patterns

In the above `not` function, both possible values for the Boolean type were checked. However, if SML can detect that an option has not been considered it will generate a system warning. The function can still be applied but may generate a run-time error.

```
— fun not false = true;

Warning: match not exhaustive false => . . .
val not = fn : bool —> bool

— not false;
val it = true : bool
```

```
— not true;
uncaught exception Match
```

More often than not, the SML system warning will come as a surprise and serve to remind the programmer of a pattern that has been forgotten. Some programmers may be tempted to ignore this warning if they think they know that a particular pattern will never arise. However, it is sensible to trap the unexpected cases with an appropriate 'default' pattern. For example, if all of the days of the week were catered for as patterns in the second version of the SolomonGrundy function, it might still be desirable to have a final pattern that dealt with any string which did not represent a day of the week.[6]

Pattern matching with wild cards

Sometimes it can be tedious to think of names for function parameters that are never used. SML allows the substitution of the *wild card* symbol _ for one or more parameter names. Thus the function fst could also have been written:

```
fun fst (x,_) = x
```

This saves the bother of naming the y which is not used in the function body. Similarly the function or could be written with explicit matching or with wild cards substituting for both x and y as demonstrated by the following three equivalent definitions:

```
fun or1 (false,false) = false
|   or1 (x,y)         = true

fun or2 (false,false) = false
|   or2 (_,_)         = true

fun or3 (false,false) = false
|   or3 _             = true
```

However, it is not legal to use _ in a function body. Indeed, _ is often used in a pattern to emphasize the fact that the corresponding formal parameter is not used in the function body.

2.5.3 Order of evaluation

It must be stressed that SML checks each alternative sequentially from the top pattern to the bottom pattern, ceasing evaluation at the first successful match. If the patterns are mutually exclusive then it does not matter in which order they are

6. See Section 2.9 for how this pattern may be dealt with by the SML **exception** mechanism.

defined. However, patterns often overlap and then the order of definition is *vital*, as is now shown:

```
fun wrong_or x              = true
 |   wrong_or (false,false) = false

- wrong_or (false,false);
val it = true : bool
```

The guideline for designing functions with overlapping alternative patterns is to arrange the patterns such that the more specific cases appear first. In the above example (false,false) was less general than x and should have been the first pattern to be matched against. This, of course, is also true for wild cards.

2.6   Type information

This section shows that it is not always possible for SML to distinguish the types of formal parameters and introduces some tools for interaction with the SML type system.

2.6.1   Type ambiguity

For all the correctly defined functions so far, the SML system has been able to work out the types of the function parameters from their context. For example, the parameters to the function quotrem (Section 2.3.3) must have integer values because the built-in functions div and mod are defined to operate on integers. Similarly the following definition for decrement:

```
fun decrement x = x - 1
```

succeeds because the constant 1 appears in the function body, thereby forcing SML to make the overloaded subtraction operator expect an integer value for the formal parameter x. However, the following attempt at defining square fails since * is overloaded; x could be either an integer or a real number and there is no information to indicate which type was intended.

```
- fun wrong_square x = x * x;

Error: overloaded variable "*" cannot be resolved
```

This kind of ambiguity can be resolved by adding *explicit* type information to the function definition.

Resolving source type ambiguity

The type of any parameter can be indicated by following the parameter with a colon and the desired type and bracketing the entire expression. Thus, the ambiguity of wrong_square can be resolved by introducing a *type constraint* in the following manner:

```
fun square (x :int) = x * x
```

The source type constraint for a formal parameter need only appear once in a function definition, regardless of the number of patterns in the definition. It may, of course, be necessary to resolve the ambiguity of more than one overloaded operator:

```
fun squares ((x, y) :(real * int)) = (x * x, y * y)

fun twices ((x :int), y) = (x + x, y * 2)
```

It is also possible to state the type of a formal parameter by placing type constraints inside expressions in the function body. Thus, equivalent definitions of square are:

```
fun square x = (x :int) * x

fun square x = x * (x :int)
```

Stating target type

It is possible to inform SML of the intended result type of a function. There are two alternative approaches:

1. By following the formal parameter with a colon and type name *without* the surrounding brackets:

    ```
    fun abstwice x :real = abs (x + x)
    ```

2. By following the function body with a colon and a type name:

    ```
    fun abstwice x = abs (x + x) :real
    ```

The above definitions declare abstwice to evaluate to a real number – even though abs is able to return either a real or an int depending on the type of its argument.

Notice that with this second approach there is an implicit bracketing of the entire function body, so that the following two examples are equivalent:

```
fun square x = x * x :real

fun square x = (x * x) :real
```

By contrast, the example below specifies the type of the parameter x:

```
fun square x = x * (x :real)
```

Stating source and target types

Explicit type constraints for both source and target types can be combined. The second of the above two methods for constraining the target type is recommended and this provides the good convention that source types are always indicated on the left-hand side of a function definition, whilst target types are always indicated on the right-hand side of a function definition. Thus, the recommended format is:

> **fun** *function_name* (*parameter_name* : *parameter_type*)
> = *function body* : *target_type*

For example:

```
fun hypotenuse ((x, y) :int * int)
    = sqrt (real ((x * x) + (y * y))) :real
```

Of course, the *parameter_type* and *target_type* may both be omitted in circumstances where the SML system can infer the type.

A further use of type constraints is in the definition of **val** names, where the type of the name can be explicitly given on either the left-hand side or the right-hand side, as follows:

```
val (z :int) = x + y

val z = (x + y) :int
```

Polymorphic type constraint

A polytype may also be included as a type constraint.[7] The functions `third_same` and `third_any` are two versions of the same function which exemplify this property. In the first version the use of the same polytypes constrains the actual parameters to be of the same type: the second version uses different polytypes to permit actual parameters to be of different types.

---

7. This book uses single lower-case characters, preceded by a quote mark. However, a type variable can be any legal name preceded by a single quote.

Same type version:

```
— fun third_same ((x,y,z) :'a * 'a * 'a) = z :'a;
val third_same = fn : 'a * 'a * 'a —> 'a

— third_same (1,2,3);
val it = 3 : int

— third_same (1,2,3.0);

Error: operator and operand don't agree (tycon mismatch)
   operator domain: int * int * int
   operand:         int * int * real
   in expression: third_same (1,2,3.0)
```

Any type version:

```
— fun third_any ((x,y,z) :'a * 'b * 'c) = z :'c;
val third_any = fn : 'a * 'b * 'c —> 'c

— third_any (1,2,3);
val it = 3 : int

— third_any (1,2.0,true);
val it = true : bool
```

There is no way to constrain the parameters to have *different* polytypes.

Exercise 2.6
Define a function intmax which takes an integer pair and returns the greater of its two components.

2.6.2   Guidelines for type constraints

Though the SML system can often deduce the types of formal parameters it is best to make this information explicit. This serves a threefold purpose:

1.   As a design aid, since the program designer is forced to consider the nature of the input and output before actually implementing any algorithm.

2.   As a documentation aid, since any programmer can immediately see the source and target types of each function.

3.   As a debugging aid, since SML will indicate differences between inferred types and declared types.

There are two approaches that can be taken to make this information explicit:

1. Preceding all function definitions with a comment to indicate the types of their source and target. This should be a minimum requirement for any program documentation.

2. Making the type information explicit in a function pattern and/or corresponding body. As seen, this approach is *essential* where SML does not have adequate information (for example in the `square` function). Notice that this is the approach that is often used for debugging, since it provides an interaction with the type system – the programmer states the type that an expression should have and the type system reports the inferred type if that is different.

Whilst some of the examples in the rest of this book do not contain explicit type constraints (for pedagogic reasons of simplicity and clarity), the second approach is encouraged as being a good programming discipline and all the extended examples will adopt this style.

2.6.3 *Type synonyms*

As a further aid to program documentation SML allows a type to be given a name. For example the tuple `(13, "March", 1066)` has the type `int * string * int`. For clarity this type could be given the name `DATE` as follows:

```
type DATE = int * string * int
```

If a value is constrained with the type name `DATE` then SML will respond with the name rather than the underlying types:

```
— val mybirthday = (1, "April", 1900) :DATE;
val mybirthday = (1,"April",1900) : DATE
```

However, for all other purposes the value `mybirthday` will be treated as an `int * string * int` aggregate type. The keyword **type** introduces a type synonym.[8] *It does not introduce a new type.* Thus values of type `DATE` and type `int * string * int` can be compared and otherwise mixed, *unlike* the strong type discipline imposed, for instance, between `int`s and `real`s. Thus, the following is legal:

```
— val abirthday = (1, "April", 1900);
val abirthday = (1,"April",1900) : int * string * int

— mybirthday = abirthday;
val it = true : bool
```

8. Sometimes known as a 'type abbreviation'.

Polymorphic type synonyms

It is also legal to have **type** synonyms that are wholly or partially comprised of polytypes. If a polytype appears on the right-hand of a declaration then it must also appear on the left-hand between the keyword **type** and the new name. For example the following type `P_TRIPLE` can be declared to be a triple of any type such as integers or real numbers by defining it as a polytype:

```
type 'a P_TRIPLE = ('a * 'a * 'a)
```

An alternative and more general type synonym would be:

```
type ('a,'b,'c) GP_TRIPLE = ('a * 'b * 'c)
```

This is more general than the first version because it does not require all the elements of the three-tuple to have the same type. The type synonym can then be used in functions as follows:

```
fun third ((x,y,z) :'a P_TRIPLE) = z :'a
```

or

```
fun third ((x,y,z) :('a,'b,'c) GP_TRIPLE) = z :'c
```

Polytypes and base types can also be declared in conjunction, with similar usage:

```
type 'a MIX2 = 'a * int
```

2.7   Simple recursive functions

SML, like other functional programming languages, uses *recursion* as its main iteration control structure; this general mechanism can achieve the same effect as the imperative language features such as 'while', 'repeat' and 'for' loops.[9] A recursive function definition is one where the name of the function being defined appears inside the function body. When the function is applied to an argument, an appearance of the function name in the function body causes a new copy of the function to be generated and then applied to a new argument. If the function name appears as part of an expression then the evaluation of the expression is suspended until the recursive function application returns a value.

---

9. See also Chapter 4.

Recursion is a very powerful and general mechanism which must be used carefully. At its simplest, it can be used to generate an infinite number of applications of the same function, for example:

```
fun loop_forever () = loop_forever ()
```

If this function[10] is ever evaluated, it will loop for ever, calling itself again and again and achieving nothing. The function loop_forever could also be defined to take an argument, but is equally useless:

```
fun loop_forever x = loop_forever x
```

Evaluating this function by hand shows that whenever loop_forever is applied to the message "BUY US A DRINK" it immediately invokes another *copy* of the function loop_forever and applies it to another *copy* of the message.

```
loop_forever "BUY US A DRINK"
== loop_forever "BUY US A DRINK"
== loop_forever "BUY US A DRINK"
== loop_forever "BUY US A DRINK"
. . .
```

To create a more useful recursive function definition, it is necessary to ensure that there is some *terminating condition* for the function and also that the recursive calls are successively applied to arguments that *converge* towards the terminating condition.

A number of recursive styles can be identified which achieve the above criteria, the rest of this section shows the most common simple recursive styles: *stack* and *accumulative* recursion.

2.7.1 Stack recursive functions

The following function printdots is an example of the recursive style known as *stack* recursion. This function prints the number of dots indicated by its parameter. Firstly, there is a terminating pattern 0. Secondly, each recursive application of printdots is to a *different* n. Thirdly, each successive n decreases towards the terminating pattern 0:

```
- fun printdots (0 :int) = "" :string
  |   printdots n        = "." ^ (printdots (n - 1));
val printdots = fn : int -> string
```

10. Notice that it is *not* possible to have a recursive **val** definition such as (val loop = loop); this would give rise to an error unless loop had previously been defined. In general, **val** definitions cannot be recursive (see Appendix B for a counter-example using the reserved name **rec**).

A hand evaluation reveals:

```
printdots 3
== "." ^ (printdots (3 - 1))
== "." ^ (printdots 2)
== "." ^ ("." ^ (printdots (2 - 1)))
== "." ^ ("." ^ ("." ^ (printdots 1)))
== "." ^ ("." ^ ("." ^ (printdots (1 - 1))))
== "." ^ ("." ^ ("." ^ (printdots 0)))
== "." ^ ("." ^ ("." ^ ("")))
== "." ^ ("." ^ ("." ^ ""))
== "." ^ ("." ^ ".")
== "." ^ ("..")
== "..."
```

This hand evaluation illustrates the appropriateness of the name *stack recursion*; the arguments of all the calculations being *stacked* (rather like a stack of playing cards) until the terminating pattern is met.

Exercise 2.7
Define a recursive function to add up all the integers from 1 to a given upper limit.

2.7.2   *Accumulative recursive functions*

An alternative style of recursive function is now shown. The following example p l u s exploits the fact that two positive numbers can be added by successively incrementing one of them and decrementing the other until it reaches zero:

```
- fun plus ((x,0) :int * int) = x :int
  |   plus (x,y)               = plus (x + 1, y - 1);

val plus = fn : int * int -> int
```

Hand evaluating the application of p l u s to the tuple (2,3) gives:

```
plus (2,3)
== plus (2 + 1,3 - 1)
== plus (3,2)
== plus (3 + 1,2 - 1)
== plus (4,1)
```

```
== plus (4 + 1,1 - 1)
== plus (5,0)
== 5
```

This function also meets the fundamental requirements of having a terminating condition and a convergent action. The terminating condition is met in the first pattern, which if matched halts the recursion and gives the result. The convergent action is satisfied by the body of the second pattern which will eventually decrement y towards the first pattern's terminating condition. It can be seen that the name *accumulative* is appropriate in that one of the component arguments is used as an *accumulator* to gather the final result.

Exercise 2.8
Write printdots in an accumulative recursive style. This will require more than one function – remember that functions must be defined before they can be applied.

Exercise 2.9
Write the function plus in a stack recursive style.

2.8 Who needs variables?

Imperative programming languages use a memory-store model with 'variables' whose names refer to memory locations. Central to the imperative style is the action of changing the values held in these variables (hence their name), yet this mechanism seems absent in the functional style.

If a purely functional subset of SML is used, there is *no assignment operator*. Furthermore, function arguments are always passed *by value* (rather than by reference) and so a function cannot change the value of its argument. Finally, although it is possible to redefine the value associated with a name, all definitions use *static* (rather than dynamic) binding and so all previous definitions will still refer to the old value and only new definitions will refer to the new value. In fact, *functional languages do not have variables*. To those who have some experience of programming in an imperative language, this may come as a shock.

In order to explain why variables are not necessary in a functional language, it is worthwhile analysing their role in imperative programs:

1. To store input and output values.

2. To control iteration.

3. To store the results of intermediate calculations.

4. To store a history of intermediate results (known as 'state' information).

All of the above imply the need to consider the nature of data storage. In functional languages, it is not necessary to think in terms of data storage locations and so it is correspondingly unnecessary to think in terms of variables or the alteration of the contents of data storage locations. The role taken by variables is either provided transparently by the SML system or is a natural consequence of the recursive style of programming:

1. Input to a program appears as the actual parameter to its topmost function and output from the program is the result of the topmost function application. The allocation of storage locations to hold these values is automatically managed by the system and the output of the topmost function application is printed to the screen without the programmer having to specify this action.

2. Iteration control is provided by recursion, the number of iterative steps being controlled by the value of the initial argument.

3. The results of intermediate calculations need not be stored (although a result can be 'remembered' as a **val** definition for later use). The automatic storage allocation mechanism of SML hides store allocation and de-allocation from the programmer, as seen in the following comparison of the imperative and functional treatments of the function swap:

An ANSI C definition of swap is:

```
void swap(int *xp, int *yp) {
        int t;

        t = *xp;
        *xp = *yp;
        *yp = t;
}
```

An alternative imperative approach is to pass the two integers as an aggregate type, for example:

```
typedef struct {
        int x;
        int y;
} PAIR;

PAIR swap(PAIR arg) {
        PAIR result;

        result.x = arg.y;
        result.y = arg.x;
        return result;
}
```

For both imperative approaches it is necessary to allocate a specific storage variable – either to hold a temporary (intermediate) value or to hold the result. By contrast, the SML approach is much simpler:

```
fun swap (x,y) = (y,x)
```

4. The storage of state information is also dealt with automatically by a functional language implementation. For example, the accumulative recursive style 'remembers' the changing state of values from one recursive application to the next by means of the 'accumulative' parameter.

Program control

It is worth noting that the three classic program control structures of imperative programming languages are also available to the functional programmer:

1. Iteration: by means of recursion.

2. Selection: by means of the conditional expression and/or pattern matching.

3. Sequencing: by means of the nesting of function applications.

2.9 Exceptions and error messages

Some functions may not have a sensible result for all of their possible argument values. For example, if the built-in function div is applied with a zero denominator then it will terminate with the error message:

```
uncaught exception Div
```

A function which has no defined result for one or more of its input values is known as a *partial function*: as illustrated in Figure 2.5.

It is often the case that a programmer will need to define a partial function. For example, the function printdots (given in Section 2.7.1) should produce an error if applied to a value of n which is less than zero. Unfortunately, in the current definition the parameter of recursion, n, will never converge to its terminating condition if it is initially negative. There are three options available to the SML programmer to handle this situation:

1. Impose a dummy answer. A negative number of dots is clearly meaningless but could be dealt with by indicating that negative values generate no dots.

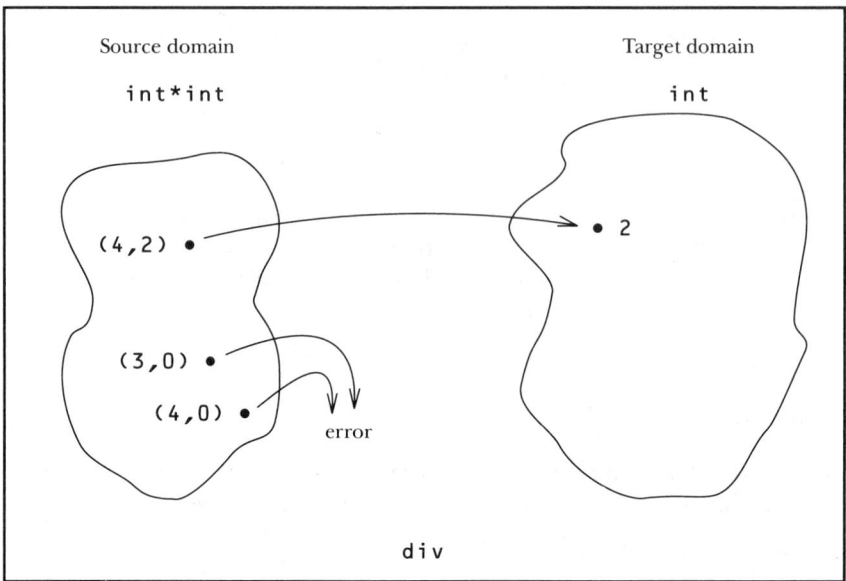

Figure 2.5. Source and target domains for the partial function **div**

2. Ignore it and let the SML system recurse for ever or generate some not very helpful error message such as:

```
Warning: can't increase heap
Ran out of memory
```

Unfortunately this will not necessarily pinpoint which function has failed inside a complex expression or program.

3. Force the SML system to give a more meaningful message by stating which function has failed.

This last option can be achieved using the keywords **raise** and **exception** as follows:

```
- exception Printdots;
exception Printdots

- fun printdots (0 :int) = "" :string
|    printdots n
     = if n < 0
       then raise Printdots
       else "." ^ (printdots (n - 1));
val printdots = fn : int -> string
```

```
- printdots ~1;
uncaught exception Printdots
```

The choice of name for the **exception** is somewhat arbitrary; this text uses the New Jersey convention that the **exception** is called by the same name as the function that **raise**s it, with its first letter in upper case. However, it is necessary to declare the exception name *before* it is **raise**d, in accordance with the SML practice of always defining something before using it.

Exercise 2.10
Write the function i n t e g e r _ d i v i d e without using the SML divide operators.

2.10 *Programming with functions*

This section shows the design of a small program to convert an integer to a string value. This mirrors the function makestring for integers, though it must be noted that due to SML's strong type system it is not possible for the user to write a program to convert both integers and real numbers. The design of this program is presented in a *top-down* manner. This technique is known as top-down design because each step, except the final step, assumes the existence of functions defined at a later step. Unfortunately, SML cannot reflect this top-down organization because it requires a function to be defined before it is used.[11] Hence, it is necessary to enter the functions in the reverse sequence to that in which they are printed in this section.

Specification

The program will take an integer as its parameter and will evaluate to a string. The string will be a denary representation of the integer; for a negative integer the string will start with the tilde character.

Design

Firstly, the sign of the input integer is determined and dealt with. Secondly, a function to process positive integers is developed. This breaks its input into two parts; an integer less than 10 (which can be represented as a single character) together with an integer greater than 10 which requires exactly the same processing.

---

11. Chapters 5 and 7 show ways to put together functions in a manner that more closely reflects their dependencies.

Implementation

Step 1:   Converting any integer to a string

Assuming that a positive number can be represented as a string, then a negative number can also be represented by taking its absolute value (using **abs**) and preceding the string representation by a ~ character. This description converts directly to the SML code for a top-level function `int_to_string` which will translate an integer value to a string value:

```
fun int_to_string (n :int)
    = if n < 0
        then    "~" ^ pos_to_string (abs n)
        else           pos_to_string n :string
```

Step 2:   Converting a positive integer to a string

The next stage of the design is to define `pos_to_string` to convert a positive integer to a string. Since only integers less than 10 have a single character ASCII representation, the integer to be converted must either be less than 10 (the terminating condition of the function) or requires further processing.

The integer must be split into two parts; the least significant digit (which can be obtained using **mod**) and the integer without its least significant digit (which can be obtained using **div**). At each step the least significant digit must be converted to a single character string using the function `int_to_char`. The rest of the integer forms the parameter to another application of `pos_to_string`. At each successive application the parameter will reduce and eventually converge to a number less than 10.

Because individual digits are discovered in the reverse order to that which they must appear, it is necessary to concatenate them on the right of any recursive application of `pos_to_string`.

This description leads directly to the following SML code:

```
fun pos_to_string (n :int)
    = if   n < 10
        then    int_to_char n
        else    pos_to_string (n div 10)
                ^ int_to_char (n mod 10) :string
```

Step 3:   Converting an integer less than 10 to a string

The code for this function is based on the same rationale as for the function **toupper** shown in Section 2.1 and should be self-explanatory:

```
fun int_to_char (n :int) = chr (n + ord "0") :string
```

Note that int_to_char is presented as a separate function because it is concerned with type *conversion* whilst pos_to_string has an *iterative* purpose.

Putting it all together

As stated before, it is necessary to enter the functions in the following sequence:

```
int_to_char
pos_to_string
int_to_string
```

One function per function

It must be stressed that each function in the above program has a single purpose. This recommended method allows *easier testing* and *easier modification* of individual parts of the program.

2.11 Summary

This chapter has discussed the definition and use of functions. Functions may have zero, one or more input parameters, with *tuples* being used to collect together multiple parameters. An alternative style that does not need tuples is discussed in Chapter 4.

There are many choices available to the designer of functions, including the following:

1. The types of the function parameters – this includes the choice of which types may be used, whether they are monomorphic or *polymorphic* and whether the function is defined for all input values.

    Functions may either be monomorphic, which means that their definition absolutely specifies the required types of the input data, or they may be polymorphic, whereby the actual types of the input data may be different for different applications of the function. Polymorphic function definitions are an important extension to the strong type system introduced in Chapter 1. Functions that are only defined for some values of their input parameter are known as *partial functions*; if they are applied to an argument for which they have no definition, the programmer may signify that the program should terminate immediately with an error message.

2. The use of recursion as a general-purpose control structure.

    The mechanism of *recursion* has been shown to provide the iterative control structures of imperative programming languages (such as 'for loops' and 'while' loops). Recursive function definition is of fundamental importance to programming in SML and in this chapter the two most common forms of recursion (*stack* and *accumulative*) have been introduced. The nature of recursive definitions is further explored in Chapters 3 and 4.

3. The use of the pattern matching style of definition.

The technique of *pattern matching* may be used when defining functions; this has many advantages, including the elimination of conditional expressions and providing a way to ensure that a programmer gives consideration to all of the possible inputs to a function.

3 · Lists

As has been shown in previous chapters, data items of types such as `int` and `bool` can only hold one data value at a time. In order to collect more than one value, *tuples* and *strings* can be used; these are known as aggregate data types. However, since they are not recursive by nature, it is not easy to manipulate data items of these types in a recursive manner. The `list` data type is introduced in this chapter as a powerful aggregate data type which is recursively defined and is used to hold many values of a single type. Built-in functions are introduced to construct and deconstruct data items of this new type.

Functions which manipulate lists are naturally recursive. This chapter provides guidelines for the design of such functions using the techniques of case analysis and structural induction; case analysis ensures that the programmer considers all possible inputs to a function, whereas structural induction is a powerful tool for developing recursive algorithms.

Recursive function definition is of such fundamental importance to the manipulation of the list data structure that the general technique is analysed further and five common modes of recursion over lists are discussed. The chapter ends with a detailed example of program design utilizing the above techniques; the program *grep*, a textual search utility, which will be used as an extended example throughout the rest of the book.

3.1 The list aggregate type

Aggregate types

It is often necessary to represent many items of data that are related in some way and it is useful to have a single name to refer to all of these related items. Any data type that allows more than one item of data to be referenced by a single name is called an *aggregate type* or a *data structure*, since the items are represented in a structured and orderly manner.

It is clear that objects of the base types `bool`, `int` or `real` have one value and are not aggregate types. One example of an aggregate type is the tuple, which allows a fixed number of data items to be represented by a single name. This chapter introduces the `list` aggregate type, which is of particular interest to functional language programmers because it is *recursively defined* and may be easily manipulated by recursive functions.

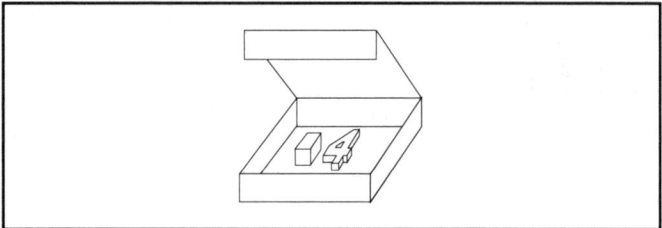

Figure 3.1. Box containing empty box and the data item 4

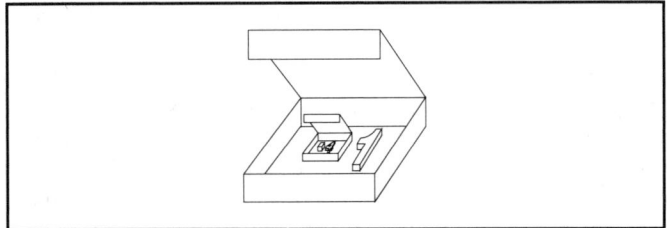

Figure 3.2. Box containing the data item 1 and another box

Lists

The important concept of the list data structure is analogous to a collection of nested boxes. There is a central ('empty') box which may be surrounded by a slightly larger box, which in turn may be surrounded by another box, and so on. The central box contains nothing and cannot be opened, whereas all other boxes contain a data item and another nested-box structure (see Figure 3.1). To inspect the first item in this data structure, it is necessary to open the outermost box – inside will be the first data item and a smaller box (the rest of the data structure). In order to inspect the second item in the list it is necessary to do two things – first open the outermost box, then open the box that is found inside. At that point, the second data item in the list is available, together with a smaller box representing the remainder of the data structure (see Figure 3.2).

In order to use such a data structure, the following operations must be provided by the language:

1. A way to construct a new structure (that is, the ability to put things inside a new box).

2. A way to deconstruct an existing structure (that is, the ability to 'open a box').

3. A way to recognize the empty box so that there will be no attempt to deconstruct it (which would be an error because it contains nothing).

The following discussion of SML lists will first present the notation used and then explain how these three operations may be performed.

3.1.1 *List syntax*

From the above analogy it should be clear that the list data structure is naturally recursive in its definition. Informally, an SML list may be defined either as being empty or containing one element together with a list (which itself is empty or consists of an element of the same type as the previous element together with a list (which itself is empty or consists of an element of the same type as the previous element together with . . . and so on . . .)).

From the above a more formal, recursive definition of a list may now be derived:

> *A list is either:*
> *empty*
> *or:*
> *an element of a given type together with*
> *a list of elements of the same type*

There are two notations that SML uses to represent lists: an *aggregate* format and a *constructed* format. The aggregate format is introduced below, whereas the constructed format is presented in Section 3.2.

The empty list is represented in aggregate format by the characters []; this corresponds to the 'empty box' which cannot be opened.

```
— [];
val it = [] : 'a list
```

For lists with one or more elements, the empty box is implicit in the aggregate format and only the data items are given explicitly. For example, a box which contains the integer 1 together with the empty box is represented by the aggregate format [1]. Further examples follow:

```
— [1,2];
val it = [1,2] : int list

— ["Standard","Meta","Language"];
val it = ["Standard","Meta","Language"] : string list

— [(1,2),(3,1)];
val it = [(1,2),(3,1)] : (int * int) list

— [[1],[2,2,2]];
val it = [[1],[2,2,2]] : int list list
```

Illegal lists

All the elements of a list *must* have the same type; the SML system will detect any attempt to define a list of mixed types. All of the following examples are therefore illegal. In each case the first element of the list is an integer and so the SML type checker expects all the other elements of the list to be integers as well:

```
— val wrong1 = [1,"1"];
Error: operator and operand don't agree (tycon mismatch)
  operator domain: int * int list
  operand:         int * string list
  in expression: 1 :: "1" :: nil

— val wrong2 = [1,[1]];
Error: operator and operand don't agree (tycon mismatch)
  operator domain: int * int list
  operand:         int * int list list
  in expression: :: 1 :: (1 :: nil) :: nil

— val wrong3 = [1,(1,1)];
Error: operator and operand don't agree (tycon mismatch)
  operator domain: int * int list
  operand:         int * (int * int) list
  in expression: 1 :: (1,1) :: nil

— val wrong4 = [1,[]];
Error: operator and operand don't agree (tycon mismatch)
  operator domain: int * int list
  operand:         int * 'Z list list
  in expression: 1 :: nil :: nil
```

3.1.2 *The empty list – nil*

The empty list may either be represented in aggregate format by the characters [] or by the name nil; these two representations are equivalent and interchangeable.

Recursive functions which operate on lists will successively deconstruct each smaller 'box' in the list structure and will converge on the empty list nil. However, it is important that such a function should not attempt to deconstruct nil since this would give an error.

The value nil is used as the starting point for constructing a list of any type; thus, nil must have the polytype 'a list. For example, when nil is used to create a list of integers it adopts the type int list, but when it is used to create a list of Booleans it adopts the type bool list. Notice that nil is a data item which can itself appear in lists: both of the following values have type 'a list list:

```
— [ [], [], [] ];
val it = [[],[],[]] : 'a list list

— [[]];
val it = [ [] ] : 'a list list
```

3.2 *Built-in operations on lists*

SML provides a number of built-in operations for list manipulation, including those for list construction and deconstruction. An empty list can simply be created by giving a name to the empty list constant nil. Other lists can be created by combining an item with an existing list using the special list constructor :: or by combining a list with another list using the built-in operator @. Typically, two functions are also provided for list deconstruction: hd and tl. The former takes a list and returns its first element; the latter takes a list and returns the list without the first element. A number of other list manipulating functions (such as extracting the nth item of a list or finding its length) may also be provided as built-in functions. However, they could easily be written by the programmer, as will be seen later in this chapter.

3.2.1 *List construction* – ::

Apart from nil, the only list operator that is actually required is the polymorphic operator :: (pronounced 'cons') which *prepends an item to an existing list of the same type as that item*. To use the nested-box analogy, :: takes a data item and a box and puts both into a bigger box; this creates a new list. The type constraint is important – the second argument must either be empty or contain items of the same type as the first argument. A list of one item can be created from a single item and nil because nil is a polytype list and so can be combined with an item of any type. The type of :: is therefore:

```
'a * 'a list -> 'a list
```

Example session:

```
- val alist = "a" :: nil;
val alist = ["a"] : string list

- val blist = "fed" :: "cb" :: alist;
val blist = ["fed","cb","a"] : string list

- val clist = "C" :: ["c", "c", "c"];
val clist = ["C","c","c","c"] : string list

- val dlist = "d" :: "dd" :: "d" :: nil;
val dlist = ["d","dd","d"] : string list

- val (front :: rest) = [3, 2, 1];
val front = 3 : int
val rest = [2, 1] : int list
```

The use of :: provides the list in its constructed format though the system responds by giving the list in its aggregate format.

The last command in the above session is similar to that of tuple matching shown in Chapter 1. The use of :: in this manner is possible because it is not a normal function or operator but is a special form of what is known as a *constructor*. It is not concerned with manipulating the values of its arguments but with constructing a new list. *One of the most important properties of constructors is that they provide a unique representation for each value of an aggregate type.* Thus, a new list can be constructed – and so deconstructed – in only one way. In the above example, the only possible value for front is the integer 3 and the only possible value for rest is the integer list [2,1].

The operator :: is also different from other operators so far seen in that it associates to the right; that is (1 :: 2 :: nil) is really (1 :: (2 :: nil)). If :: associated to the left giving ((1 :: 2) :: nil), then the construction (1 :: 2) would fail because 2 is not a list.

List construction abuse

The following examples demonstrate common mistakes. The first example is wrong in that the integer 1 is being *cons*ed to a list whose items are strings (whereas SML expects the items to be integers, to be consistent with the first argument to ::). In the second example the first argument to :: is a list of type integer and therefore SML expects the second argument to be a list whose items are themselves lists of integers. An error occurs because the second argument is in fact a list whose items are integers. The third example has a similar error in that the integer 1 is expected to be prepended to a list of integers whereas the second argument is an integer and not a list:

```
— val wrong_x = 1 :: ["a","bcd"];
Error: operator and operand don't agree (tycon mismatch)
   operator domain: int * int list
   operand:         int * string list
   in expression: :: (1,"a" :: "bcd" :: nil)

— val wrong_y = [1] :: [2,3];
Error: operator and operand don't agree (tycon mismatch)
   operator domain: int list * int list list
   operand:         int list * int list
   in expression: :: (1 :: nil, 2 :: 3 :: nil)

— val wrong_z = 1 :: 2;
Error: operator and operand don't agree (tycon mismatch)
   operator domain: int * int list
   operand:         int * int
   in expression: :: (1,2)
```

Exercise 3.1
Give the two possible correct versions of wrong_y.

Exercise 3.2
Which of the following are legal list constructions?

```
val list1 = 1 :: []
val list2 = 1 :: [] :: []
val list3 = 1 :: [1]
val list4 = [] :: [1]
val list5 = [1] :: [1] :: []
```

@ – *append*

SML provides another polymorphic list operator @ (pronounced 'append'). This takes two lists of the same type and concatenates them to create a new list of the same type. The terminating nil value of the first list is discarded. The type of @ is therefore:

```
'a list * 'a list -> 'a list
```

Sample session:

```
- [1] @ [2,3];
val it = [1,2,3] : int list

- [] @ [1];
val it = [1] : int list

- [] @ [];
val it = [] : 'a list

- 1 @ [2,3];
Error: operator and operand don't agree (tycon mismatch)
   operator domain: 'Z list * 'Z list
   operand:         int * int list
   in expression: @ (1,2 :: 3 :: nil)
```

Properties of @

Two properties of @ are worth noting:

1. The operator @ could associate from the left or from the right and produce the same result. An advantage here is that expressions involving @ do not require bracketing.

2. The operator @ is not a constructor because it cannot provide a unique representation for a list. This is demonstrated by the fact that the comparison:

```
["A","A"] = front @ rest
```

could be satisfied by both front and back having the values ["A"] or by one of them having the value nil and the other having the value ["A","A"].

Theoretically @ is unnecessary since it can be defined in terms of :: (as shown in Section 3.7.2). Nevertheless it is provided as a built-in operator because it is such a frequent programming requirement.

3.2.2 List deconstruction

Many SML implementations provide two polymorphic functions to extract items from a list, called hd and tl. Where they are not provided, they may easily be defined as shown in Section 3.4.

The function hd (pronounced 'head') operates on a list to select its first element (that is, it 'opens the box' and extracts the data item). The type of hd is therefore:

```
'a list -> 'a
```

Examples:

```
- hd [1];
val it = 1 : int

- hd [1,2,3,4];
val it = 1 : int

- hd ["Schoenfinkel","male","mathematician"];
val it = "Schoenfinkel" : string

- hd [[1,2,3],[8,9]];
val it = [1,2,3] : int list

- hd [(1,2),(7,~1),(0,0)];
val it = (1,2) : int * int
```

The function tl (pronounced 'tail') is complementary to hd in that it operates on a list to yield that list with its first element removed (that is, it 'opens the box' and extracts the inner box). The type of tl is therefore:

```
'a list -> 'a list
```

Thus, if tl is applied to an int list then it will return an int list (even if the resulting list is nil).

Examples:

```
- tl [1];
val it = [] : int list

- tl [1,2,3,4];
val it = [2,3,4] : int list

- tl ["Schoenfinkel","male","mathematician"];
val it = ["male","mathematician"] : string list

- tl [[1,2,3],[8,9]];
val it = [[8,9]] : int list list

- tl [(1,2),(7,~1),(0,0)];
val it = [(7,~1),(0,0)] : (int * int) list
```

The relationship between hd, tl and ::

Both hd and tl give rise to errors when applied to empty lists:

```
- hd [];
uncaught exception Hd

- tl [];
uncaught exception Tl
```

Thus, when programming with lists, it is necessary to use either a conditional expression or pattern matching to avoid such errors. This test often arises as a natural consequence of the fact that the empty list is the terminating condition for functions that are defined recursively over a list (as shown later in this chapter).

Apart from the case of the empty list, hd and tl and :: are related in such a way that for any list:

```
(hd anylist) :: (tl anylist) = anylist
```

Exercise 3.3
SML adopts the view that it is meaningless to attempt to extract something from nothing: generating an error seems a reasonable treatment for such an attempt. What would be the consequences if hd and tl were to evaluate to nil when applied to an empty list?

3.3   Lists and other aggregate types

This section briefly looks at the relationship between lists and the other aggregate types: tuples, strings and arrays.

3.3.1   Lists and tuples

It can be seen that lists and tuples are similar in that they are both aggregate data structures (that is, they collect together many data elements). However, they differ in three ways:

1. Their types: all the items in a list must be of the same type[1] whereas tuple elements may be of differing types. However, lists and tuples can mix; it is legal to have tuples with list components and vice versa. In the latter case it is necessary to ensure that the tuple elements of the list are of the same length and have the same component types.

    ```
    - val tuple = ([1,2,3],[true,false])
    val tuple = ([1,2,3,],[true,false]) : int list * bool list

    val wrong_list = [(1,2,3),(true,false)];
    Error: operator and operand don't agree (tycon mismatch)
      operator domain:
      (int * int * int) * (int * int * int) list
      operand:
      (int * int * int) * (bool * bool) list
      in expression: (1,2,3) :: (true,false) :: nil

    - val good_list = [(12,"June",1752), (13,"March",1066)]
    val good_list = [(12,"June",1752), (13,"March",1066)
                  : (int * string * int) list
    ```

2. A list is a *recursively defined* type (it is defined in terms of itself), and therefore the type contains no information about the number of elements in the list. By contrast, a tuple is *not* recursively defined and the type of a tuple determines exactly how many elements it will contain. It is for this reason that lists may be constructed incrementally, whilst tuples may not.

3. Equality testing: tuple comparison can only be made against tuples of the same composite type and hence the same number of components, whereas lists of any length may be compared.

---

1. See Chapter 6 for ways of creating a new type of list which may have elements of different underlying types.

Comparing tuples:

```
— (1,2,3) = (1,2);
Error: operator and operand don't agree (tycon mismatch)
  operator domain:
  (int * int * int) * (int * int * int)
  operand:
  (int * int * int) * (int * int)
  in expression: = ((1,2,3),(1,2))
```

Comparing lists:

```
— [1,2,3] = [1,2];
val it = false : bool
```

3.3.2 Lists and strings

Strings and lists of strings are semantically related, since they both represent a sequence of characters. This fact is recognized by the SML built-in function explode which converts a string to a list of single character strings, together with implode which converts a list of strings (of any length) to a single string.

```
— explode;
val it = fn : string —> string list

— explode "hallo";
val it = ["h","a","l","l","o"] : string list

— implode;
val it = fn : string list —> string

— implode ["h","a","l","l","o"];
val it = "hallo" : string

— implode ["hallo","world"];
val it = "hallo world" : string
```

Exercise 3.4
Is ^ a constructor?

Exercise 3.5
At first sight it would also appear that makestring can be bypassed by defining a function that quotes its numeric parameter:

```
fun NtoS (n :int) = "n" :string
```

Explain what the above function *actually* does.

Exercise 3.6
Explain why `(implode (explode Astring))` always evaluates to `Astring` but `(explode (implode Alist))` is not always the equivalent of `Alist`.

3.3.3 *Lists and arrays*

The favoured aggregate type for imperative programming languages is the array because it reflects the underlying computational model of those languages – that is, the direct manipulation of storage locations. The array differs from the list in two significant ways:

1. It has a fixed length.

2. It allows for direct retrieval of any of its elements – there is no need to successively deconstruct it in order to obtain a particular element.

The array aggregate type is not included in the standard definition of SML, although most implementations provide arrays (see Berry, 1991). Chapter 6 shows how a similar effect can be achieved in SML through the ability to define new data structures.

3.4 *Simple functions using lists*

Functions over lists may be defined in the same manner as all other functions; they can be recursive, polymorphic and use pattern matching. The nature of recursive, and especially polymorphic recursive, functions is dealt with in later sections; this section overviews the use of pattern matching on lists. There are four things that can appear in function patterns involving lists:

1. Formal parameters – which can be substituted by any actual value.

2. Wild cards – which can also be substituted by any actual value.

3. Constants – including the empty list `nil` (or `[]`).

4. Constructed lists using `::` notation (the aggregate form may also be used, but is not recommended for general use).

Examples of simple functions using lists:

```
fun isempty (nil :'a list) = true :bool
|   isempty anylist        = false

fun isnotempty (anylist :'a list)
    = not (isempty anylist) :bool
```

```
fun bothempty ((nil, nil) :'a list * 'a list)
    = true :bool
|   bothempty _ = false

fun startswithSML (("S" :: "M" :: "L" :: _) :string list)
    = true :bool
|   startswithSML _ = false
```

In the final example it is necessary to bracket the ("S"::"M"::"L":: _) list construction so that it is treated as a single value, which can then be pattern matched. Further examples of pattern matching using list construction include possible implementations of the built-in functions hd and tl:

```
exception Hd

fun hd (nil :'a list) = raise Hd
|   hd (front :: rest) = front :'a

exception Tl
fun tl (nil :'a list) = raise Tl
|   tl (front :: rest) = rest :'a list
```

The use of pattern matching in these examples emphasizes that there is no possible way of deconstructing nil to give component values.

3.5   Recursive functions using lists

Many of the functions over lists are recursive because the list itself is a recursive data structure. Whilst recursion involving numbers generally requires the recognition of zero to provide a terminating condition, list processing generally requires the recognition of the empty list. This section shows that the two recursive styles shown in Chapter 2 can also be used to manipulate lists.

Stack recursion over lists

The template for many functions on lists is very similar to that of stack recursive functions shown in Section 2.7.1:

> **fun**   *template* **nil**
> = *some final value*
>
> | *template (front :: rest)*
> = *do something with front and*
> *combine the result with a*
> *recursion on template applied to rest*

For example, the following function adds all the items in an integer list. It specifies that the sum of an empty list is 0, whilst the sum of any other list is the value of the front item added to the sum of the rest of the list:

```
type ILIST = int list

fun sum (nil :ILIST) = 0 :int
|   sum (front :: rest) = front + sum rest
```

Exercise 3.7
Write a stack recursive function to add all numbers less than 3 which appear in a list of integers.

Accumulative recursion over lists

The following example reworks sum to show its equivalent accumulative recursive implementation:

```
type ILIST = int list

fun xsum (nil :ILIST, total :int) = total :int
|   xsum (front :: rest, total)
    = xsum (rest, front + total)

fun sum (any :ILIST) = xsum (any, 0) :int
```

However, if it were desired to consider the sum of an empty list to be meaningless or an error, it would be sensible to validate the input list in sum and process it in the auxiliary function xsum. In the following version, if sum recognizes an empty list it treats this as an error, **raises** an **exception** and does no further processing. In contrast, when xsum recognizes an empty list it treats this as the *terminating condition* for the recursion and returns the desired total:

```
type ILIST = int list

fun xsum (nil :ILIST, total :int) = total :int

|   xsum (front :: rest, total)
    = xsum (rest, front + total)

exception Sum

fun sum nil = raise Sum
|   sum (any :ILIST) = xsum (any, 0) :int
```

It is worth noting that validation is only done once in this example and has been separated from the calculation. In contrast, the following version is undesirable in that an extra pattern is needed to detect the terminating condition and also that the validation is confused with the calculation. As discussed in Section 2.10, from a software design perspective it is generally poor practice to make a function do more than one thing:

```
type ILIST = int list

exception Muddledsum

fun xmuddledsum (nil, _)
      = raise Muddledsum

|     xmuddledsum (((item :: nil), total) :ILIST * int)
      = (item + total) :int

|     xmuddledsum (front :: rest, total)
      = xmuddledsum (rest, front + total)

fun muddledsum (any :ILIST)
      = xmuddledsum (any, 0) :int
```

A general template for accumulative recursive functions is:

> **fun** *aux* (**nil**, *accumulator*)
>   = *accumulator*
>
> | *aux* (*front* :: *rest*, *accumulator*)
>   = *aux* (*rest*, (*do something with front and accumulator*))
>
> **fun** *main* **nil**
>   = *some terminating condition*
>   *or* **raise** *an exception*
>
> | *main any* = *aux* (*any*, (*initial value of accumulator*))

Exercise 3.8
The following function listmax is accumulative recursive. Rather than using an explicit accumulator it uses the front of the list to hold the current maximum value.

```
type ILIST = int list
exception Listmax
```

```
fun listmax nil = raise Listmax

|    listmax ((front :: nil) :ILIST)
     = front :int

|    listmax (front :: next :: rest)
     = listmax (  if    front > next
                  then (front :: rest)
                  else (next :: rest))
```

Rewrite listmax so that it uses an auxiliary function and an explicit accumulator to store the current largest item in the list.

3.6   Polymorphic recursive functions on lists

Many list-handling functions are designed to explore or manipulate the list structure itself rather than the list elements. These are called 'polymorphic' functions because the elements of the source lists may be of any type; otherwise they are the same as non-polymorphic functions, as has already been shown with the simple functions isempty and bothempty. Polymorphic recursive functions on lists are particularly interesting in that they are the basis for a rich variety of tools that are of general utility for list processing. This section presents two of these functions over lists: length and drop. The treatment of drop will also demonstrate that not all software design principles are set in stone.

length

The following definition of length follows the template provided to describe stack recursive functions. Informally the length of a list can be seen as one of two possibilities: the length of an empty list (which is 0) or the length of a non-empty list. The latter can be seen to be 1 plus the length of a list containing one less item.

```
— fun length (nil :'a list) = 0 :int
  |   length (front :: rest) = 1 + length rest;

val length = fn : 'a list —> int
```

drop

The polymorphic function drop returns part of its second argument (a list of items of any type) by removing the first n items, where n is the first argument.

```
exception Drop
fun drop (0 :int, anylist :'a list) = anylist :'a list
|   drop (_, nil)                    = raise Drop
|   drop (n, (front :: rest))        = drop (n - 1, rest)
```

This function has been presented in the way that most functional programmers would probably write it. However, it goes against the advice given for the function sum. A better design might be:

```
exception Drop

fun xdrop ((0, anylist) :int * 'a list)
        = anylist :'a list
|   drop (n, (front :: rest))
        = xdrop (n - 1, rest)

fun drop ((n, anylist) :int * 'a list)
        = if (n < 0) orelse (n > (length anylist))
          then raise Drop
          else xdrop (n, anylist) :'a list
```

This definition satisfies the principle of a function only doing one kind of activity because it separates the validation from the rest of the processing. However, it is algorithmically unsatisfying in that the entire length of anylist must be calculated even though xdrop will work as desired on any list with at least n elements. For example, the length of a million item list may have to be calculated even though the programmer only wanted to discard its first element!

An alternative solution is to replace length in the conditional part of the **if .. then .. else** expression with a more finely tuned function which only checks that anylist is of the minimum necessary length.

```
fun drop (n :int, anylist :'a list)
        = if (n < 0) orelse (shorterthan (n, anylist))
          then raise Drop
          else xdrop (n, anylist) :'a list
```

Exercise 3.9
What happens if a negative value of n is supplied to the first version of d r o p?

Exercise 3.10
Write the function s h o r t e r t h a n used by the final version of d r o p.

Exercise 3.11
Write the function c o n c a t which is the equivalent of the built-in ˆ operator.

3.6.1 Restricted polymorphic functions on lists

As expected, recursive functions using lists may also be restricted polymorphic in nature. This is demonstrated in the following definition of the function `member` which checks whether an item appears in a list. The specification is simple:

1. The terminating condition where the list is empty – hence nothing can appear in it, and so `member` evaluates to `false`.

2. The terminating condition where the item to be found matches the head of the list – and so `member` evaluates to `true`.

3. The item does not match the head of the list – and so it is necessary to see if the item appears in the rest of the list.

Translation to SML is as simple as the function specification:

```
fun member (nil :''a list, _ :''a) = false :bool
|    member (front :: rest, item)
     = (item = front)
       orelse
       member (rest, item)
```

(Recall that **orelse** does not evaluate its second argument if its first argument evaluates to `true` and therefore `member` is *not* recursively applied if `item = front`).

3.7 Thinking about lists

The list-handling functions introduced so far have been simple to write because their SML code follows directly from their natural language specification. Unfortunately not all functions are so intuitively defined; to make the programmer's task easier this section discusses two important tools for designing functions and list-handling functions in particular. The first tool is commonly known as *case analysis*, which stresses the importance of looking at each expected function parameter. The second tool is known as *structural induction* and offers an important technique to aid the design of recursive algorithms.

3.7.1 Case analysis

It is impossible to consider every possible argument value to a list-handling function. In practice it is only necessary to consider a limited number of cases:

1. The empty list `nil` which must *always* be considered because it is either a terminating value or an illegal option.

2. The general list (front :: rest) which also must *always* be considered; the function body corresponding to this pattern is where the recursive application is normally found.

3. Specific 'n item' lists. For example the single item list (item :: nil), since there is a class of functions (for example listmax in Exercise 3.8) that require at least one element in the list for a meaningful result.

List reversal

This section explores the design of the function reverse which reverses the order of the items in a list (and therefore has the type 'a list —> 'a list).[2] The discussion also highlights some important properties of list manipulation using :: and a.

The function definition can be derived by case analysis of possible input values:

1. The empty list.

2. A list of one item.

3. A list of two items, which is the simplest case where the list is transformed.

4. A general list.

List reversal for the first two cases is trivial:

```
fun reverse nil    = nil
  | reverse [item] = [item]
```

Considering the third case, the desired result can be seen as simply reversing the two elements of the list. This means that the list must be deconstructed to give a name to each of the two elements and then reconstructed with the elements reversed.

The deconstruction of the list can be done using pattern matching with either the aggregate format or the constructed format for the list:

```
fun reverse1 [front, final] = ???

fun reverse2 (front :: rest) = ???
```

Remember that final and rest are not the same thing – the former refers to an item whereas the latter refers to a list (which contains both the final item and the empty list).

Similarly, there are three ways to reconstruct the list – using either the :: operator or using the list aggregate format or using the a operator. Here are the six possibilities:

2. Note that SML provides a built-in list reversal function called rev.

```
fun reverse11 [front, final] = final :: front :: []

fun reverse12 [front, final] = [final, front]

fun reverse13 [front, final] = [final] @ [front]

fun reverse21 (front :: rest) = (hd rest) :: front :: []

fun reverse22 (front :: rest) = [(hd rest), front]

fun reverse23 (front :: rest) = rest @ [front]
```

Notice that both `reverse21` and `reverse22` require `rest` to be further broken down by use of the `hd` function, and so in this situation the aggregate pattern seems to be more useful. However, `reverse13` requires both `front` and `final` to be converted into lists before they can be appended. This conversion is achieved by enclosing each in square brackets, which is equivalent to using `::` and the empty list `nil`.

As a guiding principle, the use of `::` in the pattern is preferred for the general recursive case (as will be seen below) and in the base cases either format may be used. For `reverse`, the most straightforward of the correct definitions given above is:

```
reverse [front, final] = [final, front]
```

The reader should be wary of the following two errors:

```
fun wrong_reverse1 [front, final] = final :: front

fun wrong_reverse2 [front, final] = final @ front
```

Both of the above definitions fail to compile because the operator (either `::` or `@`) does not get arguments of the correct types. The latter definition is actually legal for a list whose items are themselves lists, but it is semantically wrong because the list items are inappropriately compressed:

```
wrong_reverse2 [[1], [2]]
== [2] @ [1]
== [2,1]
```

Considering the final case, the recursive nature of list processing becomes more obvious. As a first step, reversing, for example, `[1,2,3]` can be treated as reversing `[2,3]` appended to `[1]`, that is `(reverse [2,3]) @ [1]`. Reversing `[2,3]` is, of course, covered by the third case and the list `[2,3]` can easily be extracted from `[1,2,3]` using pattern matching.

The above discussion leads to the provisional function definition:

```
fun reverse (nil :'a list) = nil :'a list

|    reverse [item] = [item]

|    reverse [front, final] = [final, front]

|    reverse (front :: rest) = (reverse rest) @ [front]
```

The provisional function evaluates in the following manner:

```
reverse [1,2,3]
== (reverse [2,3]) @ [1]
== [3,2] @ [1]
== [3,2,1]
```

Rationalization of list reversal

In practice, the above definition may be simplified in that the final three patterns can all be catered for by the final function body. Applying the final pattern to a double item list shows that both the patterns for double and single item lists are redundant. This is because the reverse of the single item list is a special case of the final pattern: [item] is just (item :: nil). The function reverse thus simplifies to:

```
fun reverse (nil :'a list)  = nil :'a list
|    reverse (front :: rest) = (reverse rest) @ [front]
```

A hand evaluation reveals:

```
reverse [1,2]
== (reverse [2]) @ [1]          (* using the final pattern *)
== ((reverse []) @ [2]) @ [1] (* using the final pattern *)
== ([] @ [2]) @ [1]           (* using the first pattern *)
== [2] @ [1]                  (* ([] @ [item]) == [item] *)
== [2,1]
```

3.7.2 Structural induction

Case analysis is a useful method of ensuring that a programmer considers all possible inputs to a function. This gives immediate solutions to all base cases which are directly provided for in the function specification and also highlights those cases which require further processing. In the previous example of reverse an intuitive recursive solution was evolved for the general list (front :: rest); however, not all problems are as amenable to such intuition. There is, therefore, a need for a more systematic method of analysis. The nature of this analysis will depend on the nature of the parameter of recursion (that is, the parameter which converges towards a terminating condition). For lists, a technique known as *structural induction* is recommended because it provides a way to reason about a list's recursive structure.

Structural induction requires two steps:

1.   Consider all the base cases as for case analysis.

2.   Consider the general case. The design of the function body may be facilitated by the following technique: assume that a function body exists for a list `rest` and then construct a definition for the case `(front :: rest)`. The assumption is normally known as the *induction hypothesis*.

The use of structural induction to design two functions (`startswith` and `append`) is now presented. The first function `startswith` will be used in the extended example later in this chapter.

Specification of `startswith`

The function `startswith` takes two lists and returns a Boolean value. If the first list is an initial sublist of the second list then the function evaluates to `true` otherwise it evaluates to `false` (for example, `startswith ([1,2,3], [1,2,3,4,5])` evaluates to `true`). By definition an empty list is an initial sublist of any list.

Design of `startswith`

The function `startswith` will take two lists whose elements may be compared for equality. It therefore has the type `(''a list * ''a list) -> bool`.

The design will consider the general case and then the base cases. In this example, it helps to consider the general case first in order to determine the parameter of recursion. However, the program designer may consider the base cases first if appropriate.

The general case is where neither list is empty – there is no direct solution from the specification and so this requires further processing. The general form of the first list is `(front1 :: rest1)` and the general form of the second list is `(front2 :: rest2)`. In this general case, the induction hypothesis is that the application `startswith (rest1, rest2)` will evaluate to the appropriate truth value. Given this assumption, the creative step is to realize that the general case should evaluate to `true` if `startswith (rest1, rest2)` evaluates to `true` and also `front1` is the same as `front2`. This highlights the fact that both lists converge and both are parameters of recursion. The design translates directly to the following incomplete SML code:

```
startswith (front1 :: rest1, front2 :: rest2)
= (front1 = front2)
    andalso
    startswith (rest1, rest2)
```

The base cases are:

1. An empty first list – by definition this case always returns `true`. This is the terminating case for successful matches:

```
startswith (nil, _) = true
```

2. An empty second list – which always evaluates to `false`. This is the terminating case for unsuccessful matches because there is still some of the first list to be compared. If the first list had also been empty this would have been matched by the first base case:

```
startswith (_ , nil) = false
```

The complete definition is

```
fun startswith (nil :''a list, _ :''a list) = true :bool
  | startswith (_, nil) = false
  | startswith (front1 :: rest1, front2 :: rest2)
     = (front1 = front2)
        andalso
        startswith (rest1, rest2)
```

List append

The following discussion emphasizes the advantages of using structural induction rather than case analysis, especially when a large number of cases arise, since the philosophy of structural induction is to generalize rather than specialize.

The infix operator `@` may itself be defined as a prefix function, in terms of `::`. The specification of the following function `append` is exactly that of `@` as stated earlier in this chapter: it takes two lists of the same type and concatenates them to create a new list of that type (that is, it has the type `'a list * 'a list -> 'a list`). The `nil` component of the first list is always discarded; hence if the first list is empty the function evaluates to the second list.

An attempt at defining `append` using case analysis is to write down the possible combinations of types of lists to be appended:

```
fun append (nil,                nil)              = Body_1
  | append (nil,                (item2 :: nil))   = Body_2
  | append (nil,                (front2 :: rest2)) = Body_3
  | append ((item1  :: nil),    nil)              = Body_4
  | append ((item1  :: nil),    (item2 :: nil))   = Body_5
  | append ((item1  :: nil),    (front2 :: rest2)) = Body_6
  | append ((front1 :: rest1),  nil)              = Body_7
  | append ((front1 :: rest1),  (item2 :: nil))   = Body_8
  | append ((front1 :: rest1),  (front2 :: rest2)) = Body_9
```

It is clear that providing function bodies for each of these possible cases will involve a lot of programmer effort. Much of this effort can be saved if structural induction is employed.

A definition for the general case `Body_9` is based on the induction hypothesis that there is already a definition for append (rest1, (front2 :: rest2)). The induction step is to produce a definition for append ((front1 :: rest1), (front2 :: rest2)) which uses the property that front1 must become the first item of the resultant list:

```
append ((front1 :: rest1), (front2 :: rest2))
= front1 :: append (rest1, (front2 :: rest2))
```

It is clear that the parameter of recursion is the first list – the second list never alters. Hence (front2 :: rest2) could be written more simply as anylist. There is now only one base case to consider: when the first list is empty (`Body_3`). By definition this evaluates to the second list. The full SML code is thus:

```
fun append (nil :'a list, anylist :'a list)
      = anylist :'a list

|     append ((front1 :: rest1), anylist)
      = front1 :: append (rest1, anylist)
```

All the other cases can be removed from consideration; in particular, it can be seen that the single item list is not a special case. *In general, single (or n-item) lists should only be treated in a special manner by the function definition if they are treated as special cases by the function specification.*

Exercise 3.12
Use structural induction to design the function t a k e, which works similarly to d r o p but takes the first n items in a list and discards the rest.

Exercise 3.13
Write a function f r o m t o which takes a list and two integers and which outputs all the elements in the list starting from the position indicated by the first integer up to the position indicated by the second integer. For example:

```
— fromto (3, 5, ["a","b","c","d","e","f"]);
val it = ["c","d","e"]
```

3.7.3 Problem solving using structural induction and top-down design

This section looks at a slightly larger problem, the solution to which illustrates the use of structural induction in conjunction with the top-down design technique (discussed in Section 2.10).

The problem to be considered is that of sorting information in an ascending order. There is a wealth of literature on how this may be best achieved (for example, Standish, 1980); one of the simplest methods known as *insertion sort* is now presented.

Sorted list specification

1. An empty list is defined as already sorted.

2. A list of only one element is defined as already sorted.

3. A list of the form (front :: rest) is sorted in ascending order if front is less than all the items in the rest of the list and the rest of the list is sorted in ascending order.

4. For the purposes of this example, only integer lists will be considered.

Top-down design

There are a number of strategies to achieve insertion sort; the approach taken here is to start with an unsorted list and an empty list, and then insert the items of the former into the latter one at a time, thereby ensuring that the latter list is always sorted. This approach makes the assumption that it is possible to insert one item into an already sorted list to give a new sorted list. For example, to sort the list [3,1,4,6,2,4] the following changes will occur to the two lists:

	unsorted list	sorted list
Initially	[3,1,4,6,2,4]	[]
First pass	[1,4,6,2,4]	[3]
Second pass	[4,6,2,4]	[1,3]
Third pass	[6,2,4]	[1,3,4]
Fifth pass	[2,4]	[1,3,4,6]
Sixth pass	[4]	[1,2,3,4,6]
Final pass	[]	[1,2,3,4,4,6]

Insertion sort implementation

To meet the above design, the function isort must employ an accumulator (which is initialized to be empty) to build the final sorted list. There is also the need for a function to insert each element from the unsorted list into the accumulator. This leads directly to the SML code:

```
type ILIST = int list

fun xsort (nil :ILIST, sortedlist :ILIST)
    = sortedlist :ILIST

|   xsort ((front :: rest), sortedlist)
    = xsort (rest, insert (front, sortedlist))

fun isort (anylist :ILIST) = xsort (anylist, nil) :ILIST
```

Insert design

The design of the function insert is simple: the item to be inserted is compared against each element of the sorted list in turn, until its correct position is found.

Insert implementation

The base case is that of inserting an item into an empty list which just gives a singleton list of that item:

```
fun insert ((item, nil) :int * int list)
    = [item] :int list
```

The general case is that of inserting an item into a non-empty sorted list:

```
fun insert (item, (front :: rest)) = ???
```

This involves finding the first item in that list which is greater than the item to be inserted and placing the new item before it. There are two sub-cases to consider:

1. The front of the list is greater than the new item. The new sorted list is now the new item constructed onto the existing sorted list:

    ```
    if item < front
    then item :: front :: rest
    else ???
    ```

2. The front of the list is not greater than the new item, and so it is necessary to place the new item somewhere in the rest of the sorted list. The inductive hypothesis is to assume that insert works correctly for the smaller list rest. The inductive step is to use this assumption to form the general function body so that insert will work correctly for the larger list (front :: rest). This gives:

```
front :: insert (item, rest)
```

Note that if the new item is larger than any existing list member then eventually the rest of the list will converge towards nil; this has already been covered in the base case.

Piecing all this together gives:

```
type ILIST = int list

fun insert (item :int, nil :ILIST) = [item] :ILIST

|   insert (item, (front :: rest))
    = if item < front
        then item :: front :: rest
        else front :: insert (item, rest)
```

Insertion sort limitations

This sorting algorithm is not particularly efficient, nor is it very general (it will only sort integers in ascending order). Chapter 4 presents a more general purpose version that will sort a list of any type in any order. Chapter 5 presents a more elegant algorithm known as *quicksort*.

3.8   Modes of recursion

This section reviews the two familiar styles of recursive functions over lists (stack and accumulative recursion) and introduces three new styles (filter, tail and mutual recursion). The different styles of recursion may often be mixed to form even more expressive control structures. However, the programmer should choose the style which most closely mirrors the natural specification of the problem.

Stack recursive functions

Stack recursion was first introduced in Chapter 2, where the printdots function was used as an example. In general, stack recursive functions such as length have a growing stage where evaluation is suspended, and a reducing stage where the final result is evaluated. The reducing stage can only arise when the parameter of recursion reaches the value that causes the non-recursive option to be taken. At this point, the parameter of recursion is said to have *converged* and the reducing stage is triggered by the fact that the non-recursive option returns a value instead of causing another function application.

A further example of a stack recursive function is occurs which counts how many times a particular item appears in a given list. There are three cases to consider:

1. The terminating condition of the empty list which has no occurrences of any item and so evaluates to zero.

2. The item matches the head of the list and so the number of occurrences is one plus the number of occurrences in the rest of the list.

3. The item does not match the head of the list and so the number of occurrences is zero plus the number of occurrences in the rest of the list.

Translating the above specification to a stack recursive implementation gives:

```
fun occurs (nil :''a list, item :''a) = 0 :int

|    occurs ((front :: rest), item)
     = (if item = front then 1 else 0)
       + occurs (rest, item)
```

Two alternative recursive implementations of the above specification are now discussed.

Filter recursive functions

A variation on the stack recursive approach is filter or partial stack recursion, which is demonstrated in the following implementation of occurs. The definition just presented is inelegant in that the artificial value 0 was invented to denote the non-occurrence of an item in a list. For example, the application occurs ([0,22,3, 5,0,1,1,9,101,0],0) recursively expands to (1 + 0 + 0 + 0 + 1 + 0 + 0 + 0 + 0 + 1 + 0) whereas it would be more elegant to have an algorithm that recursively expanded to just (1 + 1 + 1), thereby dropping the superfluous zeros.

The stack recursive algorithm for the function occurs can be modified to adopt a filter recursive approach as follows:

1. If the list is empty, the result is the same as for stack recursion.

2. If the item matches the head of the list, the result is the same as for stack recursion.

3. If the item does not match the head of the list, the number of occurrences is just the number of occurrences in the rest of the list.

As with the stack recursive version, the new version eventually reaches an empty list and evaluates to zero; thus there is no danger of a 'dangling' addition:

```
fun occurs (nil :''a list, _ :''a) = 0 :int
|   occurs ((front :: rest), item)
    = if front = item
      then 1 + occurs (rest, item)
      else      occurs (rest, item)
```

Applying this version of occurs on the above example almost filters out all of the unwanted zeros – there is still the trivial case of a final addition for the empty list.

Accumulative recursive functions

The recursive style using *accumulators* (introduced in Section 2.7.2) is also applicable to list-handling functions and, as already shown in the definitions of sum and xsum, it is often necessary to provide a main and auxiliary function definition. The main function normally provides any necessary preliminary validation and initializes the accumulator. Rewriting the function occurs in this style gives:

```
fun xoccurs (nil :''a list, _ :''a, total :int)
    = total :int
|   xoccurs ((front :: rest), item, total)
    = if front = item
      then xoccurs (rest, item, total + 1)
      else xoccurs (rest, item, total)

fun occurs (any :''a list, item :''a)
    = xoccurs (any, item, 0) :int
```

This version of occurs will achieve the same results as the two previous versions but is more difficult to read and reason about, probably because its definition is more procedural in nature and further away from its natural language specification.

Tail recursive functions

The restricted polymorphic definition of the function member in Section 3.6.1 is an example of a *tail recursive* function. A tail recursive function is one where at no stage is evaluation suspended.[3] Another example is the function last which selects the final item in a non-empty list or **raises** an **exception** if the list if empty:

```
exception Last
fun last nil = raise Last
|   last ((front :: nil) :'a list) = front :'a
|   last (front :: rest) = last rest
```

---

3. This has an important consequence for functional language implementation because many implementations detect tail recursive functions and produce code which uses constant stack storage space (MacLennan, 1990; Aho *et al.*, 1983; Field and Harrison, 1988).

The functions `member` and `last` are 'pure' tail recursive functions: they exhibit neither stack nor accumulative recursive style. Accumulative recursive functions are also tail recursive when they do not suspend any evaluation. By contrast, stack recursive functions can never be tail recursive.

Mutual recursion

A function must be predefined before use by another function. This means that if two or more functions are defined in terms of one another (that is, these functions are mutually recursive) then they must be dealt with in a special manner. This is demonstrated by the following (illegal) program, which takes an SML program in the form of a list of single character strings and returns a program with all its (unnested) comments stripped:

```
fun wrong_skipcomments nil
    = nil

|   wrong_skipcomments ("(" :: "*" :: rest)
    = incomments rest

|   wrong_skipcomments (front :: rest)
    = front :: wrong_skipcomments rest

fun incomments ("*" :: ")" :: rest)
    = wrong_skipcomments rest

|   incomments (front :: rest)
    = incomments rest
```

The SML system would reject the first function definition, reporting that `incomments` is not known to `wrong_skipcomments`.[4]

The intended meaning can be expressed by using the keyword **and** which allows for simultaneous definitions:

```
type SLIST = string list

fun skipcomments (nil :SLIST)
    = nil :SLIST

|   skipcomments ("(" :: "*" :: rest)
    = incomments rest
```

---

4. See Chapter 5 for a fuller explanation.

```
|    skipcomments (front :: rest)
     = front :: skipcomments rest

and

incomments (("*" :: ")" :: rest) :SLIST)
     = skipcomments rest :SLIST

|    incomments (front :: rest)
     = incomments rest
```

Is mutual recursion desirable?

Mutually recursive solutions are often considered undesirable because it is generally unclear which function is calling the other with any particular values. Furthermore, it is also impossible to test each individual function separately! Fortunately, it is often the case that the mutual dependencies can be eliminated.

In the following (correct) program, the function skipcomments scans the text until it finds the start of an SML comment. At this point it passes the remainder of the input text to incomments, which strips the rest of the current comment and returns the remaining text. The function skipcomments can now use this result to find the next comment:

```
type SLIST = string list

fun incomments (("*" :: ")" :: rest) :SLIST)
     = rest :SLIST

|    incomments (front :: rest)
     = incomments rest

fun skipcomments (nil :SLIST)
     = nil :SLIST

|    skipcomments ("(" :: "*" :: rest)
     = skipcomments (incomments rest)

|    skipcomments (front :: rest)
     = front :: skipcomments rest
```

Exercise 3.14
Modify the skipcomments program to cater for nested comments.

3.9 Extended example – grep

This section introduces the development of the UNIX program *grep* which will be used as an extended example throughout this book. The rest of this chapter shows how the SML facilities already demonstrated may be used to develop a real software tool. The program will be developed incrementally as new features of SML are introduced in subsequent chapters to make the design easier to understand and of more general utility.

Grep specification

Grep is a UNIX program which displays each line from its input that contains an instance of a given pattern. As such, it is clearly very useful for a number of different tasks, including the location of keywords and **val** names within a program or selecting interesting parts of a document. For example, assuming the file called 'textbook' contains the lines:

```
Programming in SML
by C.Myers, C.Clack and E.Poon
```

then typing:

```
grep "SML" "textbook"
```

will result in the first line of the file 'textbook' being displayed.

In practice *grep* is more than a simple pattern matching tool; it also caters for what are known as *regular expressions* (Aho *et al.*, 1974; Kernighan and Pike, 1984). In a regular expression certain characters may be *meta-characters*, which have special meanings. In the case of *grep* the meanings of characters, in order of precedence, are given in Table 3.1.[5] Thus, it is possible to search for a pattern that is anchored at the

Table 3.1. Options for the UNIX *grep* facility

Character	Meaning
c	Any non-special character c matches itself
\\c	Turn off any special meaning of character c
^	Beginning of line
$	End of line
.	Any single character
[...]	Any one of characters in ... ; ranges like a–z are legal
[^...]	Any one of characters not in ... ; ranges are legal
r*	Zero or more occurrences of a regular expression r
$r1r2$	Regular expression $r1$ followed by regular expression $r2$
	No regular expression matches a new line

5. The table was adapted from Section 4.1 of *The UNIX Programming Environment* (Kernighan and Pike, 1984). The actual UNIX tool has several more options.

beginning or end of a line and more importantly to search for patterns that contain 'wild cards'. For example:

```
^S.L
```

will match any line starting with 'S' followed by any character and with 'L' as the third character. Similarly

```
S.*L
```

will match:

```
SML or S.L or SXL or SAAAAAAL or SABCL or SL
```

anywhere on the searched line, and

```
[a-zA-Z][a-zA-Z_1-9]*
```

will match any line that starts with an alphabetic character, followed by zero or more occurrences of an alphabetic character, digit or underscore, *in any combination*, such as:

```
fun
SML
legal_name
aux1
aux2_fun
```

It should be clear from the above why *grep* is sometimes known as a 'filter' program: only the part of the input that matches the pattern is output, all other parts are filtered out.

Development considerations

The development of *grep* will be presented in five stages:

1. A simple program to indicate if a given pattern appears in a line. This is *grep* without any meta-characters. This version of *grep* will deal with just one line of input, and merely return the Boolean value true or false depending on whether the given pattern has been matched or not.

2. A program to allow the * meta-character to appear in the pattern. The rationale for considering this as the next case is that if zero or more occurrences of a normal character can be matched then it is likely that zero or more occurrences of a wild card can also be matched.

3. An extended program to cater for many lines of input returning the text of each line that has a successful match. This is presented in Chapter 4.

4. A program to cater for the other regular expression meta-characters. This is presented in Chapter 7.

5. A version that deals with file handling is presented in Appendix A.

3.9.1 A simple version of grep

Specification

The *grep* program will return the truth value of whether the first component of its tuple pair argument is a substring of the second component. Therefore it has the type:

```
(string * string) -> bool
```

Design

The requirement for a successful *grep* search is that the regular expression (the pattern) either matches from the front of the searched line, or it matches from the front of the rest of the searched line. This is the general case of the structural induction. The terminating cases are:

1. The empty regular expression, which matches any line.

2. The empty searched line, which only matches an empty regular expression.

Implementation

Since SML cannot directly extract the individual elements of a string, it is necessary to explode the two string components to enable the recursion. In practice it is worthwhile providing a simple front-end to perform this action before any further processing:

```
fun grep (regexp :string, line :string)
      = sublist ((explode regexp), (explode line)) :bool
```

The rest of the design translates directly to the SML code:

```
type SLIST = string list

fun sublist (nil :SLIST, _ :SLIST) = true :bool

 |    sublist (_, nil) = false
```

```
|    sublist (regexp, line)
   = startswith (regexp, line)
     orelse
     sublist (regexp, (tl line))
```

It is important that the two base cases are defined in the above sequence. The cases are not mutually exclusive; if they were swapped then matching an empty regular expression and an empty input line would incorrectly evaluate to **false.**

Design of startswith

This has already been done in Section 3.7.2.

Exercise 3.15
It would appear that sublist now no longer needs its first function pattern because this is checked as the first pattern in startswith. Explain why this is incorrect, and also whether the second pattern of sublist can safely be removed.

Exercise 3.16
An incorrect attempt to optimize the startswith program would combine startswith and sublist in one function:

```
type SLIST = string list

fun sublist ((nil, _) :SLIST * SLIST)
    = true :bool
|   sublist (_, nil) = false
|   sublist ((regfront :: regrest), (lfront :: lrest))
    = ((regfront = lfront)
       andalso
       sublist (regrest, lrest))
      orelse
      sublist ((regfront :: regrest), lrest)
```

This follows the general inductive case that the result is true if the front two items of the lists are equal and the result of a sublist search of the rest of the two lists is also true. Alternatively the entire regular expression matches the rest of the search line.
   Show why this approach is wrong.

3.9.2 Incorporating zero or more occurrences

The next stage of the development is to allow for zero or more occurrences of a given character to appear in the searched line. For example:

```
A*BC       appears  in        AAABC
                              ABC
                              BC
                              AAABAAABC

A*A        appears  in        AAAAAA
                              AA
                              A
```

At this point it is also worth recalling that * itself can be matched by preceding it with a \ which turns off its special meaning.

```
A\*B       appears  in        A*B

A\*B       does  not  appear  in AABC
                              ABC
                              BC
                              AAABAAABC
```

The need for lexical analysis

The design of *grep* is now made more complex by the necessity of always checking for the * meta-character following any other character. There are two approaches to handling this. One approach is that the auxiliary function startswith could look ahead for the meta-character *. However, this *confuses* the activity of recognizing the meta-characters in the regular expression with the activity of comparing the regular expression with the current search line. This makes the resultant function startswith very complicated and will go against the advice in Chapter 2 that a function should only do one thing.

In preference, the regular expression could be preprocessed to attribute every character with a 'match-type token' to indicate whether it is to be matched *once only*, as a normal character, or whether it is to be matched *zero or more* times.[6] For this version of *grep* a new function called lex is used to do the preprocessing; this function will initially recognise \ and *, but will be extended later to deal with the other meta-characters.[7] The easiest way of representing the two attributes is probably a tuple of the form (*MATCH_TYPE, actual_value*). For example, ("ONCE", "A") or ("ZERO_ MORE", "B") as shown in Figure 3.3.

Pattern matching can now be employed to convert the raw regular expression into a list of regular expression elements:

6. With this approach, startswith is also saved the bother of checking for the escape sequence \c, where c is any character.
7. This technique of transforming the regular expression into a sequence of actual values and their match-type token is known as 'lexical analysis' (Aho and Ullman, 1984; Kernighan and Pike, 1984); hence the name of the function lex.

```
type MTYPE    = string
type REGTYPE  = MTYPE * string
type REGLIST  = REGTYPE list
type SLIST    = string list

fun lex (nil :SLIST) = nil :REGLIST

|    lex ("\\" :: ch :: "*" :: rest)
     = ("ZERO_MORE", ch) :: lex rest
     (* note: SML interprets the two-character '\\'
     as the single character '\' *)

|    lex ("\\" :: ch :: rest)
     = ("ONCE", ch) :: lex rest

|    lex ("\\" :: nil)
     = [("ONCE", "\\")]

|    lex (ch :: "*" :: rest)
     = ("ZERO_MORE", ch) :: lex rest

|    lex (ch :: rest)
     = ("ONCE", ch) :: lex rest
```

The reader is also referred to Chapter 6 for a more elegant treatment using *enumerated types*.

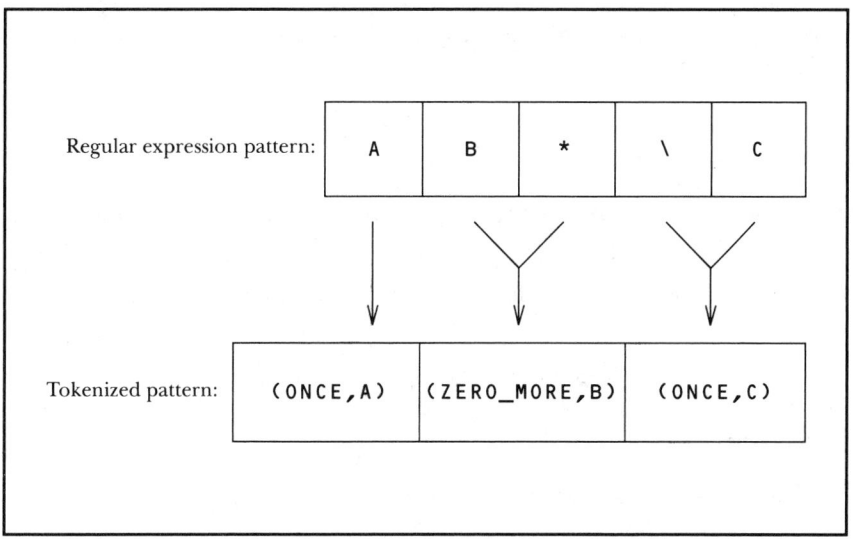

Figure 3.3. Example of a regular expression in tokenized form

3.9.3 Redesign of startswith

Matching strategy

Incorporating "ZERO_MORE" match-types into the startswith function requires the careful consideration of two additional factors:

1. Each element of the regular expression list may be either a "ONCE" match-type or a "ZERO_MORE" match-type and it is necessary to treat them separately because they lead to different inductive hypotheses.

2. There are many possible sub-lines within a line that can match a regular expression, especially one involving a "ZERO_MORE" match-type; for example, "A*A" matches both "A" and "AAAAAAAAAA". In order to continue the design it is necessary to adopt a strategy to deal with all possibilities in a consistent manner. The most common strategies are:

    (i) Look for the shortest possible match; for example, to match the regular expression "A*A" it is only necessary to inspect the first character in the string "AAAAAAA". (Notice, however, that matching "A*B" against "AAAAAAAB" still requires the inspection of the entire second string.)

    (ii) Look for the longest possible match; for example, to match the regular expression "A*A" it is necessary to inspect all of the characters in the string "AAAAAAA".

Since the function grep only returns a Boolean value either strategy is valid; the efficiency of the strategy depends mainly on the nature of the regular expression and the searched line. The program presented in this book will follow the strategy of the shortest possible match.[8]

Design and implementation

The design proceeds by identifying the important cases for analysis:

1. The general case, where both the searched list and the regular expression list are non-empty. This must be split into two sub-cases to cater for the two different match-types.

2. The base cases; for the empty regular expression list and for the empty searched list. In the latter case, once again there is a need to cater for the two different match-types.

This leads to the following five alternative patterns:

---

8. However, many text editors with a 'search-and-replace' command adopt the longest possible match strategy.

```
fun startswith (nil, _)
    = Body_1
|   startswith (("ONCE", ch) :: regrest, nil)
    = Body_2
|   startswith (("ZERO_MORE", ch) :: regrest, nil)
    = Body_3
|   startswith (("ONCE", ch) :: regrest, (lfront :: lrest))
    = Body_4
|   startswith (("ZERO_MORE", ch) :: regrest,
                (lfront :: lrest))
    = Body_5
```

Finally, in accordance with the advice given in Chapter 2, a default pattern is added to help with debugging:

```
|   startswith _ = raise Startswith
```

The definitions of `Body_1`, `Body_2` and `Body_4` are essentially the same as those for the previous version of `startswith` (as explained in Section 3.7.2). However, the other definitions need further attention.

Body_5 – "ZERO_MORE" *general case*

Given the pattern `(("ZERO_MORE", ch) :: regrest, (lfront :: lrest))`, there are two successful matching possibilities; either to *zero* occurrences of `ch` or to the *first* of *one or more* occurrences of `ch` (which requires further processing to determine how many more occurrences of `ch` exist). The 'shortest possible' match strategy first assumes a match to zero occurrences of `ch` and has the inductive hypothesis that `(startswith (regrest, (lfront :: lrest))` will operate correctly. If the recursion evaluates to `true` then the entire search evaluates to `true`. Otherwise, the strategy is to 'backtrack' to consider the possibility of a single occurrence match. This search will be successful if `ch` matches `lfront` and also if all of the current regular expression matches the rest of the search line.[9] This leads to the following SML code for `Body_5`:

```
startswith (regrest, (lfront :: lrest))
orelse
((ch = lfront)
 andalso
 startswith (("ZERO_MORE",ch) :: regrest, lrest))
```

It is interesting to observe that if **orelse** did not delay the evaluation of its second argument then the function would evaluate all possible matches for the regular

---

9. Note that if the searched list contains a long sequence of `ch` characters then this could lead to a large number of delayed decisions, and indeed backtracking may occur many times before the appropriate match is found.

expression to the searched list. By contrast, any actual evaluation is limited to a sequential search from the shortest to the longest, stopping when an overall match is found.

Body_5 at work

The following shows the code for `Body_5` at work on two exemplary cases:

1. A successful match of the regular expression `"A*A"` against the input line `"AAB"` which demonstrates the shortest possible match strategy.

2. A successful match of the regular expression `"A*B"` against the input line `"AAB"` which demonstrates the backtracking mechanism.

For clarity the hand evaluation is shown using the 'raw' regular expression and searched-line strings rather than their tokenized list versions.

Shortest match strategy:

```
grep ("A*A", "AAB")
== startswith ("A*A", "AAB")          i.e. Pattern_5
== startswith ("A", "AAB")            i.e. Pattern_4
== true
```

Backtracking mechanism:

```
grep ("A*B", "AAB")
== startswith ("A*B", "AAB")          i.e. Pattern_5
== startswith ("B", "AAB")            i.e. Pattern_4
== false
 orelse
 (
 "A" = "A"
    andalso
    startswith ("A*B", "AB")          i.e. Pattern_5
    == startswith ("B", "AB")         i.e. Pattern_4
    ==false
    orelse
    (
    "A" = "A"
      andalso
      startswith ("A*B", "B")         i.e. Pattern_5
      == startswith ("B", "B")        i.e. Pattern_4
      == true
    )
    == true
 )
 == true
```

Body_3 – "ZERO_MORE" *at end of line*

This leaves the case for `Body_3`, which can be considered as a successful zero-occurrence match. One of the parameters of recursion has reached termination (or was `nil` to start with) but the other still needs further processing to handle regular expressions of the form `"A*B*"` (which can successfully match an empty search list). The inductive hypothesis is the same as for `Body_5`: the inductive step is therefore to recurse using the rest of the regular expression. The evaluation will either converge towards an empty regular expression and succeed or a `"ONCE"` match-type will be found in the regular expression and the overall search will fail. The code is:

```
startswith (("ZERO_MORE", ch) :: regrest, nil)
= startswith (regrest, nil)
```

Final code for startswith

Piecing this all together gives:

```
exception Startswith

type MTYPE   = string
type REGTYPE = MTYPE * string
type REGLIST = REGTYPE list
type SLIST   = string list

fun startswith (nil :REGLIST, _ :SLIST)
    = true :bool

|   startswith (("ONCE", ch) :: regrest, nil)
    = false

|   startswith (("ZERO_MORE", ch) :: regrest, nil)
    = startswith (regrest, nil)

|   startswith (("ONCE", ch) :: regrest,
                (lfront :: lrest))
    = (ch = lfront)
      andalso
      startswith (regrest, lrest)
```

```
|    startswith (("ZERO_MORE", ch) :: regrest,
                    (lfront :: lrest))
    = startswith (regrest, (lfront :: lrest))
      orelse
      ((ch = lfront)
       andalso
       startswith (("ZERO_MORE", ch) :: regrest, lrest))

|    startswith _ = raise Startswith
```

In order to complete the implementation, the sublist function needs a little modification so that a regular expression such as "A*" matches the empty string (as is shown in the answer to Exercise 3.19). The grep and sublist functions just need amending to preprocess the raw regular expression:

```
fun sublist (nil :REGLIST, _ :SLIST) = true :bool
|    sublist (_, nil) = false
|    sublist (regexp, line)
    = startswith (regexp, line)
      orelse
      sublist (regexp, (tl line))

fun grep (regexp :string, line :string)
    = sublist (lex (explode regexp), explode line) :bool
```

Exercise 3.17
Explain the presence of the final pattern in the function startswith, even though it should never be encountered.

Exercise 3.18
What would happen if the second and third pattern in startswith were swapped?

Exercise 3.19
Alter the sublist function so that "A*" matches the empty string.

3.10 *Summary*

This chapter has introduced a recursively defined aggregate data type called the list. A new list may be created from an existing list and a new value by use of the *constructor* ::. Chapter 6 will extend this concept to user-defined recursive types with user-defined constructors.

The techniques of *case analysis* and *structural induction* were introduced as an aid to designing list-handling functions. Recursive function definition is of such fundamental importance to the manipulation of the list data structure that the general technique was analysed further and five common modes of recursion over lists were discussed: tail recursion, stack recursion, filter recursion, accumulative recursion and mutual recursion. Chapter 4 shows how higher order functions may be used to encapsulate common recursive forms.

This chapter ended with the design and development of the *grep* program, using the tools and techniques learned so far. At later stages in the book we will show how more advanced techniques can be applied to the same real-world example to produce a better design.

4 · Curried and Higher Order Functions

Chapter 2 has shown that functions are values in themselves and can be treated as data items (see Section 2.2). This chapter shows that functions may in fact be passed as parameters to other functions; a function that either takes another function as an argument or produces a function as a result is known as a *higher order function*.

Two further concepts are introduced in this chapter: *currying* and *function composition*. Currying (named in honour of the mathematician Haskell Curry) enables functions to be defined with multiple parameters without the need to use a tuple. A curried function also has the property that it does not have to be applied to all of its parameters at once; it can be *partially applied* to form a new function which may then be passed as a parameter to a higher order function. Function composition is used to chain together functions (which may themselves be partial applications) to form a new function.

Several powerful 'families' of higher order functions on lists are shown; these functions can be combined and composed together to create new higher order functions. Higher order functions may be used to avoid the use of explicit recursion, thereby producing programs which are shorter, easier to read and easier to maintain.

4.1 Currying

It is sometimes tedious to use tuple notation to deal with functions that require more than one parameter. An alternative way of writing the function definition and application is to omit the tuple notation as is shown in the definition for `get_nth` (which selects the *n*th item from a list):[1]

```
exception Get_nth

— fun get_nth _ nil            = raise Get_nth
   |    get_nth 1 (front :: _)  = front
   |    get_nth n (_ :: rest)   = get_nth (n — 1) rest
```

---

1. Note that the brackets around `(front :: _)` are not tuple brackets but part of the list construction and must not be removed.

The system response is new:

```
val get_nth = fn : int -> 'a list -> 'a
```

This is different from previous responses for function definition, which had a single arrow in the type. In the curried definition shown above, there are two arrows which implies that two functions have been defined. These type arrows always associate to the right,[2] so that an equivalent type response is:

```
val get_nth = fn : int -> ('a list -> 'a)
```

This illustrates that get_nth is a function which has an integer source type and generates an intermediate result which is itself a function; this second, but anonymous, function translates a polytype list into a polytype.

The presence of multiple arrows in the type indicates that get_nth is a *curried* function. This curried version of get_nth may now be applied to two arguments, without using tuple brackets, giving the desired result:

```
- get_nth 2 ["a","b","c"];
val it = "b" : string
```

In practice, any uncurried function could have been defined in a curried manner, regardless of the number of components in its argument. *From now on most functions will be presented in a curried form.*

4.1.1 Partially applied functions

Although currying allows a simpler syntax, its real advantage is that it provides the facility to define *partially applied functions*. This is useful because it enables the creation of new functions as specializations of existing functions. For instance, the function get_nth may be used with just one argument to give rise to a new function:

```
- val get_second = get_nth 2;
val get_second = fn : 'a list -> 'a

- val get_fifth = get_nth 5;
val get_fifth = fn : 'a list -> 'a

- get_second ["a","b","c"];
val it = "b" : string
```

A hand evaluation of the above application of get_second shows:

---

2. Remember that function *application* associates to the left.

```
get_second ["a","b","c"]
== (get_nth 2) ["a","b","c"]
== get_nth 2 ["a","b","c"]
== get_nth 1 ["b","c"]
== "b"
```

The partial application of (get_nth 2) thus generates an intermediate function, waiting for application to a final argument in order to generate a result. A partial application may also be used as an actual parameter to another function;[3] the expressive power of this feature will become evident later in this chapter during the discussion of *higher order functions*.

4.1.2 *Converting uncurried functions to curried form*

The user-defined functions presented in the first three chapters of this book have been defined in an uncurried format. This is a sensible format when the functions are intended to be used with all of their arguments but it is not as flexible as the curried format. If curried versions are required then it would be possible to rewrite each function using curried notation; however, this would involve a lot of programmer effort (and consequently would be prone to programmer error).

A more pragmatic approach is to write a function that will generate curried versions of uncurried functions – this function could be written once and then used as and when necessary. Unfortunately, it is impossible to write a single conversion function to deal with functions with different numbers of parameters. This is because all functions must have a well-defined source type and therefore must have either a fixed number of curried arguments or a tuple of fixed size. A separate conversion function is therefore necessary for all the uncurried functions with two arguments, and another for all the uncurried functions of three arguments, and so on. It is, of course, unnecessary to convert monadic functions (which take only one non-tuple argument) because in this case the curried and uncurried formats are identical.

This section presents a function, make_curried, which will convert any uncurried, dyadic function (that is, a function which takes a tuple with two components) to curried format. The programmer can then use this function as a template for further conversion functions as required.

The conversion function make_curried is itself in curried form and takes three parameters. The first parameter stands for the uncurried function and the next two parameters stand for that function's arguments. All that the function body needs to do is apply the input function to these last two parameters collected into a tuple (since an uncurried function only works on a single argument):

```
- fun make_curried ff x y = ff (x,y);
val make_curried = fn : ('a * 'b ->'c) -> 'a -> 'b -> 'c
```

---

3. If the partial application is only going to be used once, then the keyword **fn** provides a way to define such a function without binding it to a name. For further discussion of **fn**, see Appendix B.

The type of make_curried is new; the bracketed first parameter ('a * 'b -> 'c) indicates that ff is a polymorphic, uncurried function which takes two arguments. In general, if an arrow appears inside brackets in a function's type then this indicates that it takes a function as one of its arguments.

Now, given the definition:

```
fun max (x :int, y :int)
= if x > y
    then x
    else y :int
```

then clearly the application max 1 2 will fail, as the function max expects an integer pair. Using make_curried gets around this problem:[4]

```
make_curried max 2 3
== max (2,3)
== 3
```

Similarly, new curried versions of existing functions can be created with the minimum of programmer effort:

```
val newmax = make_curried max
```

The function make_curried is an example of a *higher order function*. In general, any function that takes a function as at least one of its parameters or returns a function as its result is known as a higher order function.

Exercise 4.1
Write the function make_uncurried which will allow a curried, dyadic function to accept a tuple as its argument.

4.1.3 *Converting operators to curried form*

The SML arithmetic and relational operators all have an underlying uncurried format. This means that they cannot be partially applied; for example, both of the following definitions will fail:

---

4. This is an excellent example of the fact that function application associates from the left, to give (((make_curried max) 2) 3) rather than (make_curried (max (2 3))) which would be an error.

```
val inc = 1 +

val inc = + 1
```

It is, of course, possible to define simple, prefix, curried functions which do the same as their operator equivalents and can then be partially applied:

```
fun plus (x :int) (y :int) = x + y :int

val inc = plus 1
```

As there are not many operators, this approach provides a brief, simple and pragmatic solution. An alternative approach is to use the function `make_curried`, which has just been defined. However, before `make_curried` can be used to provide a curried form for an operator, it is firstly necessary to transform that infix operator into a prefix function. This may be achieved for *any* dyadic operator by preceding it with the keyword **op**. For example, the two following expressions are equivalent:

```
- 1 + 2;
val it = 3 : int

- (op + ) (1,2)
val it = 3 : int
```

The latter firstly demonstrates that the syntactic form `(op + )` is a prefix function, and secondly that it takes its two arguments as a two-tuple (and hence is uncurried).

The following definitions show that using `make_curried` in conjunction with the keyword **op** and an operator achieves the same effect as using `make_curried` on its own with user-defined functions:[5]

```
- val inc = make_curried (op + ) 1;
val inc = fn : int -> int

- val twice = make_curried (op * ) 2;
val twice = fn : int -> int
```

Some further examples of curried, prefix operators are:[6]

5. Notice that `(op *)` is illegal because the two-character sequence `*)` already means 'end of comment'. However, `(op * )` is perfectly legal and this style is therefore used consistently whenever **op** is applied to an operator.
6. However, the use of relational operators on values of type `string` is not part of the language definition of SML as published in Milner *et al.* (1990).

```
val plus
    = (make_curried (op + )) :int -> int -> int
val real_plus
    = (make_curried (op + )) :real -> real -> real

val times
    = (make_curried (op * )) :int -> int -> int
val real _times
    = (make_curried (op * )) :real -> real -> real

val concat   = (make_curried (op ^ ))
val cons     = (make_curried (op :: ))

val equal    = (make_curried (op = ))
val notequal = (make_curried (op <> ))

val isitgreaterthan
    = (make_curried (op < )) :int -> int -> bool
val greaterthan
    = (make_curried (op > )) :int -> int -> bool

val isitlessthan
    = (make_curried (op > )) :int -> int -> bool
val lessthan
    = (make_curried (op < )) :int -> int -> bool
val str_lessthan
    = (make_curried (op < )) :string -> string -> bool
```

Notice that integer comparison has two variants, for example `isitlessthan` and `lessthan`.[7] These two functions are quite different:

1. `isitlessthan` is normally used in a partially applied manner to provide a predicate, for example:

    ```
    - val is_negative = isitlessthan 0;
    val is_negative = fn : int -> bool;

    - is_negative ~1;
    val it = true : bool
    ```

2. `lessthan` is normally used as a prefix replacement for the infix operator <:

---

7. The following discussion applies equally to the functions `isitgreaterthan` and `greaterthan`.

```
— lessthan 0 ~1;
val it = false : bool
```

The partial application (lessthan 0) is interpreted as 'is 0 less than some integer?'. This kind of distinction applies to all *non-commutative* operators.

Curried Boolean operators

It is not possible to curry the Boolean operators **andalso** and **orelse** in the above manner because SML treats them as special variants of the conditional **if .. then .. else** construct. To use them in a partially applied manner, it is necessary to write explicit curried versions:

```
fun both   x y = x andalso y

fun either x y = x orelse y
```

However, these are no longer lazy because x and y are always evaluated *before* the function body is evaluated!

4.2   Simple higher order functions

Higher order functions are a powerful extension to the function concept and are as easy to define and use as any other function. The rest of this section shows a number of simple higher order functions, whilst the next section extends the principle to higher order functions over lists.

4.2.1   Function composition

The built-in operator o (pronounced 'compose') is different to previously shown built-in operators in that it takes two functions as its parameters (and hence is also a higher order function). A frequent programming practice is to apply a function to the result of another function application. For instance, using the function twice (defined in the previous section):

```
fun quad x = twice (twice x)

fun many x = twice (twice (twice (twice x)))
```

In this sort of function definition, the use of bracket pairs is tedious and can lead to errors if a bracket is either misplaced or forgotten. The operator o enables most of the brackets to be replaced:

```
fun quad x = (twice o twice) x

fun many x = (twice o twice o twice o twice) x
```

Not only is this notation easier to read but it also emphasizes the way the functions are combined. The outermost brackets are still necessary because o has a lower precedence than function application.

The compose operator is specified by:

$$(f \ o \ g) \ x = f \ (g \ x)$$

where the source type of the function f must be the same as the result type of the function g.

Function composition provides a further advantage beyond mere 'syntactic sugaring' in that it allows two functions to be combined and treated as a single function. As shown in Chapter 1, the following intuitive attempt at naming many fails because twice expects an integer argument rather than a function translating an integer to an integer:

```
- val wrong_many = twice twice twice twice;

Error: operator and operand don't agree (tycon mismatch)
   operator domain: int
   operand:          int -> int
   in expression: twice twice
```

The correct version uses o:

```
- val many = twice o twice o twice o twice;
val many = fn : int -> int

- many 3;
val it = 48 : int
```

The use of o is not limited to combining several instances of the same function (which itself must have identical source and target types) – it can be used to combine any pair of functions that satisfy the specification given above. For example:

```
val neg_many = ~ o many

val sqrt_dbl = sqrt o real o (plus 1) o twice
```

Note that in the final example (plus 1) is a monadic function (it takes just one parameter); the use of plus on its own is inappropriate for composition because it is dyadic.

Exercise 4.2
Give the types of the following compositions:

```
tl o (op a)
abs o fst
chr o chr
```

4.2.2 *Combinatorial functions*

The following functions are similar to o and `make_curried` in that they facilitate the use of higher order functions. Traditionally these functions are known as *combinators* (Diller, 1988; Field and Harrison, 1988) and are given single upper-case letter names. This text only introduces the combinators B, C and K, which are of general utility. There are many more possible combinators which have mainly theoretical interest and serve as the basis for many implementations of functional languages. For more information the reader is referred to the Bibliography.

B – *Compose*

The prefix equivalent of o is the combinator B which is defined below:

```
fun B ff gg x = ff (gg x)
```

B can now be used in the same way and with the same advantages as its built-in equivalent.

C – *Swap*

The C combinator is known as 'swap' and serves to exchange the arguments of a (curried) dyadic function:

```
fun C ff x y = ff y x
```

K – *Cancel*

The K combinator is known as 'cancel' because it always discards the second of its two arguments and returns its first argument:

```
fun K x y = x
```

For example, the function `fst` (introduced in Chapter 2) may be written as:

```
val fst = make_uncurried K
```

A hand evaluation reveals:

```
fst (1,2)
== make_uncurried K (1,2)
== K 1 2
== 1
```

whilst the function snd can be thought of as fst with its parameters swapped, that is:

```
val snd = make_uncurried (C K)
```

A hand evaluation reveals:

```
snd (1,2)
== make_uncurried (C K) (1,2)
== C K 1 2
== K 2 1
== 2
```

4.2.3 *Iteration*

An important advantage of the functional approach is that the programmer can create a rich set of iterative control structures and hence be more likely to chose one which represents the problem specification. This sub-section illustrates this point in the definition of a 'repeat' loop construct. The following (non-robust) function repeatedly applies its second parameter to its final parameter, which serves as an *accumulator* for the final result. The parameter of recursion is n which converges towards zero:

```
fun repeat (0 :int) (ff :'a -> 'a) (state :'a)
    = state :'a

|   repeat n ff state
    = repeat (n — 1) ff (ff state)
```

The function **repeat** can be used to give a non-recursive definition of any function that bases its recursion on a fixed number of iterations. For example, the function **printdots** (from Chapter 2) may be defined as:

```
fun printdots n = repeat n (concat ".") ""
```

In `printdots` the empty string is the `state` parameter or accumulator, which changes at each recursive step. A hand evaluation of (`printdots 2`) reveals:

```
printdots 2
== repeat 2 (concat ".") ""
== repeat 1 (concat ".") ((concat ".") "")
== repeat 1 (concat ".") ("." ^ "")
== repeat 1 (concat ".") (".")
== repeat 0 (concat ".") ((concat ".") ".")
== repeat 0 (concat ".") ("." ^ ".")
== repeat 0 (concat ".") ("..")
== ".."
```

If the function to be repeated also requires the iteration count as a parameter, the following variant `repeatc` may be used (assuming the iteration counter counts down towards zero):

```
fun repeatc (0 :int) (ff :'a -> int -> 'a) (state :'a)
    = state :'a

|   repeatc n ff state
    = repeatc (n - 1) ff (ff state n)
```

Exercise 4.3
Explain why `repeat` is non-robust and provide a robust version.

Exercise 4.4
Define a function to achieve a result similar to an imperative programming language 'while' loop. Do not name the function 'while' because this is a reserved word (as shown in Appendix C).

4.3   Higher order functions on lists

Many of the list-handling functions presented in Chapter 3 exhibit similar forms of recursion but use different operations to achieve their results. SML provides the facility to generalize these functions and removes the need to program with explicit recursion.

This section shows three families of curried, polymorphic, higher order functions on lists:

1.   The 'map' family which retains the list structure but transforms the list items.

2. The 'fold' family which distributes an operator over a list, typically to produce a single value result.

3. The 'select' family which retains the list structure but may delete items from the list, according to a given predicate.

4.3.1 The map family

It is often useful to apply a function to each item in a list, returning a list of the consequences. For example `map_inc` will apply inc to each item in a given integer list and `map_twice` will apply `twice` to each item in a given integer list:

```
val inc = plus 1
val twice = times 2

fun map_inc nil
    = nil
|   map_inc (front :: rest)
    = (inc front) :: (map_inc rest)

fun map_twice nil
    = nil
|   map_twice (front :: rest)
    = (twice front) :: (map_twice rest)
```

A template for any function of this form is:

fun map_ff **nil = nil**
    | map_ff $(front :: rest) = (ff\ front) :: (map\_ff\ rest)$

It can be seen from this template that the only important difference between `map_inc` and `map_twice` is the name of the function that is applied to the `front` item (represented by ff in the template). Rather than having to define functions of this form using explicit recursion it is possible to define them using the built-in higher order function `map`. This function has ff as its first argument and the list to be transformed as its second argument:

```
— map inc [1,3,2,6];
val it = [2,4,3,7] : int list
```

The behaviour of the function `map` is further illustrated in Figure 4.1 and the following examples.

```
— map (make_curried (op + ) 1) [1,2,3];
val it = [2,3,4] : int list
```

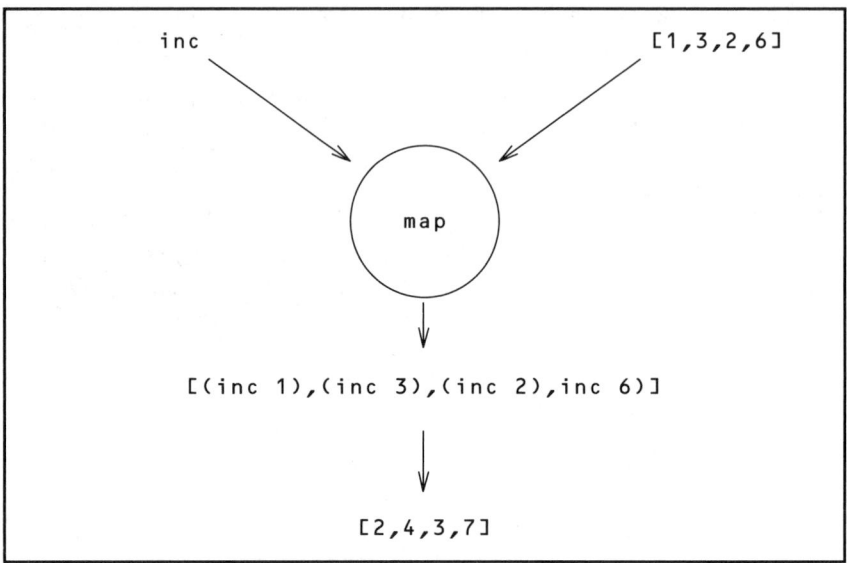

Figure 4.1. The behaviour of the function `map`

```
— map (twice o inc) [1,2,3];
val it = [4,6,8] : int list

— map (plus 2) [1,2,3];
val it = [3,4,5] : int list

— val list_inc = map inc;
val list_inc = fn : int list —> int list

— list_inc [1,2,3];
val it = [2,3,4] : int list
```

It is important to note that `(map inc)` is a partially applied function (where `inc` is a function argument to `map`) and is *not* a function composition!

```
— map inc;
val it = fn : int list —> int list

— map o inc;
Error: operator and operand don't agree (tycon mismatch)
  operator domain:
  (('Z —> 'Y) —> 'Z list —> 'Y list) * (int —> 'Z —> 'Y)
  operand:
  (('Z —> 'Y) —> 'Z list —> 'Y list) * (int—> int)
  in expression: o (map, inc)
```

Designing map

In fact, map is very easy to write. All that is necessary is to generalize from the *map_ ff* template by passing *ff* as an additional argument:

```
fun map ff nil           = nil
|   map ff (front :: rest) = (ff front) :: (map ff rest)
```

The function map is polymorphic, as can be seen from its type:

```
- map;
val it = fn : ('a -> 'b) -> 'a list -> 'b list
```

The function can transform a list of any type provided that the source type of ff matches the type of the items in the list.

Mapping over two lists

The principle of list transformation using map can be extended to cater for more than one list. For example, the following function takes two lists and recursively applies a dyadic function to the corresponding front items:

```
exception Map_two

fun map_two (ff :'a -> 'b -> 'c) (nil :'a list) (nil :'b list)
    = nil :'c list

|   map_two ff (front1 :: rest1) (front2 :: rest2)
    = (ff front1 front2) :: map_two ff rest1 rest2

|   map_two ff _ _
    = raise Map_two   (* lists of unequal length *)


- map_two (make_curried max) [1,2,3] [3,2,1];
val it = [3,2,3] : int list
```

Exercise 4.5
In the definition of map_two source lists of unequal length have been treated as an error. It is an equally valid design decision to truncate the longer list; amend the definition to meet this revised specification.

Exercise 4.6
Explain why the following definitions are equivalent:

```
fun f1 x alist = map (plus x) alist
fun f2 x = map (plus x)
val f3 = (map o plus)
```

4.3.2   List folding – reduce and accumulate

This subsection discusses how a dyadic function can be distributed so that it works over a list, typically evaluating to a single value, for example to give the sum of all the numbers in a list. As with the discussion of `map` it will be shown how explicit recursion can be removed by means of a single higher order function. Two strategies are used:

1. Stack recursion, to define a function called `reduce`, (also known as `foldr`).

2. Accumulative recursion, to define a function called `accumulate`, (also known as `foldl`).

The higher order function reduce

On inspecting the structure of the following definitions of `sumlist,` `divall` and `anytrue` it can be seen that they share a common structure:

```
fun sumlist nil              = 0
|   sumlist (front :: rest)  = front  +  (sumlist rest)

fun divall nil               = 1.0
|   divall (front :: rest)   = front  /  (divall rest)

fun anytrue nil              = false
|   anytrue (front :: rest) = front orelse (anytrue rest)
```

Functions of this form place the dyadic operator between each of the list items and substitute a terminating value for the empty list. For example, the sum of the list [1,2,5,2] may be thought of as the result of $1 + 2 + 5 + 2 + 0$. Generalizing gives the template:

fun *reduce_ ff* **nil** = *default*
| *reduce_ ff* (*front* :: *rest*) = *front* $\oplus$ (*reduce_ ff rest*)

This template is appropriate for all dyadic infix functions $\oplus$. In the above examples the default value has been chosen such that the following specification holds:

$$any \oplus default = any$$

When the default value has this property it is formally known as the *identity* element of the dyadic function, as illustrated in Table 4.1.

Table 4.1   Identity elements of common dyadic functions

any	$\oplus$	Identity	=	any
any_int	+	0	=	any_int
any_real	/	1.0	=	any_real
any_bool	orelse	false	=	any_bool
any_string	~	" "	=	any_string
any_list	@	nil	=	any_list

Notice that it is not always necessary to choose the identity as the default. For example:

```
fun product_times_ten nil
        = 10
|   product_times_ten (front :: rest)
            = front * (product_times_ten rest)
```

Furthermore, many dyadic functions do not have an identity and so great care must be taken in the choice of a sensible default value. For example, it is not obvious what would be a sensible default value for the operator mod.

SML does not normally provide a built-in higher order function to generalize *reduce_ff*; however, a user-defined version can easily be written using a similar approach to that taken with the design of map.

Designing reduce

The above examples considered the distribution of built-in infix operators over lists. However, reduce will be designed to accept prefix functions, for two reasons:

1. As user-defined functions are normally defined in prefix form, reduce should deal with functions in this form.

2. It is not possible to pass the built-in operators *directly* as arguments to a function; they must either be passed in prefix, curried form (by using the keyword **op** and the function make_curried) or replaced with their prefix, curried equivalents (as suggested in Section 4.1.3).

The design proceeds by replacing $\oplus$ with a prefix version *ff* in the template:

fun   *reduce_ff* **nil**   = *default*
| *reduce_ff* (*front :: rest*)   = *ff front* (*reduce_ff rest*)

All that is now necessary is to make *ff* and *default* become explicit arguments:

```
- fun reduce ff default nil
      = default
  |   reduce ff default (front :: rest)
      = ff front (reduce ff default rest);

val reduce = fn : ('a -> 'b -> 'b) -> 'b -> 'a list -> 'b
```

Examples of partial applications which use reduce are now presented (employing the curried functions defined in Section 4.1.3):

```
val anytrue           = reduce either false
val sumlist           = reduce plus 0
val divall            = reduce (make_curried (op / )) 1.0
val product_times_ten = reduce times 10

- reduce plus 0 [1,2,3];
val it = 6 : int

- sumlist [1,3,5];
val it = 9 : int
```

A hand evaluation of the last application shows:

```
sumlist [1,3,5]
== reduce plus 0 [1,3,5]
== plus 1 (reduce plus 0 [3,5])
== plus 1 (plus 3 (reduce plus 0 [5]))
== plus 1 (plus 3 (plus 5 (reduce plus 0 [])))
== plus 1 (plus 3 (plus 5 0))
== plus 1 (plus 3 5)
== plus 1 8
== 9
```

The function reduce is stack recursive in that it stacks a growing unevaluated expression until the empty list is encountered. At this point it unstacks from the innermost right to the outermost left, combining them pairwise by means of application of the function parameter ff. In the unstacking phase, this can be seen as 'folding' the list from the right, usually into a single value; hence the alternative name foldr.

The function reduce is not restricted to a single value result; it can also return an aggregate type as illustrated in the following example:

```
- val do_nothing = reduce cons nil;
val do_nothing = fn : 'a list -> 'a list
```

```
— do_nothing [1,5,8];
val it = [1,5,8]
```

A hand evaluation shows how this works:

```
do_nothing [1,5,8]
== reduce cons nil [1,5,8]
== cons 1 (reduce cons nil [5,8])
== cons 1 (cons 5 (reduce cons nil [8]))
== cons 1 (cons 5 (cons 8 (reduce cons nil [])))
== cons 1 (cons 5 (cons 8 nil))
== cons 1 (cons 5 [8])
== cons 1 [5,8]
== [1,5,8]
```

The overall result is an aggregate type because the dyadic function being distributed (in this case cons) returns an aggregate type. Notice that the target type of the function being distributed must be the same as the source type of its second argument (that is, it must have type 'a —> 'b —> 'b). Also notice that cons has no identity – however, nil was chosen as the sensible default value because it produces a list as required.

It is also possible to use **reduce** to distribute partial applications and function compositions across lists, as demonstrated below:

```
— fun addup_greaterthan (x :int) (y :int) (z :int)
    = if   (x < y)
      then (y + z)
      else z : int;
val addup_greaterthan = fn : int —> int —> int —> int

— reduce (addup_greaterthan 3) 0 [1,7,3,9,8,4,1];
val it = 28 : int

— reduce (cons o inc) nil [1,2,3];
val it = [2,3,4] : int list
```

The final example above is particularly interesting as it has the same action as map inc [1,2,3]. A hand evaluation shows how it works:

```
reduce (cons o inc) nil [1,2,3]
== (cons o inc) 1 (reduce (cons o inc) nil [2,3])
== cons (inc 1) (reduce (cons o inc) nil [2,3])
== cons 2 (reduce (cons o inc) nil [2,3])
== cons 2 ((cons o inc) 2 (reduce (cons o inc) nil [3]))
```

```
== cons 2 (cons (inc 2) (reduce (cons o inc) nil [3]))
== cons 2 (cons 3 (reduce (cons o inc) nil [3]))
== cons 2 (cons 3 ((cons o inc) 3 (reduce (cons o inc)
   nil [])))
== cons 2 (cons 3 (cons (inc 3) (reduce (cons o inc)
   nil [])))
== cons 2 (cons 3 (cons 4 (reduce (cons o inc) nil [])))
== cons 2 (cons 3 (cons 4 nil))
== cons 2 (cons 3 [4])
== cons 2 [3,4]
== [2,3,4]
```

The higher order function accumulate

It is possible to define a very similar function to reduce that makes use of the accumulative style of recursion. This function, known as accumulate or foldl, starts evaluating immediately by recursing on the tail of the list with the default value being used as the accumulator:

```
- fun accumulate ff default nil
      = default

  |   accumulate ff default (front :: rest)
      = accumulate ff (ff default front) rest;

val accumulate = fn : ('a -> 'b -> 'a) -> 'a -> 'b list -> 'a
```

Equivalence of reduce and accumulate

On many occasions reduce can be substituted with accumulate, as is shown in the next three examples which rework the previous reduce examples. However, this is not always the case, as will be demonstrated in the subsequent treatment for reverse:

```
val anytrue          = accumulate either false

val sumlist          = accumulate plus 0

val product_times_ten = accumulate times 10
```

A hand evaluation of sumlist [1,3,5] reveals that the same answer is obtained as for the reduce version, but in a very different manner:

```
sumlist [1,3,5]
== accumulate plus 0 [1,3,5]
== accumulate plus (plus 0 1) [3,5]
== accumulate plus 1 [3,5]
== accumulate plus (plus 1 3) [5]
== accumulate plus 4 [5]
== accumulate plus (plus 4 5) []
== accumulate plus 9 []
== 9
```

By contrast, it is not possible to substitute accumulate for reduce in the divall example, nor reduce for accumulate in the following definition of reverse:

```
val reverse = accumulate (C cons) nil
```

Comparing reduce and accumulate

The reason why reduce cannot be substituted for accumulate in the above definition of reverse is best illustrated through a diagrammatic comparison of the two functions. The following example compares the distribution of the infix + operator across the list [1,2,3], with a default value of 0. If the reduce function is used then this may be considered diagrammatically as placing the default value at the right-hand end of the list and bracketing the expression from the right (hence the alternative name foldr):

```
1   : :   2   : :   3   : :   nil
↓         ↓         ↓
1   +    (2   +    (3   +   0))
```

By contrast, if the accumulate function is used then this may be considered diagrammatically as placing the default value at the left-hand end and bracketing the expression from the left (hence the alternative name foldl):

```
         1   : :   2   : :   3   : :   nil
             ↓         ↓         ↓
((0   +   1)   +   2)   +   3
```

Of course, reduce and accumulate are defined to take curried, prefix functions rather than infix operators and so the actual diagrams would be slightly more complex. For example, (reduce plus 0 [1,2,3]) would actually produce (plus 1 (plus 2 (plus 3 0))) and (accumulate plus 0 [1,2,3]) would actually produce (plus (plus (plus 0 1) 2) 3). However, the above two diagrams provide a better visual mnemonic.

In general, it is only safe to substitute one of the *fold* functions with the other if the function parameter ff is associative and also commutative (at least with its identity).

As explained in Chapter 1, an infix operator $\oplus$ is associative if the following holds for all possible values of x, y and z:

$$x \oplus (y \oplus z) = (x \oplus y) \oplus z$$

Similarly, a prefix function ff is associative if the following holds for all possible values of x, y and z:

$$ff \ x \ (ff \ y \ z) = ff \ (ff \ x \ y) \ z$$

A prefix function is commutative with its identity value if the following holds for all possible values of x:

$$ff \ Identity \ x = ff \ x \ Identity$$

It can now be seen that substituting `reduce` for `accumulate` in the definition of `reverse` will fail because both of the two conditions given above are violated. The function `(C cons)` is neither associative nor does it have an identity value. The relevance of these two criteria can also be illustrated diagrammatically. By using the rules of

1. Associativity

2. Commutativity with the identity

and by reference to the diagrams used above, it is possible to transform the diagram for `reduce plus 0 [1,2,3]` into the diagram for `accumulate plus 0 [1,2,3]` (once again infix form is used in the diagram for clarity):

```
                                  1  +  (2   +  (3   +  0))
        by rule 1  =                   (1   +   2)  +  (3   +  0)
        by rule 1  =                  ((1   +   2)  +   3)  +  0
        by rule 2  =          0  +  ((1   +   2)  +   3)
        by rule 1  =        (0  +   (1   +   2)) +   3
        by rule 1  =      ((0  +    1)  +   2)  +   3
```

Exercise 4.7
Some functions cannot be generalized over lists as they have no obvious default value for the empty list; for example it does not make sense to take the maximum value of an empty list. Write the function `reduce1` to cater for functions that require at least one list item.

Exercise 4.8
Write two curried versions of `member` (as specified in Section 3.6.1), using `reduce` and `accumulate` respectively and discuss their types and differences.

4.3.3 *List selection*

There are a large number of possible list selection functions, which remove items from a list if they do not satisfy a given predicate (that is, a function that evaluates to a Boolean value). This subsection presents two functions which are typical of this family of functions.

List truncation

The following function takes a list and a predicate as arguments and returns the initial sublist of the list whose members all satisfy the predicate:

```
fun takewhile (pred :'a -> bool) (nil :'a list)
    = nil :'a list

|   takewhile pred (front :: rest)
    = if   pred front
      then front :: (takewhile pred rest)
      else nil
```

Example:

```
val words = "how_long_is_a word"

- implode (takewhile (notequal " ") (explode words));
val it = "how_long_is_a" : string
```

List filter

The next example is the function `filter` which uses a predicate that is based on the item's value. This function may be specified in terms of filter recursion, as shown in Section 3.8.

```
fun filter (pred :'a -> bool) (nil :'a list)
    = nil :'a list

|   filter pred (front :: rest)
    = if   pred front
      then front :: (filter pred rest)
      else filter pred rest
```

Examples:

```
- filter (isitlessthan 3) [1,7,2,9,67,3];
val it = [1,2] : int list
```

```
fun rm_dups (nil :''a list)
      = nil :''a list
  |   rm_dups (front :: rest)
      = front :: (rm_dups (filter (notequal front) rest))
```

Grep revisited

Using filter, the *grep* program shown in Section 3.9 can now be extended to mirror the UNIX *grep* behaviour, whereby only those lines which match the regular expression are printed from an input stream. It should be noted that the code is presented in curried form and assumes that sublist is also curried:

```
fun xgrep regexp line
      = sublist (lex (explode regexp)) (explode line)

fun grep regexp = filter (xgrep regexp)
```

Exercise 4.9
Define the function dropwhile which takes a list and a predicate as arguments and returns the list without the initial sublist of members which satisfy the predicate.

Exercise 4.10
The *set* data structure may be considered as an unordered list of unique items. Assuming the existence of the function member (as defined in Section 3.6.1) then the following function will yield a list of all the items common to two sets:

```
fun intersection (aset :''a list) (bset :''a list)
      = filter ((make_curried member) aset) bset :''a list
```

Write a function union to create a set of all the items in two sets.

4.4   Program design with higher order functions

This section shows how programming with higher order functions leads to more general purpose programs. Higher order functions eliminate explicit recursion and so lead to programs that are more concise and often nearer to the natural specification of a problem.

4.4.1   Making functions more flexible

Many functions can be made more general by substituting explicit predicate functions with a parameter; the decision as to which predicate is actually employed is thereby deferred until the function is applied. In the following example *insertion sort* (presented in Section 3.7.3) is generalized so that it will sort a list of any type in either ascending or descending order. The only alteration that is required to the original specification is to substitute a comparison function in place of the infix < operator for `insert` and `isort`. The following code reworks the example presented in Chapter 3.7.3 in curried form:

```
type 'a ORDERING = 'a -> 'a -> bool

fun insert (order :'a ORDERING)
           (item :'a)
           (nil :'a list)
    = [item] :'a list

|   insert order item (front :: rest)
    = if order item front
      then item :: front :: rest
      else front :: (insert order item rest)

fun xsort (order :'a ORDERING)
          (nil :'a list)
          (sortedlist :'a list)
    = sortedlist :'a list

|   xsort order (front :: rest) sortedlist
    = xsort order rest (insert order front sortedlist)

fun isort (order :'a ORDERING) (anylist :'a list)
    = xsort order anylist nil :'a list
```

The extra parameter `order` provides the comparison function, whilst also dictating the type of the list. In this manner the functionality of `isort` has been increased significantly since a different `order` can be slotted in place by a simple **val** declaration. For example, using the functions defined in Section 4.1.3:

```
val intsort = isort lessthan

val stringsort = isort str_lessthan
```

As a bonus it is possible to remove some of the explicit recursion from these function definitions by replacing the explicitly defined `isort` with `reduce` as follows:

```
val stringsort = reduce (insert str_lessthan) nil
```

Exercise 4.11

An equivalent version of stringsort using accumulate would require that the arguments to insert str_lessthan be reversed. Why is this the case?

4.4.2 *Combining higher order functions*

This subsection briefly looks at some of the many ways of combining higher order functions.

Example – *combining* accumulate *and* map

The following is a simple example using map and accumulate to convert a string to an integer:

```
fun ctoi (x :string)
    = (ord x) — (ord "0") :int

fun map_ctoi (astring :string)
    = map ctoi (explode astring) :int list

fun string_to_int (astring :string)
    = accumulate (plus o (times 10))
                 0
                 (map_ctoi astring) :int
```

This may be simplified, using function composition, as follows:

```
fun ctoi (x :string) = (ord x) — (ord "0") :int

val string_to_int
    = (accumulate (plus o (times 10)) 0)
      o (map ctoi)
      o explode :string —> int
```

This example reinforces the observation that function composition is the equivalent of sequencing in an imperative style of programming, though here the program sequence should be read from the rightmost composition towards the leftmost.

Example – *combining* map *and* filter

The functions filter and map may be combined to give a function which takes a list of items, each of type (STUDENT * GRADE), and outputs the names of all students with a grade less than 50%.

```
type STUDENT = string
type GRADE   = int
type RESULTS = (STUDENT * GRADE) list
type MAPPING = RESULTS -> STUDENT list

val weak_students
    = (map fst) o filter ((isitlessthan 50) o snd) :MAPPING
```

Different approaches to combining functions

There are a number of approaches to combining functions and higher order functions; to illustrate this point, two of the many possible versions of the function length are now shown.

The first version has an underlying design that considers the length of a list as the sum of a list which has had all of its items transformed into the integer 1. Hence the implementation must *firstly* transform each of its argument's list elements into 1 and *secondly* perform the summation. This can be written using accumulate, map and the combinator K as follows:

```
val length = (accumulate plus 0) o (map (K 1))
```

An alternative design is to think in terms of function composition and consider the length of a list as the *on-going* summation of each list element transformed into the integer 1:

```
val length = reduce (plus o (K 1)) 0
```

There are no rigid rules concerning which style to use. The best advice is to choose the definition which most closely mirrors the natural specification; however, this will differ from problem to problem and from program designer to program designer. Probably the biggest danger is to be tempted to go too far with the facilities shown in this chapter; the following code is nasty because there has been no attempt to make it intelligible:

```
val guesswhat = reduce (make_curried (op + ) o (K 1)) 0
```

Exercise 4.12
A function foldiftrue which reduces only those elements of a list which satisfy a given predicate could be defined as:

```
fun foldiftrue (pred :'a -> bool)
               (ff :'a -> 'b -> 'b)
               (default :'b)
               (nil :'a list)
  = default :'b

| foldiftrue pred ff default (front :: rest)
  = if pred front
      then (ff front (foldiftrue pred ff default rest))
      else foldiftrue pred ff default rest
```

Write this function in terms of a composition of reduce and filter.

4.5 *Summary*

Much of the power of SML derives from its ability to treat functions themselves as objects to be manipulated as easily as single values and data structures; a function that either takes a function as an argument or returns a function as its result is known as a *higher order function*.

All the functions introduced in this chapter are higher order functions. They make extensive use of a functional programming language feature known as *currying*; this technique allows the programmer to express the *partial application* of a function to only a few of its arguments (maybe none). Since a partial application is itself a function, this provides a simple and uniform mechanism for treating functions as values; they may be passed as arguments to other functions and they may be returned as the result of a function.

In order to emphasize the treatment of functions as values, a number of *combinators* have been introduced. These combinators are higher order functions that manipulate other functions. They may often help to simplify code by providing simple, general-purpose manipulation of functions and their arguments. In particular, *functional composition* encapsulates the common practice of using the result of one function application as the input parameter to a second function. The composition operator facilitates the repeated use of this technique, producing a 'pipeline' style of programming.

Higher order functions provide an elegant mechanism to remove the need for explicit recursion. To demonstrate this facility for lists, three families of curried, polymorphic higher order functions on lists have been introduced:

1. The map family which retains the list structure but transforms the list items.

2. The fold family which distributes an operator over a list, generally to produce a single value result.

3. The select family which may select items from a list, according to a given predicate.

5 · *Managing Environments*

The main theme of this chapter is *modularity*; it will be seen that the programmer has considerable control over the accessibility of names and may use restricted environments to produce code that is easier to understand, easier to maintain and more re-usable.

5.1 *Environments*

As an SML session proceeds the system builds what is known as an *environment*, which incrementally records all the function and **val** name definitions with their associated values. Each new definition is said to *bind* a name to a value. When a new object is defined it has access to all of these bindings. Subsequently the new object name, together with its associated value, is added to the existing environment.

When a function is defined, its body has a *new* environment consisting of the inherited environment at the point of definition together with the names of the function's formal parameters (which are only bound to actual values when the function is applied). This new environment is specific to the function body and does not affect subsequent function definitions.

5.1.1 *Free and bound names*

In order to determine the value of a name that appears in a function's body one of two rules is applied:

1. Any appearance of a formal parameter name takes its value from the actual parameter to which the function is applied. In other words, the local environment ignores any previous binding for that name in the inherited environment. Formally, the name is said to be *bound* in that function.

    This rule also holds for the name of the function itself.

2. Any other name that appears in the function body takes its value from the inherited environment; formally, it is said to be *free* in that function. Any function that does not have any free values is said to be closed or to exhibit *closure*.

133

Scope

The region of program text in which a binding is effective is known as its *scope*. Thus, the two rules presented above are often known as the *rules of scope*. Outside the scope of a particular binding, the name for that binding has no value and any reference to the name will result in an error (as will be demonstrated below). Notice that the environment of an expression (that is, the set of names that are accessible to the expression) depends only on the *textual position* of the expression in the program.

The terms 'bound' and 'in scope' are often interchangeable, as are the terms 'unbound' and 'out of scope'. For example, if a name that is free in a function does not appear in the inherited environment then SML will report that it is *unbound*, as shown in Figure 5.1. The error message displayed in Figure 5.1 means that SML cannot find a meaning for y in the environment of the function not_bound, although SML may have a meaning for y in the local environment of another function. In this case there was a value previously associated with the name y but this was bound in the function both_bound.

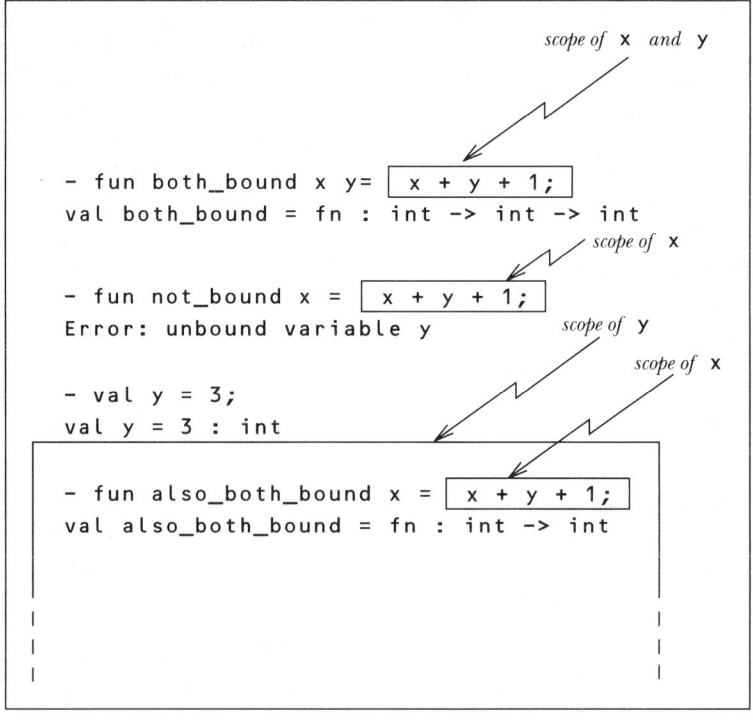

Figure 5.1. The scope of bindings

What can be bound?

Reserved names[1] *cannot* be re-bound, whilst it is recommended that function names and type names *should not* be re-bound. Thus, the following example, which rebinds predefined names, is legitimate but deplorable in that it is not immediately obvious what the function does:

```
fun nasty nil string = false

  |   nasty (hd :: tl) string
      = if   hd = string
         then    true
         else    nasty tl string
```

Even though `string` is a basic type and `hd` and `tl` are functions that are normally provided by SML, their original meanings are suspended throughout the scope of the function `nasty`. The function happens to work because the names `string,` `hd` and `tl` are bound as formal parameters in the local environment for the function `nasty`. However, it must again be stressed that this style is dangerous and definitely *not* recommended.

5.1.2 Scope implications

The discussion of the SML rules of scope should clarify two important constraints on SML programs:

1. Mutual recursion – without the keyword **and** it would be impossible to define mutually recursive functions. This is because the first function to be defined would not have any of the other functions (which are subsequently defined) in scope.

2. Displaying a top-down design – it is not directly possible to present the results of a top-down design in a top-down manner. This is because all functions must have their subsidiary functions in scope.

5.1.3 Re-using names

The fact that SML is an interactive system that uses incremental program construction has advantages for the rapid development of new ideas. However, the misuse of this interactive nature of SML can cause severe difficulties when attempting to construct permanent programs, mainly because the programmer cannot expect referential transparency in an SML session.

1. See Appendix D.

In order to ensure understandable, maintainable and re-usable code, it must be stressed that the redefinition of functions or **val** names should *never* occur as a part of the final version of a program. For small programs, any potential name clashes can easily be avoided. This program development is normally only undertaken by one person who can keep track of the limited number of names. For larger programs it is much harder to guarantee the uniqueness of names because of their increased number and the fact that more than one programmer will normally be involved in the software development process. In this context, it is certainly unreasonable to expect a programmer to invent new names for every new object in the system. Similarly, programmers should not be expected to know the names of objects that they are not directly interested in.

The rest of this chapter shows that unique names are not really a problem because names can be limited to a particular scope; that is, programmers can control their own program environment.

5.2 Modularity – local and let

A function's formal parameters are only in scope within the function body; this enhances modularity by providing a local environment. However, this does not really give much control. What is really needed is a means of defining a function or value to have a limited scope; that is, to have expressions that are not generally free from their point of definition, but are in scope for a number of other specified expressions only.

The simple example of reverse shown in Figure 5.2 makes use of an auxiliary accumulative function xrev. The latter is not robust (as it does not validate its parameter) nor is it reasonable to expect someone to know that it requires its second parameter to be instantiated to nil. In this context the requirement for safe programming can be met by binding xrev to reverse such that the existence of xrev is concealed from any other function. In SML this may be achieved by using one of the keywords **local** or **let**. As a rule of thumb, **local** definitions will be shown as useful to restrict the scope of auxiliary definitions and **let** expressions will be shown as useful for defining sub-expressions or providing a means for textual substitution. However, as with many other programming language features, it will be seen that the choice of one form or the other is often a matter of individual style.

5.2.1 local definitions

Figure 5.3 introduces the keywords **local**, **in** and **end**. The auxiliary function xrev is in scope only from its point of definition to the terminating keyword **end**. The fact that xrev is bound in the function reverse is emphasized by the SML response (which makes no mention of the name xrev). Unless xrev had already been defined

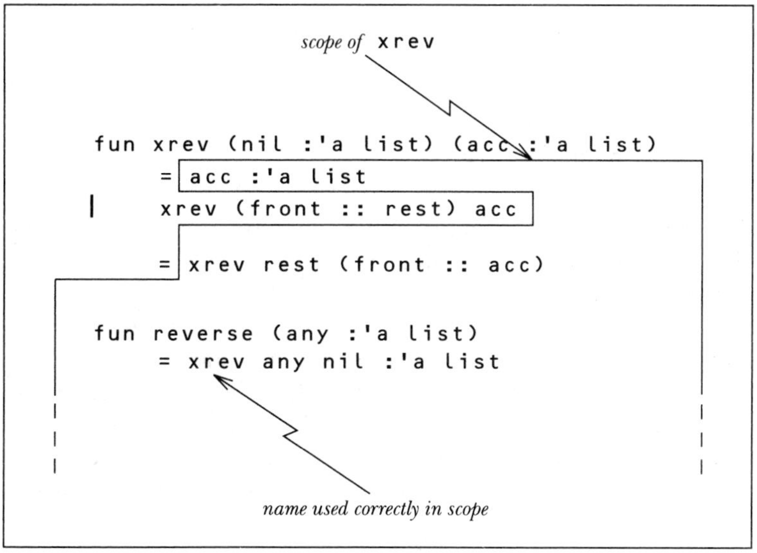

```
                    scope of xrev

    fun xrev (nil :'a list) (acc :'a list)
        = | acc :'a list
      |   xrev (front :: rest) acc

        = | xrev rest (front :: acc)

    fun reverse (any :'a list)
        = xrev any nil :'a list




                name used correctly in scope
```

Figure 5.2.   Subsidiary function in scope

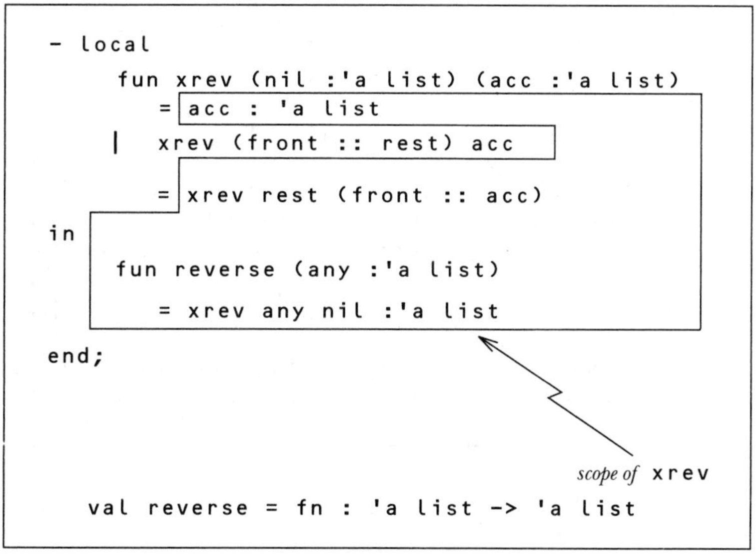

```
-  local
      fun xrev (nil :'a list) (acc :'a list)
          = | acc : 'a list
        |   xrev (front :: rest) acc

          = | xrev rest (front :: acc)
  in
          fun reverse (any :'a list)
              = xrev any nil :'a list

  end;


                                    scope of xrev

      val reverse = fn : 'a list -> 'a list
```

Figure 5.3.   Scope of a **local** function definition

in another context, an attempt to apply it would give rise to the error that xrev is not bound:

```
— xrev [1,2,3] nil;
Error: unbound variable xrev
```

Thus the function xrev is unknown to anything but reverse; if reverse were used from another file by a different programmer, he or she would not even be aware that reverse employs this auxiliary function in its implementation.

Similarly, more than one function can be made local to another function or functions can be nested within functions. This is demonstrated in the example shown in Figure 5.4, borrowed from Chapter 2, where the hierarchical organization of the program design is now accurately reflected by limiting the scope of the auxiliary functions. However, it may be clearer to combine the two **local** definitions in the actual code and demonstrate the top-down design as part of the program documentation, as shown in Figure 5.5.

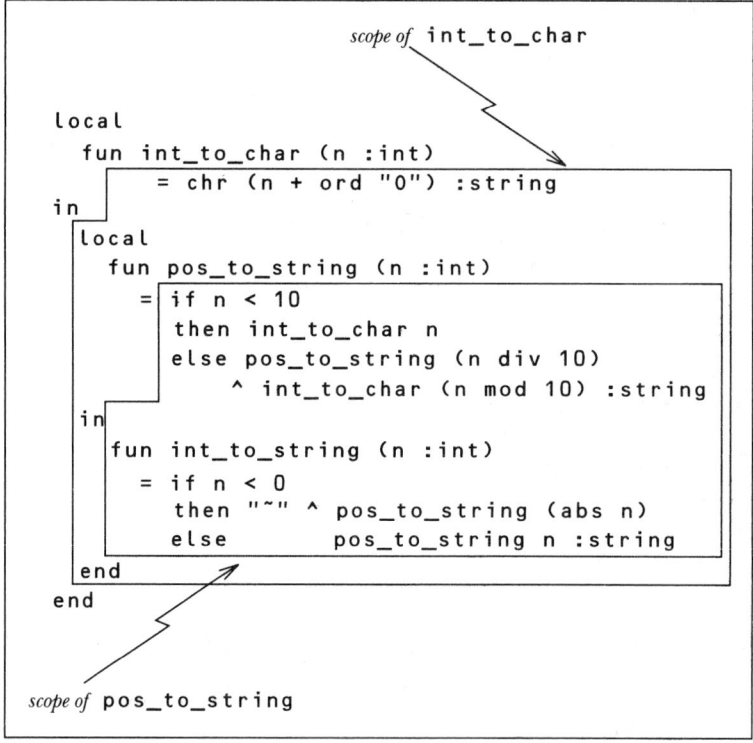

Figure 5.4. Scope of nested **local** function definitions

```
(* int_to_string displays an integer as a
character string.

Dependencies:

int_to_string uses pos_to_string
pos_to_string uses int_to_char


*)

local
    fun int_to_char (n :int)
        = chr (n + ord "0") :string

    fun pos_to_string (n :int)
        = if n < 10
          then int_to_char n
          else pos_to_string (n div 10)
               ^ int_to_char (n mod 10) :string
in
    fun int_to_string (n :int)
        = if n < 0
          then "~" ^ pos_to_string (abs n)
          else         pos_to_string n :string

end
```

scope of int_to_char

scope of pos_to_string

Figure 5.5. Alternative definition for int_to_string

As can also be seen in the following example[2] **local** definitions may contain **val** names as well as **fun** definitions and may also bind more than one function. It should also be noted that where more than one definition appears within a **local** environment then the environment is built in exactly the same way as the top-level environment:

2. This algorithm was adapted from 'Random number generators: good ones are hard to find', by S.K.Park and K.W.Miller, *Communications ACM*, vol. 31, 1988, pp.1192–1201.

```
(* Program to generate a list of random numbers
real number version for systems with 46-bit
mantissas together with function to constrain
the result to integer limits
*)

type RLIST = real list

exception Randomize
local
    val C1 = 16807.0
    val MAX = 2147483647.0

    fun nextseed (seed :real)
        = (C1 * seed) — MAX
          * real (floor ((C1 * seed) / MAX)) :real

    fun genlist (0 :int) (seed :real) (rlist :RLIST)
        = (seed, rlist) :real * RLIST
    |   genlist n seed rlist
        = genlist (n — 1) (nextseed seed) (seed :: rlist)
in

    (* generate N random numbers and a
       new seed from an initial seed
    *)
    fun randomize (n :int) (firstseed :real)
        = if (n < 0)
             then raise Randomize
             else genlist n firstseed nil :real * RLIST


    (* constrain random real number to acceptable
       integer range
    *)
    fun constrain (k :int) (r :real)
        = 1 + floor ((r / MAX) * (real k)) :int
end


(* the function could be used in the following manner:

  map (constrain 3) (snd (randomize 50 1.1))

*)
```

Exercise 5.1
Write a function, using **local** definitions, to return the string that appears before a given sublist in a string. For example: b e f o r e s t r i n g (" a n d " , " S t a n d a r d M L ") will return the string " S t ".

5.2.2 *let expressions*

The following examples demonstrate the use of the keywords **let**, **in** and **end** in a number of contexts. Figure 5.6 shows one of the simplest uses of **let** which is to make code more readable by replacing long expressions with shorter ones. In this example, the single names l o w and h i g h replace the unwieldy expressions f s t (s p l i t p r e d r e s t) and s n d (s p l i t p r e d r e s t). As with **local** definitions, the new binding is not available outside of the restricted scope.

```
fun split (pred : 'a -> bool) (nil :'a list)
    = (nil, nil) :'a list * 'a list

|   split pred (front :: rest)
    = let
          val (low, high) = split pred rest
      in
          if pred front
          then (front :: low, high)
          else (low, front :: high)
      end

            scope of low and high
```

Figure 5.6. The scope of names in a **let** expression

The next example shows that **let** expressions can also contain function definitions. Here r e v e r s e is written with an accumulator hidden in an auxiliary function. The style is similar to that of a **local** definition, except that the visual emphasis is now on the main function rather than the **local** keyword:

```
fun reverse (alist :'a list)
   = let
      fun xrev (nil :'a list) (acc :'a list)
         = acc :'a list

      |   xrev (front :: rest) acc
         = xrev rest (front :: acc)
      in
         xrev alist nil :'a list
      end
```

As with **local** definitions, there is also no restriction on the number of definitions that can appear within a **let** expression and, as expected, if more than one definition appears then the **let** sub-environment is built in exactly the same way as the top-level environment. This is demonstrated in the following program (part of a text justifier) which throws away all leading white-space characters in a string and which compresses all other occurrences of multiple white-space characters into a single space.

```
type SLIST = string list

fun compress (astring :string)
   = let
         val SPACE     = " "
         val TAB       = "\t"
         val NEWLINE   = "\n"
         val EOS       = ""

         fun isspace (c :string)
            = (c = SPACE)
               orelse (c = TAB)
               orelse (c = NEWLINE) :bool
(* this drop differs from the Chapter 3 version *)
         fun drop (nil :SLIST) = nil :SLIST
         |   drop (front :: rest)
            = if isspace front
              then drop rest
              else (front :: rest)

         fun squeeze (nil :SLIST) = EOS :string
         |   squeeze (front :: rest)
            = if isspace front
              then SPACE ^ squeeze (drop rest)
              else front ^ squeeze rest
      in
       squeeze (drop (explode astring)) :string
      end
```

```
type 'a ORDERING = 'a -> 'a -> bool

fun qsort (order :'a ORDERING) (nil :'a list)
    = nil :'a list
    | qsort order (front :: rest)
    = let
        fun split pred nil = (nil, nil)
        |    split pred (front :: rest)
            = let
                val (low, high) = split pred rest
            in
                if pred front
                then (front :: low, high)
                else (low, front :: high)
            end
        val (low, high) = split (order front) rest
    in
        qsort order low
        @ [front]
        @ qsort order high

    end
```

scope of inner definitions for low *and* high

scope of outer definitions for low *and* high

Figure 5.7. Scope of names in nested **let** expressions

The implementation of 'quicksort'[3] shown in Figure 5.7 uses the split function to decompose the unsorted list to yield a tuple pair of those values that satisfy the ordering function[4] and those that do not. This example demonstrates how **let** expressions may be nested, with the effect that the names low and high can be used in two different contexts. In general, this is considered to be bad style because of the

3. Quicksort is a recursive sorting algorithm which works by choosing one of the values in the list as a pivot; the list is then split into all values less than the pivot, the pivot itself, and all values greater than the pivot; the quicksort algorithm is then applied to each of the two sublists just generated (choosing a new pivot for each sublist). Empty sublists are ignored and eventually every value will have been considered as a pivot – all the pivots are now in order and can be collected together to form the sorted list, as required. For more details see Standish (1980).
4. To sort integers in ascending order the ordering function should be isitlessthan since it is used in a partially applied manner within split.

possible confusion over names. However, the example serves to illustrate the point that it is possible, and indeed this technique is unfortunately quite common amongst programmers.

The programmer may often choose whether to use **let** or **local** definitions, as demonstrated by the following reworking of the `split` function. There are no absolute rules to guide the programmer in this choice; it is a question of style and the programmer should aim to produce clear, obvious and uncluttered code:

```
type 'a PREDICATE = 'a -> bool
type 'a LISTPAIR  = 'a list * 'a list

local
    fun pair (pred :'a PREDICATE)
             (nil :'a list)
             (any :'a LISTPAIR)
        = any :'a LISTPAIR
      | pair pred (front :: rest) (low, high)
        = pair pred rest (if pred front
                          then (front :: low, high)
                          else (low, front :: high))
in
    fun split (pred : 'a PREDICATE) (any :'a list)
        = pair pred any (nil, nil) :'a LISTPAIR
end
```

Exercise 5.2
As Exercise 5.1 but use **let** expressions instead of **local** declarations.

Eliminating unnecessary sub-expressions

Using **let** can also produce more modular code when a sub-expression appears more than once in another expression. For instance, the function `oklength` checks to see if a given string is of at least a specified size `lowerbound` and not larger than `upperbound`:

```
fun oklength (s :string) (lowerbound :int) (upperbound :int)
    = size s >= lowerbound
      andalso
      size s <= upperbound :bool
```

However, `size s` appears twice and might have to be altered twice if the function specification changed. If a **let** definition is used then the alteration can be done in one place only, thereby making the programmer's task easier and the code safer.

```
fun oklength (s :string) (lowerbound :int) (upperbound :int)
   = let
          val slen = size s
       in
          slen >= lowerbound
          andalso
          slen <= upperbound :bool
       end
```

The advantage of this modular approach becomes increasingly more apparent as the sub-expression occurs more often in the main expression.

Eliminating unnecessary parameters

The following curried version of the sublist function from the *grep* program (shown in Chapter 3) uses an auxiliary function xsublist whose binding is confined to sublist but does not carry around the regexp parameter on each of its recursive applications. Although regexp is free in xsublist it is in scope and hence accessible to xsublist:

```
type SLIST   = string list
type MTYPE   = string
type REGTYPE = MTYPE * string
type REGLIST = REGTYPE list


fun sublist (regexp :REGLIST) (line :SLIST)
   = (startswith regexp line)
         orelse
           let
             fun xsublist (nil :SLIST) = false :bool
             |   xsublist ( _ :: lrest)
                 = (startswith regexp lrest)
                   orelse
                   (xsublist lrest)
           in
                xsublist line :bool
           end
```

This is quite a common functional programming style because it is generally easier to read functions with less parameters. Unfortunately, this style can easily be abused; the following definition of map also saves on passing a parameter (ff) but may be considered less clear because it is not obvious from where xmap expects its list parameter:

```
fun map (ff :'a -> 'b)
    =   let
            fun xmap (nil :'a list) = nil :'b list
            |   xmap (front :: rest)
                = (ff front) :: xmap rest
        in
            xmap :'a list -> 'b list
        end
```

A clearer version would include the list parameter to `map`:

```
fun map (ff :'a -> 'b) (anylist :'a list)
    =   let fun xmap (nil :'a list) = nil :'b list
        |   xmap (front :: rest)
            = (ff front) :: xmap rest
        in
            xmap anylist :'b list
        end
```

Exercise 5.3

Explain the scope of the various values of and evaluate the application of `silly` to the argument `"silly"`:

```
fun silly (silly :string) =
let
        val silly = silly ^ silly
        val silly = silly ^ silly
in
        silly ^ silly :string
end
```

5.3 *Simultaneous definitions – and*

The keyword **and** has already been shown as a means of permitting mutually recursive function definitions. This section shows some of its other uses and potential abuses for:

1.   Linking closely related utilities.

2.   Reflecting a program's top-down organization.

3.   Controlling the scope of bindings within a sub-expression.

Linking utilities

The keyword **and** is sometimes used to stress the semantic dependencies between two or more closely related functions. This is because the reader is obliged to consider, as a whole, all those functions that have been **and**ed together. For example, the functions `fstsame` and `sndsame` are not mutually recursive: however, the two functions are complementary in that they cover the two selection possibilities on a tuple of type `'a * 'a`. The use of **and** helps to document this fact:

```
fun fstsame ((x, _) :'a * 'a) = x :'a
and
    sndsame ((_, y) :'a * 'a) = y :'a
```

Generally, however, it is better practice to rely upon appropriate *comments* to emphasize this form of tight-coupling. For example:

```
(* fstsame and sndsame are complementary functions
   Always define them together.
*)
fun fstsame ((x, _) :'a * 'a) = x :'a
fun sndsame ((_, y) :'a * 'a) = y :'a
```

Displaying a top-down design

The keyword **and** is also sometimes unwisely used to reflect the top-down design of a program because it relaxes the requirement that a function must be defined before use.[5] For example:

```
fun reverse (any :'a list) = xrev any nil :'a list
and
    xrev (nil :'a list) (acc :'a list)
    = acc :'a list
|   xrev (front :: rest) acc
    = xrev rest (front :: acc)
```

However, it must be emphasized that this style of programming is *not safe*; the auxiliary function `xrev` has not had its scope restricted and is just as available as `reverse`.

Furthermore, this style is misleading and may give rise to errors when employed with polymorphic functions, as demonstrated by the following example:

---

5. Chapter 7 shows how the above program could be made safe by enveloping it in what is known as a **structure** and only allowing `reverse` to be known to other programmers.

```
— fun wrong_firsts (x :real * real) (y :int * int)
    = (fst x, fst y) : (real * int)
  and
    fst (x,y) = x;

Error: operator and operand don't agree (tycon mismatch)
operator domain: real * real
operand:         int * int
in expression:
  fst y
```

The above example fails because the polymorphic nature of fst can only be utilized *after* it has been defined. Thus, because wrong_firsts and fst are defined simultaneously, fst may only appear in the function body for wrong_firsts as a function of fixed, non-polymorphic type. The initial application of fst in the function body will determine which type it has. However, in any subsequent definition or application fst will be polymorphic.

This restriction on the use of polymorphic functions is apparent in the above example because the types of the input parameters to wrong_firsts are explicitly stated. In the following example, the types are not given and so the definition does not produce an error – it may however produce an error when the function is applied:

```
— fun sometimes_wrong_firsts x y
      = (fst x, fst y)
  and
      fst (x,y) = x ;

val sometimes_wrong_firsts
    = fn : 'a * 'b —> 'a * 'b —> ('a * 'a)
val fst = fn : 'a * 'b —> 'a

— sometimes_wrong_firsts (1, 3) (2, 4);
val it = (1, 2) : (int * int)

— sometimes_wrong_firsts (2.0, 2.8) (2.3, 2.3);
val it = (2.0, 2.3) : (real * real)

— sometimes_wrong_firsts (1, 3) (1.0, 3.45);
Error: operator and operand don't agree (tycon mismatch)
operator domain: int * int
operand:         real * real
in expression:
    sometimes_wrong_firsts (1, 3) (1.0, 3.45)
```

In fact, SML provides a strong hint that the usual polymorphism has been restricted – the reader is encouraged to compare the type which SML has inferred for sometimes_wrong_firsts above and that for always_correct_firsts below:

```
— fun fst (x,y) = x ;
val fst = fn : 'a * 'b—> 'a

— fun always_correct_firsts x y = (fst x, fst y);
val always_correct_firsts = fn : 'a * 'b —> 'c * 'd —> 'a * 'c
```

The use of **and** with **val** definitions

Perhaps contrary to expectations, the following may give rise to an error or return a result other than the value 6:

```
— val x = 3
  and y = x;
  ...
— x + y;
```

The reason is that **val** definitions are not recursive (see Appendix B). A recursive definition would allow x to appear within the definition body: however, the above only makes x available *after* the simultaneous definitions of both x and y. Hence, x would have to have been already defined for this definition to be legal. For example, the following evaluates to 4 rather than 6 because y takes its value from the 'outer' binding of x:

```
val x = 1        (* outer binding *)
let
    val x = 3    (* inner binding *)
    and y = x
in
    x + y
end
```

As a guideline, this sort of definition should be *avoided*. Assuming that a programmer wishes to bind y to the value of the outer x, it does not take too much effort to think of another name for the inner x in the above expression.

Exercise 5.4
Explain the system response to the following:

```
fun x _ = 3
and
val y = x
```

5.4 *Summary*

One of the very first features of SML to be covered in this text is the ability to allocate **val** names to expressions. These names are useful because the values of their expressions may be recalled by using the names in subsequent expressions. There are strict rules which govern the binding of names to values and which dictate how these names are made accessible to subsequent expressions. Firstly, every expression has access to those names that exist in its *environment*; secondly, the environment of an expression (that is, the set of names that are accessible to the expression) depends on the textual position of the expression in the program; thirdly, the various environments in the program may be explicitly augmented using **local** and/or **let** definitions.

The main advantage of using **let** or **local** expressions is that closely related functions and definitions may be self-contained and so not rely on values bound outside the expression (that is, they exhibit closure). They are consequently safer and easier to re-use. This principle is further explained in Chapter 7 where the concept of the **structure** is introduced to enable module definition.

6 · User-defined Types

Chapter 1 introduced the idea of categorizing program data into various types and the importance of a strong type system has been emphasized throughout this book. However, the available built-in types are somewhat limited in that they do not always directly model the complex relationships inherent in 'real-world' data. This chapter presents a mechanism by which a programmer can create new types. This allows the creation of data structures which are better able to model real-world relationships and it encourages the use of the type system to provide *built-in validation* of data.

The chapter first discusses the **datatype** keyword, which defines a new type, and then introduces the **abstype** keyword, which defines a new type together with the operations which are valid for that type. The former provides a simple data structuring mechanism, whereas the latter provides abstraction by hiding the underlying representation (that is, by hiding the definitions of the primitive operations for the type). The ability to take an abstract view of both code and data leads to a better appreciation of the overall meaning and structure of a program.

6.1 The need for new types

This section illustrates the need for new types through several examples. A type may be defined with precision by listing the collection of values which belong to the type (that is, the values which exist in the type domain). For example, the type `bool` is precisely defined by listing the two values in its domain: `true` and `false`. The examples in this section therefore concentrate on the collection of values which define a type; this approach is further utilized in the next section, where a general mechanism for creating new types will be presented.

New types

SML provides a small number of useful built-in types. However, the choice of built-in types is a matter for the language designer and it is likely that some other useful types have not been provided. This is often true in other languages where, for example, there may not be a built-in Boolean type. If the type `bool` did not already exist in SML, it could be created by specifying the permitted values as `true` or `false`. For brevity, this can be written *true | false*, where the vertical bar is used to separate the alternative values.

If the type `int` did not already exist, an attempt could be made to create it in a similar way: *1 | 2 | 3 | 4 | 5* . . . However, this type presents some difficulty because of the very large number of alternative values (in practice limited by the computer architecture). The solution to the problem of a large number of values is to describe the values recursively, as will be seen later in this chapter (Sections 6.4 and 6.5).

Special versions of types

Although the type `bool` is a built-in type for SML, it is possible that a programmer might wish to create several special versions of the type and make use of the fact that the type system will ensure that they are used consistently in the program and will not be mixed. For example, *windows_true | windows_false* could be used to indicate whether the program is connected to a display which supports a windowing environment, whilst *multi_user_true | multi_user_false* could be used to indicate whether the program is available to a single user or to many users.

This facility for specialization is not limited to Boolean values. For instance, dice-playing games require special meaning to be given to the numbers from one to six, so *dice_one | dice_two | dice_three | dice_four | dice_five | dice_six* could be used to indicate the full range of values for a new type called *DICE*.

By using these new types, not only can a program be made more readable but there is the considerable advantage that the type system can be used to provide built-in validation (so that *windows_true* and *true* can never be confused).

Structured types and constructors

In the pursuit of well-structured data, it is desirable to be able to specify new types in terms of previously defined types. In particular, it should be possible to build upon existing types (including previously specified user-defined types) in order to produce a new type which is able to represent the structured data which occurs in many applications.

A convenient mechanism to achieve this aim is to allow each constant value of a user-defined type to be combined with a type name to indicate a further sub-level of values. This principle may then be extended to allow many different levels, whereby at each level the choice of data value determines what underlying values are available at the next (that is, the lower) level. For example, it is possible to define a single type which contains information about whether multiple simultaneous users are allowed, with each of the two values having a further underlying value to indicate whether a windowing system is being used (here the word 'of' introduces each underlying type): *multi_user of bool | single_user of bool*. In this example, the domain for the new type is fully defined by the values *multi_user false, multi_user true, single_user false* and *single_user true*. However, the underlying types need not have finite domains, as shown by the following example: *discrete of int | continuous of real*.

In the above example the constant values *discrete* and *continuous* provide a unique way to determine the structure of a particular value in the domain of this type; for this reason they are often referred to as *constructors*. Notice that there need not be any underlying type to be 'constructed': true and false are both simple data values and are also known as constructors. Furthermore, the different constructors for a type can have mixed structure – some may have a complex underlying type, whereas others may have no underlying type at all.

Mixed types

A programmer might wish to create a new type whose values could be drawn from any one of a mixture of built-in types. For example, a company might describe a customer using a string if the customer is an individual, by an int or (int list) if the customer is an internal department or group of departments, or by a (string * int) or (string * (int list)) pair if the customer is a department or group of departments of an external company. In this example, the programmer may wish to encapsulate these options into a new type with the alternatives: (*individual of string | department of int | group of (int list) | ext_dept of (string * int) | ext_group of (string * (int list))*). Examples of values of this new type are individual "Winston", department 45 and group [1,3,67]; thus the domain for this new type contains all the values of the string domain *and* all the values of the int domain *and* all the values of the (int list) domain and so on.

Towards type abstraction

A programmer might wish to specify which values of an existing type are legal for a particular task; for example a twenty-four hour *CLOCK* type should only allow numbers in the range 0 to 24. If the number of alternative values is small then a new type can be generated such as *clock_one | clock_two | clock_three | . . . | clock_twenty_three | clock_twenty_four*.

An alternative would be to create a new type which uses all the values of an underlying type (such as int). However, in this case it would be necessary to define a set of operations for the new type so that values outside the range 0 to 24 are considered illegal and so that inappropriate operations (such as multiplying together values which represent the hours of the day) are not allowed. Later in this chapter there will be a discussion of the **abstype** mechanism which allows a programmer to package a new type together with the operations which are appropriate for that type.

The next section will present the full SML syntax for creating new types, which is based on a general mechanism for describing and creating types by means of *defining the permitted values of the type*.

6.2 Datatypes

In SML a user-defined type is known as a **datatype** and is created by a general purpose mechanism based on the idea of *constructors*, which were first discussed in Section 3.2.1. The fundamental principle is that each permitted value of a new type is distinguished from permitted values of other types by means of a special tag, known as a constructor. This gives a *unique and unambiguous* representation for every value of a user-defined type, in exactly the same way that the built-in constructors `::` and `nil` give a unique and unambiguous representation of any list.

The general format for a new type definition is:

> **datatype**   *new_type_name*
>   = *value1*
> | *value2*
>   . . .
> | *valueN*

A new type must have at least one value; alternatives are denoted by the vertical bar and each value may either be *nullary* or may be constructed from an underlying type. A nullary value is a constant value, such as `true` or `false`, and is represented by a *nullary constructor* (sometimes known as a 'constant constructor' for self-evident reasons). A value therefore has one of two formats:

> *nullary_constructor_name*

or

> *constructor_name* **of** *underlying_type*

The *underlying_type* may be simple or aggregate, built-in or another **datatype** previously defined in the program.

New **datatype**s are characterized by two important features:

1. They are *not* type synonyms. A type synonym is merely a shorthand denotation for an already existing type, whereas a **datatype** is a totally new type; a type synonym may be mixed with its actual type, whereas **datatype**s may not be mixed with other types. Thus, in the definition:

    ```
    datatype POSITIVE = Positive of int
    ```

    the new type name is `POSITIVE`, the constructor name is `Positive`, and the value (`Positive 3`) may *not* be substituted for the value `3` because they are of different types.

2. The existing properties of any underlying types are *not* inherited; equality is the only operation which may be legal upon two instances of a **datatype**. For example, although the operator `<` is defined for the built-in type `int`, it is not defined for the type `POSITIVE` and therefore the expression (`Positive 3`) `<` (`Positive 5`) is meaningless.

Further examples:

```
datatype SWITCH = On | Off
datatype COLOUR = Rgb of (real * real * real)
                     (*Red, Green, Blue*)
                | Hsl of (real * real * real)
                     (*Hue, Saturation, Luminance*)
```

```
datatype RADIUS = Radius of real

datatype SPHERE = Sphere of (RADIUS * COLOUR)

datatype CUSTOMER = Individual of string
                  | Department of int
                  | Group of int list
                  | Company of (string * int)
```

The rest of this section discusses the various kinds of new **datatype**s that can be defined, including **datatype**s firstly with just one constructor and one underlying type through to **datatype**s with many constructors with different underlying types, and **datatype**s which do not have an underlying type.

6.2.1 *Simple datatype definition and usage*

Datatype *definition*

```
— datatype COORDS = Coords of real * real * real;

datatype COORDS
con Coords : real * real * real —> COORDS
```

This definition serves two related purposes:

1. To create a new type named **COORDS**.

2. To create a new prefix constructor named **Coords** (as indicated by the system response **con**).

This new constructor takes a real number triple[1] and converts it to the new **datatype**; as such, a constructor might be considered as a special form of function without a function body. However, there are many differences between constructors and functions; for example, SML constructors are always *uncurried*. The differences between functions and constructors are explored in more depth in Section 6.3.

Datatype *naming*

Constructors must be legal SML identifiers; they must conform to the rules for SML names, but there are no further restrictions and constructor names may look just like any other **val** name. However, in an attempt to promote readable code this book

---

1. Notice that the triple in the definition must be a *type* and therefore the type operator * is used, rather than the tuple expression format with brackets and commas.

adopts a consistent naming policy; wherever appropriate, it follows the convention that a new **datatype** is defined with an entirely UPPER CASE name and new constructors have their initial letter in Upper case. Though this is not a requirement of SML, it should help the reader to differentiate between constructors and other values.

Legal SML identifiers cannot start with a digit. Thus, in particular, it is not possible to model the integers with the definition:

```
datatype WRONG_DICE = 1 | 2 | 3 | 4 | 5 | 6
```

It is equally wrong to use strings as constructors, since a string is not a legal SML identifier:

```
datatype WRONG_DICE
    = "One" | "Two" | "Three" | "Four" | "Five" | "Six"
```

A legal definition would be:

```
datatype LEGAL_DICE = One | Two | Three | Four | Five | Six
```

Care must be taken to ensure that the constructor names of each new **datatype** are unique within a program. If this were not the case, and if two definitions were to employ the same constructor name, then the latter definition would take precedence over the former.

Datatype *instantiation*

New instances of COORDS may be created by supplying the Coords constructor with its expected argument (the keyword **of** is not required).

```
— val point_origin = Coords (0.0, 0.0, 0.0);
val point_origin = Coords (0.0,0.0,0.0) : COORDS

— val point_max = Coords (1000.0, 1000.0, 1000.0);
val point_max = Coords (1000.0,1000.0,1000.0) : COORDS
```

The Coords constructor is used in the same manner as the built-in list constructor ::. This is illustrated by comparing its use with that of the prefix version of the latter ((op ::)):

```
— (op ::) (1, [2,3]);
val it = [1,2,3] : int list

— Coords (3.0, 4.0, 5.0);
val it = Coords (3.0,4.0,5.0) : COORDS
```

Datatype *usage*

Using new types in functions is just as easy as using existing types and constructors. If there is a requirement to write a function to find the midpoint of two COORDS then they may be deconstructed to their underlying type using pattern matching:

```
- fun midpoint (Coords (x1,y1,z1)) (Coords (x2,y2,z2))
      = Coords ((x1 + x2)/ 2.0,
                (y1 + y2)/ 2.0,
                (z1 + z2)/ 2.0);
  val midpoint = fn : COORDS -> COORDS -> COORDS
```

In the application of the function midpoint to the two parameters point_origin and point_max:

```
- midpoint point_origin point_max;
  val it = Coords (500.0,500.0,500.0) : COORDS
```

the formal parameters (Coords (x1,y1,z1)) and (Coords (x2,y2,z2)) will be substituted with the actual values: (Coords (0.0, 0.0, 0.0)) and (Coords (1000.0, 1000.0, 1000.0)) respectively, and so will be success-fully matched.

It can be seen that constructors are used in function patterns in order to *deconstruct* a **datatype** and that they are used in function bodies to *construct* a value of a **datatype**. Thus, for deconstruction purposes there is no practical difference between the extraction of the head of a list front from the constructed list (front :: rest) and the extraction of the real numbers x1, y1 and z1 from the constructed instance (Coords (x1,y1,z1)). Similarly, for construction purposes there is no practical difference between the creation of a new list (front :: rest) from the item front and the list rest and the creation of a new COORDS instance by means of the application (Coords (x1,y1,z1)).

Note that, just as with patterns involving the list constructor ::, it is necessary to bracket the Coords constructor with its argument otherwise a syntax error will occur. This is because a constructor pattern must always be complete (see Section 6.3.1).

Exercise 6.1
Write a function to calculate the distance between a pair of COORDS.

Datatypes *are strongly typed*

It must be emphasized that using the keyword **datatype** creates a *new* type which conforms to the SML strong typing philosophy. This has the considerable advantage that the system will perform data validation and automatically catch any accidental attempts to use a new type in an illegal manner. In the above example, it is assumed that the programmer wishes to express the relationship between three real numbers as a new type and does *not* wish to mix a real number triple with a value drawn from this new type. Hence, a value that has been defined as a real number triple cannot be legally tested against an instance of a COORDS for equality:

```
— point_origin = (0.0, 0.0, 0.0);

Error: operator and operand don't agree (tycon mismatch)
   operator domain: COORDS * COORDS
   operand:         COORDS * (real * real * real)
   in expression: = (point_origin, (0.0,0.0,0.0))
```

In a similar manner, any function defined over a tuple of type (real * real * real) (even if given a name using a type synonym) cannot be applied to COORDS arguments.

6.2.2   Datatypes with multiple constructors

A **datatype** may also have more than one constructor. This is shown in the following two examples, the first of which shows a new type with more than one constructor over the same underlying type: the second shows the benefit of having constructors with different underlying types.

Multiple constructors over the same type

A new type FLUID is now defined to express the fact that fluid measurements are different in different countries. The subsequent definition of the function addFluids is designed to eliminate the possibility of a programmer attempting to mix operations on fluid measures of differing kinds:

```
datatype FLUID = USgallons of real
               | UKgallons of real
               | Litres of real

exception AddFluids
fun addFluids (USgallons x :FLUID) (USgallons y :FLUID)
    = USgallons (x + y) :FLUID
|   addFluids (UKgallons x) (UKgallons y)
    = UKgallons (x + y)
|   addFluids (Litres x) (Litres y)
    = Litres (x + y)
|   addFluids _ _ = raise AddFluids
```

It is now guaranteed that inappropriate operations such as adding amounts of different measurements or attempting to multiply two fluid measurements are not performed accidentally. Thus, the following applications will fail:

```
- addFluids (USgallons 3.0) (Litres 54.0);
uncaught exception AddFluids

- (USgallons 3.0) * (Litres 54.0);
Error: overloaded variable "*" not defined at type: FLUID

- (USgallons 3.0) + (Litres 54.0);
Error: overloaded variable "+" not defined at type: FLUID
```

The last two applications fail because the standard arithmetic and relational operators are not overloaded for user-defined types. Once again programmers are obliged to think carefully about their intentions and are helped to avoid mistakes by the type checker.

Multiple constructors over different types

It is also possible to have a **datatype** with different underlying types, as is now demonstrated with NUMBER:

```
datatype NUMBER = Int of int
                | Real of real
```

By using NUMBER, an attempt can be made to overcome what is sometimes an inconvenient barrier between integers and real numbers. For example, the function NumLess will take a pair of NUMBERs and simulate the overloaded < operator.

```
- fun NumLess (Int x :NUMBER) (Real y :NUMBER)
      = (real x) < y :bool
  |     NumLess (Real x) (Int y)
      = x < (real y)
  |     NumLess (Real x) (Real y)
      = x < y
  |      NumLess (Int x) (Int y)
      = x < y;

val NumLess = fn : NUMBER -> NUMBER -> bool
```

This new comparison function, NumLess, can now be used as any other function, for instance as a parameter to the sorting function, shown in Section 4.4.1:

```
— val NumSort = reduce (insert NumLess) nil;
val NumSort = fn : NUMBER list —> NUMBER list
```

Of course, it is still necessary to explicitly state the intended constructor for each new **NUMBER** and SML will always respond by echoing the constructor as well as the actual values:

```
— NumSort [Int 3, Real 3.1, Int 2, Real 1.9];
val it = [Real 1.9,Int 2,Int 3,Real 3.1] : NUMBER list
```

6.2.3   Underlying types for datatypes

There is no restriction on the underlying types for new constructors; they can be simple types, aggregate types, polymorphic types, functions or previously defined **datatype**s. This section shows some of these possibilities.

Polymorphic datatypes

The **datatype** facility parallels the **type** facility in that it is also legal (and often very useful) to have polymorphic **datatype**s. For example, **COORDS** could be made more general to allow for integer or real number instances:

```
datatype 'a PCOORDS = Pcoords of ('a * 'a * 'a)
```

As with **type** synonyms, it is necessary to precede the **datatype** name with a declaration of the names of the polytypes involved in the right-hand side of the definition. If there are many different polymorphic types then the name must be preceded with a tuple of all the relevant polytypes:

```
datatype ('a, 'b) PAIR = Pair of ('a * 'b)
```

New types from old

So far, all the examples of constructors have had built-in underlying types; however, it is often useful to build upon user-defined types to create more complex types that better represent the real-world data. The following example uses the polymorphic **datatype** **PCOORDS** to create a new **datatype** **LINE** which represents a straight line in three-dimensional space:

```
datatype LINE
      = Line of ((real PCOORDS) * (real PCOORDS))
```

The following example using LINE shows both:

1. A **val** name definition using the constructor Pcoords inside the constructor Line.

2. A function definition (line_midpoint) where the function pattern only needs to deconstruct the outer layer and therefore only uses the constructor Line:

```
val line = Line (Pcoords (0.0,0.0,0.0),
                 Pcoords (10.0,10.0,10.0))

fun pmidpoint ((Pcoords (x1,y1,z1)) :real PCOORDS)
              ((Pcoords (x2,y2,z2)) :real PCOORDS)
     = Pcoords ((x1 + x2)/ 2.0,
                (y1 + y2)/ 2.0,
                (z1 + z2)/ 2.0) :real PCOORDS

fun line_midpoint ((Line (x,y)) :LINE)
     = pmidpoint x y :real PCOORDS
```

Functional **datatypes**

Just as functions have been considered as values that may appear as the components of lists or tuples it is possible for them to provide the underlying type for **datatypes**, which is often useful when trying to model a dynamic relationship between objects. This is demonstrated in the following example where a new type is created to hold both a list of COMPONENTs together with a function which operates on their price to cater for accounting details such as calculating profit margins:

```
type COMPONENT = (int * string * real)
type COMPLIST = COMPONENT list
(* the type synonym COMPLIST represents a list of
   key, description and price *)

(* sample COMPONENT list *)
val net_stock_list
    = [
         (1, "yoghurt", 0.84),
         (2, "peas", 1.30),
         (3, "icecream", 2.50)
      ] :COMPLIST

datatype STOCK =
    Stock of (COMPLIST * (COMPLIST -> COMPLIST))
    (* a STOCK item represents a COMPONENT list
       together with a function to change the value
       of each item in the list *)
```

New instances of **STOCK** can be created as follows:

```
val gross_stock_list = Stock (net_stock_list, addTAX)
```

where **addTAX** has already been defined, for example, in terms of the general-purpose function **adjust**:

```
fun adjust factor (nil :COMPLIST) = nil :COMPLIST
  | adjust factor ((key, description, price) :: rest)
    = (key, description, price * factor)
      :: (adjust factor rest)

val addTAX = adjust 1.175
```

The following function will now generate the information details of a particular **STOCK** instance:

```
fun stockdetails ((Stock (slist, acc_fn)) :STOCK)
    = acc_fn slist :COMPLIST
```

The advantage of this approach is that each instance of a **STOCK** can have a different accounting function, as long as it is of the correct type. Thus, it is possible to associate different taxation ratings or retail prices to a particular list of components. For example,

```
val taxrate = stockdetails gross_stock_list
```

6.2.4 Enumerated types

The keyword **datatype** can also be used to create *enumerated* (or extensional) types, which provide a set of names representing the full range of values for the type.[2] This facility has already been seen with the built-in names **true** and **false** which are the only values for the **bool** type. In fact, they are instances of *nullary constructors*; that is, constructors which have no parameters. By contrast, constructors which take a single tuple argument are known as *unary constructors*. There is no way in SML to define a constructor with more than one argument – constructors are always *uncurried* with multiple arguments packaged into a single tuple.

Enumerated **datatype** definition

The following example introduces a **datatype** representing the possible states of a set of traffic lights. In the UK a set of traffic lights has three colours (red, amber and green) and cycles between four states; the two primary states 'green' (go) and 'red'

---

2. This is very similar to enumeration in imperative programming languages.

(stop), plus two intermediate states 'amber' and '(red + amber)'.[3] The sequence of states is *green, amber, red, (red + amber)*:

```
— datatype TRAFFIC_LIGHT = Green | Amber | Red | Red_amber;

datatype TRAFFIC_LIGHT
con Amber : TRAFFIC_LIGHT
con Green : TRAFFIC_LIGHT
con Red : TRAFFIC_LIGHT
con Red_amber : TRAFFIC_LIGHT
```

The SML system response `con` indicates that `Green, Amber, Red` and `Red_amber` are actually constructors for `TRAFFIC_LIGHT`, though in this new sort of construction the constructors construct nothing but themselves!

Enumerated **datatype** usage

The following session shows that enumerated types may be used in the same manner as any other type:

```
fun next_state (Green :TRAFFIC_LIGHT) = Amber :TRAFFIC_LIGHT
|    next_state Amber               = Red
|    next_state Red                 = Red_amber
|    next_state Red_amber           = Green

— map next_state [Green, Amber, Red, Red_amber];
val it = [Amber,Red,Red_amber,Green] : TRAFFIC_LIGHT list
```

It must be also noted that pattern matching on enumerated types follows the same rules as for all other types, in that every possible enumeration must be matched. For example, the type system will produce a warning if a function using `TRAFFIC_LIGHT` did not contain a function pattern for `Red`:

```
— fun prior_state (Green :TRAFFIC_LIGHT)
        = Red_amber :TRAFFIC_LIGHT
|    prior_state Amber
        = Green
|    prior_state Red_amber
        = Red;
```

3. The combination of two colours for one of the intermediate states makes it possible to predict the next state in the sequence without the expense of adding a fourth coloured light. Although four states could be represented by only two coloured lights, there would be an ambiguity between one of the states and a power failure!

```
Warning: match not exhaustive
Green : TRAFFIC_LIGHT => ...
Amber => ...
Red_amber => ...
val prior_state = fn : TRAFFIC_LIGHT -> TRAFFIC_LIGHT
```

In this way, convenient consistency checks are inextricably linked with the data structure.

Exercise 6.2
Given the **datatype**

```
datatype ACTION = Stop I No_change I Start
               I Slow_down I Prepare_to_start
```

write a function to take the appropriate action at each possible change in state for TRAFFIC_LIGHT.

Exercise 6.3
A Bochvar three-state logic has constants to indicate whether an expression is true, false or meaningless. Provide a **datatype** definition for this logic together with functions to perform the equivalent three-state versions of **andalso**, **orelse** and logical *implication*. Note that if any part of an expression is meaningless then the entire expression should be considered meaningless.

Grep revisited

Enumeration can be used to improve the *grep* program by representing the "ZERO_ MORE" and "ONCE" *match types* as follows:

```
datatype MTYPE = ZERO_MORE I ONCE
```

This is a more elegant solution than using strings to represent the match types. It is also safer and guarantees consistency across functions because SML will only allow pattern matching with the two constructors. Otherwise, using the approach shown in Chapter 3, it would be possible accidentally to enter a meaningless string, such as "ZERO_MORE" (where the digit 0 is mistakenly used instead of the character O) in one of the function patterns for startswith. This is a legal string – but it will never be matched. Enumeration ensures that only legal options are considered.

6.3   Constructors and functions

This section summarizes how constructors differ from functions in their use in function patterns and how they are similar for other purposes. Finally there is a discussion of the consequences of having too many constructors in a **datatype**.

6.3.1 Pattern matching with constructors

There are four kinds of object that can appear in a valid pattern:

1. Constants, such as integers and strings.

2. Constructors, either nullary or unary. However, a constructor pattern *must be complete*; that is, a unary constructor pattern must contain a valid pattern for its parameter.

3. Formal parameter names, which cannot be constants or constructors

4. Wild cards (for example _) which stand for any of the above.

It must be emphasized that although the application of a constructor to its argument may appear as a pattern, the application of a function *is not* a legal pattern.

The above constraints mean that the following two definitions are incorrect; the first because `Measure1` has not been previously defined as a constructor; the second because `Litres` does not have its parameter:

```
fun wrong_convert_to_litres (Measure1 x)
    = if Measure1 = USgallons
      then Litres (x * 3.7852)
      else
          (* etc *)

fun wrong_general_convert (USgallons x, Litres)
    = Litres (x * 3.78532)
      (* etc *)
```

6.3.2 Constructors as functions

Constructors are similar to functions in that:

1. They translate values from one type to another.

2. Equality is only defined upon a **datatype** value. This means that two nullary constructors can be compared because they each represent a legal value of the **datatype**, but two unary constructors cannot be compared because they do not represent any value until they are given the value of their underlying type. Thus `True = Meaningless` is a legal comparison, but `USgallons = UKgallons` is illegal. Comparisons of the form `USgallons x = UKgallons y` are legitimate but will only return `true` if both constructors are the same and both underlying values are the same.

3. The constructor name can be composed or passed as a parameter to other functions, for instance:

```
— map Litres [1.0,2.0,3.0];
val it = [Litres 1.0, Litres 2.0, Litres 3.0]
        : FLUID list
```

However, since a constructor is always uncurried, it cannot be partially applied to a subset of its underlying parameters.

4. They have no sense of order. Unlike the approach of most imperative programming languages, SML does not have a built-in order for **datatype** values. It does not make sense to attempt to evaluate expressions such as:

```
— Green < Red;
Error: overloaded variable "<" not defined
    at type: TRAFFIC_LIGHT
```

Hence, it is not sensible to treat constructor names as representing some underlying ordinal type. The constructors are simply symbols.

6.3.3 The dangers of too many constructors

There is sometimes a temptation when programming with **datatypes** to define a new type which represents too many things; that is, it has too many constructors. Consider the problem of providing a mechanism for the **FLUID datatype** to enable values of any one of the three constructors to be converted to values of any one of the other constructors. The sledgehammer approach is to define a function for each conversion, giving rise to six functions; UStoUK, UStoLitre, UKtoUS etc. The more elegant approach is to provide one general-purpose function; now the problem is how best to parameterize the conversion function to indicate the target constructor. One tempting approach has already been discounted – that of wrong_general_convert, shown in Section 6.3.1:

```
fun wrong_general_convert (USgallons x, Litres)
    = Litres (x * 3.78532)
        (* etc *)
```

The approach was correct in attempting to represent the target as a constructor name but was syntactically illegal because constructor patterns must be complete. A variation on this approach is to represent the target constructor as an enumeration, as is now shown:

```
datatype FLUID = USgallons of real
               | UKgallons of real
               | Litres of real
               | fluid_USGALLONS
               | fluid_UKGALLONS
               | fluid_LITRES

fun convert ((USgallons x) :FLUID) (fluid_UKGALLONS :FLUID)
    = UKgallons (x * 0.8327) :FLUID
  | convert (USgallons x) fluid_LITRES
    = Litres (x * 3.78532)
(* and similarly for the other combinations *)
```

This solves the problem but is rather unwieldy. Furthermore, in the above solution, SML will give a warning that not all the possible patterns have been considered (because the first parameter does not consider the nullary constructors, whilst the second parameter does not consider the unary constructors). What has happened is that the pattern matching requirements having been extended from three constructors to six for every function. Yet for this function not every permutation is necessary, and for many other functions the enumerations are not at all necessary. In brief, FLUID has been 'semantically overloaded'.[4]

In the above example, it is probably more natural to have types that are less tightly linked. This can be achieved using the keyword **and** in the same manner as it is used to define top-level simultaneous functions (as discussed in Section 5.3):

```
datatype FLUID = fluid of FLUID_NAME * real
and FLUID_NAME = fluid_USGALLONS
               | fluid_UKGALLONS
               | fluid_LITRES
```

Here, the two meanings are represented by two separate types but the use of the **and** keyword provides the great advantage that the two definitions are textually *tied together* so that the programmer is unlikely to modify one without the other.

6.4 Recursive datatypes

This section extends the principle of creating types that are closer models of the real world to show how recursive **datatype**s may be defined. Recursive types provide a mechanism to define new types with very many (potentially infinitely many) values. The first example shows how the built-in aggregate list type could be implemented: the second example shows the tree type, which is a more complex data structure.

---

4. Notice, having too many constructors often interacts badly with an inductive style of program development because of the cumbersome number of base cases to consider.

6.4.1 *Simple recursive datatypes*

The built-in type list, has already been semi-formally specified in Section 3.1 as:

1. *empty or*
2. *an element of a given type*
   together with a list of that given type.

This type is defined recursively and there is no restriction on the number of items in a list (other than the amount of memory available in the computer). The specification meets the structural induction requirements of having a terminating case (the empty list) and a general case (the non-empty list). The built-in constructor for the empty list is nil and the built-in constructor for the non-empty list is :: which, considered as a prefix operator, takes a tuple consisting of an item and a list, and constructs a new list from it.

This built-in recursive type may be denoted using the general mechanism described for **datatype** definition; all that is required is to use the name of the new type being defined as the underlying type for one of the constructors. Thus, in order to provide a user-defined type called LIST which mimics the built-in list type, all that is necessary is to translate the above specification directly into the following SML definition:

```
— datatype 'a LIST = Nil
                    | Cons of ('a * 'a LIST);

datatype 'a LIST
con Nil : 'a LIST
con Cons : 'a * 'a LIST —> 'a LIST
```

The tuple type operator * serves to form the Cartesian product of the single item represented by 'a with the 'a LIST. Instances of lists constructed in this manner are displayed with their construction made explicit:[5]

```
— val alist = Nil;
val alist = Nil : 'a LIST

— val blist = Cons (1,alist);
val blist = Cons (1,Nil) : int LIST

— val clist = Cons (2,blist);
val clist = Cons (2,Cons (1,Nil)) : int LIST
```

---

5. As complex **datatype** definitions are built using the tuple type operator * it is not possible to avoid the above representation and hence it is impossible to simulate SML's alternative square bracket notation. However, for all other purposes SML lists and user-defined LISTs are exactly the same.

6.4.2 Tree recursive datatypes

A more general data structure that is not an SML built-in type is the tree. Of the numerous variations on the tree concept, the following informal specification introduces one of the definitions of a *binary tree* (Standish, 1980):

> 1. *empty or*
> 2. *a node which contains a value,*
>   *together with a left and a right sub-tree*

This definition differs from the list which is essentially a linear structure wherein each element may follow the next in only one way. With a binary tree, there are two branches at each node and therefore a choice has to be made at each node as to which branch to follow. The consequence is that tree creation, traversal and manipulation are more complex than their equivalent list operations.

The main advantage of the binary tree structure is for searching: the average number of inspections to extract a given element from a linear list is half the length of the list. However, the average number of inspections to find a member of a sorted binary tree is significantly less,[6] as can be seen from Figure 6.1. The worst case involves four comparisons (that is, half the number of items in the tree) and the average number of comparisons is three.

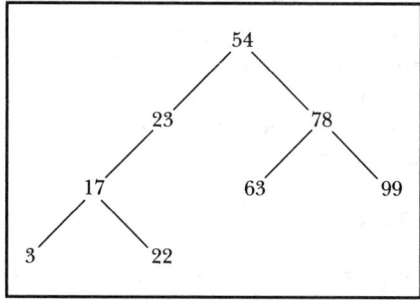

Figure 6.1. Sample tree

Tree definition

The following translates the informal specification of a tree directly into an SML definition of a polymorphic tree, the ordering of which has not yet been determined:

```
datatype 'a TREE = Tnil
               | Tree of ('a TREE * 'a * 'a TREE)
```

There are a number of possibilities as to how this kind of tree can be organized; the most common organization being that of a sorted tree. The tree presented below

---

6. It is actually $\log_2 N$ where N is the number of items in the tree (Standish, 1980).

meets the recursive specification that all the elements of a node's left sub-tree have a value that is less than the node value itself. Similarly all the elements of a node's right sub-tree must have a value that is not less than the node's value. The base case of such a tree is the empty tree Tnil which is defined to be sorted.

Growing a tree

The process of making a new (sorted) tree is very similar to that of making a sorted list using *insertion sort*, first described in Section 3.7.3. There, starting from an empty (sorted) list, elements are inserted one at a time to create an increasingly larger sorted list. Hence, to create a sorted tree, it is firstly necessary to create an empty (sorted) tree and then provide a function that takes any already sorted tree together with a new item and returns a new sorted tree.[7]

The only real difference between tree insertion sort and list insertion sort is that the structure of a tree does not require that the existing tree is re-ordered when a new element is added. All that is necessary is to traverse the tree (according to its ordering specification) until an appropriate empty sub-tree is encountered and then add the new element. Naturally, for a polymorphic tree it is also necessary to provide an ordering function as a parameter (as with isort, in Section 4.4.1).

The following two definitions show how an empty tree may be defined and how an item may be inserted into an already sorted tree. Note that the insertleaf function is drawn directly from the definition of the tree. It has the terminating condition of an empty tree and the choice at each non-empty tree as to whether to inspect the left or right sub-tree. To make this choice requires that the tree be deconstructed to obtain the node value. Afterwards a new tree must be reconstructed using the item, the node and the rest of the tree:

```
type 'a ORDERING = 'a -> 'a -> bool

fun insertleaf (order :'a ORDERING)
               (Tnil :'a TREE)
               (item :'a)
    = Tree (Tnil, item, Tnil) :'a TREE

|    insertleaf order (Tree (ltree, node, rtree)) item
    = let
          val put = insertleaf order
      in
          if (order item node)
          then
              Tree (put ltree item, node, rtree)
          else
              Tree (ltree, node, put rtree item)
      end
```

---

7. It should, of course, be stressed that *tree insertion* is a figurative term; the original tree is not actually altered, but a fresh copy is generated for each additional element.

From list to tree

Just as with isort in Chapter 4, it is possible to make use of a higher order function to grow a tree from a list without explicit recursion:

```
fun list_to_tree (order :'a ORDERING) (itemlist :'a list)
    = accumulate (insertleaf order)
                 Tnil
                 itemlist :'a TREE
```

Or, more concisely:

```
fun list_to_tree (order :'a ORDERING)
    = accumulate (insertleaf order)
                 Tnil :'a list –> 'a TREE
```

From tree to list

The complementary function tree_to_list follows even more directly from the TREE definition. In effect the constructor Tree has been replaced by the tree_to_list function and the tuple type operator * has been replaced by the append operator a:

```
fun tree_to_list (Tnil :'a TREE) = nil :'a list

|   tree_to_list (Tree (ltree, node, rtree))
    = tree_to_list ltree
      a [node]
      a tree_to_list rtree
```

Because the tree's branching nature has been eliminated, this function is often known as flatten.

Exercise 6.4
Explain why it is not sensible to attempt to mirror the tree data structure using nested lists.

Exercise 6.5
A number of useful tree manipulation functions follow naturally from the specification of a binary tree. Write functions to parallel the list manipulation functions map and length (in terms of how many nodes exist in the tree).

Exercise 6.6
What would have been the consequence of writing the function l i s t_t o_t r e e as:

```
fun list_to_tree order
    = reduce (insertleaf order) Tnil
```

Exercise 6.7
Write a function to remove an element from a sorted tree and return a tree that is still sorted.

6.5   Abstract types – abstype

This section extends the principle of structured programming discussed in Chapter 5 to show how a programmer can have safer and more re-usable code by packaging a **datatype** along with a set of operations on it, by means of the keyword **abstype.**[8] For example, if one programmer develops a number of functions that manipulate string lists (such as find_substring and drop_substring) then it is wasteful for other programmers to develop the same functions *and even unnecessary for them to understand how they are implemented.* All that is necessary is for other programmers to be able to use them in the manner intended! If these operations are also linked with the creation of a new string list **datatype** then the advantages of built-in validation are also available. Furthermore, if all the code required to manipulate the new type is collected in one place it is easier to test, modify or maintain and to make accessible to other programmers. In one way, an **abstype** definition can be viewed as a program definition in its own right, as can be seen by the following general template:

> **abstype**   *name*
> $\qquad$ = *Constructor Value1*
> $\qquad$ | *Constructor Value2*
> $\qquad\qquad$ . . .
> $\qquad$ | *Constructor ValueN*
> **with**
> $\qquad$ *definitions, including val, fun, type, datatype,*
> $\qquad$ *let and local, and exception definitions*
> **end**

The above template shows that abstract types can be treated as a form of program encapsulation – a **datatype** together with a program body. The functions defined in the **abstype** provide the public interface to the new type; values of this type can only be manipulated via the public interface functions.

---

8. The SML **abstype** facility differs from that of the *abstract data type* found in some other languages, in that the type signature and implementation are not separable.

6.5.1 *Simple abstype definition and usage*

The following example shows how the natural numbers (that is, the non-negative integers) can be considered as an **abstype** package, consisting of a **datatype** together with frequently required associated functions. This package would typically be used to manipulate anything for which a negative representation would be meaningless, *prices* and *quantities* being two very common cases.

It should be noted that the number of functions in the package is limited to mimic those provided by the built-in arithmetic and relational operators; as with the built-in types there is no need to provide functions for every possible user-specified operation involving natural numbers.[9] The functions that are provided are often known as *primitives* because they can be considered the raw building blocks for the type.

Abstype *definition*

```
abstype NAT = Nat of int
with
    exception MakeNat
    fun makeNat (x :int)
      = if x < 0
          then raise MakeNat
          else Nat x :NAT

    fun showNat ((Nat x) :NAT) = x :int

    local
        type RELOP = int * int -> bool
        type INTOP = int * int -> int

        fun relOp (ff :RELOP)
                  ((Nat x) :NAT)
                  ((Nat y) :NAT)
            = ff (x, y) :bool

        fun intOp (ff :INTOP)
                  ((Nat x) :NAT)
                  ((Nat y) :NAT)
            = makeNat (ff (x, y)) :NAT
    in
        val natEqual = relOp (op = )
        val natPlus = intOp (op + )
        val natMinus = intOp (op - )
        (* and similarly for the other arithmetic
           and relational operators *)
    end
end
```

9. See Section 6.5.4 for guidelines on which functions should be packaged.

Abstype *usage*

The following session shows how the `makeNat` function can be used to create new instances of `NAT`s. The function `NatPlus` is then used to add these two instances:

```
― val quantity1 = makeNat 3;
val quantity1 = ― : NAT

― val quantity2 = makeNat 3;
val quantity2 = ― : NAT

― natPlus quantity1 quantity2;
val it = ― : NAT
```

In all the above cases, the system response ― is new, indicating that the actual representation is hidden. The programmer cannot be tempted to bypass these primitives and attempt direct manipulation of the **datatype**. This has the considerable benefit that the underlying types and implementation details may be changed without any need to change any application programs that use the **abstype** primitives.

Hiding the implementation means that the only way to access actual values is by means of one of the `NAT` primitives:

```
― showNat (natPlus quantity1 quantity2);
val it = 6 : int

― showNat (natMinus quantity1 quantity2);
val it = 0 : int

― natEqual quantity1 quantity2;
val it = true : bool
```

Sequences – another simple example

Another simple example is a double-ended list (sometimes known as a *sequence*), where all the operations normally occurring at the front of a list have mirror operations occurring at the end of the list. The basic set of operations provided are `nilseq` (which returns an empty sequence), followed by `consLseq`, `consRseq`, `hdLseq`, `hdRseq`, `tlLseq` and `tlRseq` (which provide the normal list operations at both ends of the sequence); two further functions `appendseq` and `showseq` are also provided for convenience. This could be defined recursively or, as is shown below, by extending operations on the built-in list type:

```
abstype 'a SEQUENCE = Seq of 'a list
with
    val nilseq
        = Seq nil :'a SEQUENCE

    fun consLseq (item :'a) ((Seq aseq) :'a SEQUENCE)
        = Seq (item :: aseq) :'a SEQUENCE

    fun consRseq ((Seq aseq) :'a SEQUENCE) (item :'a)
        = Seq (aseq @ [item]) :'a SEQUENCE

    fun hdLseq ((Seq aseq) :'a SEQUENCE)
        = hd aseq :'a

    fun hdRseq ((Seq aseq) :'a SEQUENCE)
        = hd (rev aseq) :'a

    fun tlLseq ((Seq aseq) :'a SEQUENCE)
        = Seq (tl aseq) :'a SEQUENCE

    fun tlRseq ((Seq aseq) :'a SEQUENCE)
        = Seq ((rev o tl o rev) aseq) :'a SEQUENCE

    fun appendseq ((Seq aseq) :'a SEQUENCE)
                  ((Seq bseq) :'a SEQUENCE)
        = Seq (aseq @ bseq) :'a SEQUENCE

    fun showseq ((Seq s) :'a SEQUENCE)
        = s :'a list

end
```

Exercise 6.8
Provide function definitions for the NAT primitives if a recursive underlying data representation is used as follows: `abstype NAT = Zero | Succ of NAT.`

6.5.2 Properties of abstypes

This section highlights the fact that the internal representation (that is the constructors) of **abstype**s are hidden from other programmers.

Constraints imposed by abstypes

Two important restrictions are imposed on the use of **abstype**s:

1. Two **abstype** values may not be directly compared for equality:

    ```
    — quantity1 = quantity2;

    Error: operator and operand don't agree
           (equality type required)
        operator domain: '' Z * '' Z
        operand:             NAT * NAT
        in expression: = (quantity1,quantity2)
    ```

2. The **abstype** constructors are hidden; hence it is *not possible* to use them anywhere outside the definition body. The following is illegal because the constructor `Nat` is not in scope:

    ```
    — fun wrong_equal_numbers (Nat quantity) (x :real)
          = (quantity = floor x);

    Error: non—constructor applied to argument in pattern
    ...
    ```

These restrictions mean that it is quite common to provide an equality primitive inside definition bodies.

Converting between abstract types

Sometimes there will be a requirement to convert from one abstract type to another. Initially this may seem difficult because it is not possible to use an **abstype**'s constructors outside of the definition body. For example, if a program contains a `TREE` **abstype** (see Section 6.5.3) and a `SEQUENCE` **abstype**, where should the function `tree_to_sequence` be defined? It cannot be defined inside `TREE` because it will not have access to the `SEQUENCE` constructors; similarly, it cannot be defined inside `SEQUENCE` because it will not have access to the `TREE` constructors.

This apparent limitation is solved pragmatically in one of two ways:

1. If the two abstract types are not closely linked semantically then it is likely that the conversion mentioned above will not occur often and in this case it is sufficient to provide a 'show' function and a 'make' function for each; these two functions will use an intermediate form based on built-in types in order to provide the conversion. The function `sequence_to_tree` can thereafter be defined externally to both **abstype**s, as is shown in the following program extract:[10]

10. Section 7.3 shows a way to *guarantee* that the two **abstype**s will share a common intermediary type.

```
abstype 'a TREE
    = Tnil | Tree of ('a TREE * 'a * 'a TREE)
with
    fun showTREE (Tnil :'a TREE) = nil :'a list

    |   showTREE (Tree (ltree, node, rtree))
        = showTREE ltree @ [node] @ showTREE rtree
    fun makeTREE (order :'a -> 'a -> bool)
                 (alist :'a list)
        = accumulate (insertleaf order)
                     Tnil
                     alist :'a TREE
    ....
end

abstype 'a SEQUENCE = Seq of 'a list
with
    val showSEQUENCE (Seq s) = s
    ....
end

fun sequence_to_tree (order :'a -> 'a -> bool)
    = (makeTREE order) o showSEQUENCE
      : 'a SEQUENCE -> 'a TREE
```

2. By contrast, if conversion between two abstract types is a very frequent requirement then this implies that they are in fact very closely linked semantically and should therefore be defined in tandem. The function `sequence_ to_tree` can then be defined inside the combined **abstype** body and will have access to all the necessary constructors:

```
abstype 'a TREE = Tnil
                | Tree of ('a TREE * 'a * 'a TREE)
and       'a SEQUENCE = Seq of 'a list
with
    ....

    fun sequence_to_tree (Seq nil) = Tnil
    |   sequence_to_tree (Seq (front :: rest)) =
        ....
    fun tree_to_sequence Tnil = Empty
    |   tree_to_sequence (Tree (ltree, node, rtree)) =
        ....

end
```

Exercise 6.9
What is the difference between:

```
abstype PAIR = Pair of (int * int)
with
    fun makepair x y = Pair (x,y)
    fun swap (Pair (x,y)) = Pair (y,x)
    ...
end

makepair 3 4 = makepair 5 6
```

and

```
local
    datatype PAIR = Pair of (int * int)
in
    type PAIR = PAIR
    fun makepair x y = Pair (x, y)
    fun swap (Pair (x,y)) = Pair (y,x)
    ...
end

makepair 3 4 = makepair 5 6
```

6.5.3   *Further examples of abstract types*

This section now presents two more examples of the use of **abstype**s. The first example collects together the functions over a binary tree and presents an elegant method for providing a generic package for trees. The second, larger example, shows how an *array* data structure might be implemented in more than one way without affecting the way it is used in any existing programs.

*Trees as **abstype**s – generic packaging*

The major disadvantage of defining a polymorphic tree is that the ordering function must always be passed as an explicit parameter to the interface functions for tree modification and manipulation. This difficulty can be overcome by incorporating the ordering function into the constructor definition; thus, it is only necessary to specify the ordering function when a tree is first created and thereafter all other interface functions can find the ordering function by inspecting the data structure.

If the tree is represented as an **abstype** then its primitives can obtain the ordering function through pattern matching:

```
type 'a ORDERING = 'a -> 'a -> bool


abstype 'a ATREE
          = ATree of ('a ORDERING * 'a TREE)
and       'a TREE
            = Tnil
            | Tree of ('a TREE * 'a * 'a TREE)
with

  fun newtree (order :'a ORDERING)
      = ATree (order, Tnil) :'a ATREE

  fun insertleaf ((ATree (order, tree)) :'a ATREE)
                 (item :'a)
      = let
        fun insert (Tnil :'a TREE)
            = Tree (Tnil, item, Tnil) :'a TREE
        |   insert (Tree (ltree, node, rtree))
            = if (order item node)
              then
                 Tree (insert ltree, node, rtree)
              else
                 Tree (ltree, node, insert rtree)
        in
            ATree (order, (insert tree)) :'a ATREE
        end

  fun flatten ((ATree (order, tree)) :'a ATREE)
      = let
        fun inorder (Tnil :'a TREE) = nil :'a list
        |   inorder (Tree (ltree, node, rtree))
            = inorder ltree @ [node] @ inorder rtree
        in
            inorder tree :'a list
        end
  end
```

Thus, an int ATREE in increasing numeric order might be as shown in Figure 6.2.

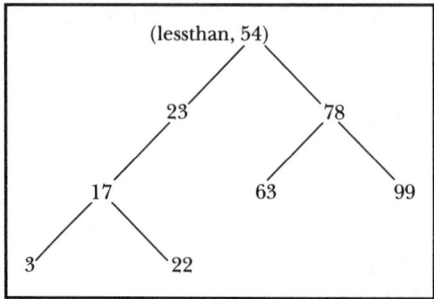

Figure 6.2. Sample ATREE

Exercise 6.10
An alternative representation of the ATREE could be to drop the TREE constructors and
have the **abstype** constructors:

```
abstype 'a OTHER_TREE
      = Anil of ('a -> ('a -> bool))
      | ATree of (('a -> 'a -> bool)
                    * 'a OTHER_TREE * 'a * 'a OTHER_TREE)
   with
         (* implementation *)
   end
```

What would be the consequences for the **abstype** implementation?

Arrays as **abstypes** – alternative implementations

The following example demonstrates the usefulness of concealing a particular
representation of a type from the programmer. The first implementation of ARRAY
could be replaced by an implementation as a list of tuples, however the interface with
other functions and values is not altered.

An array as a list of lists

This implementation shows an **abstype** representation of a two-dimensional array,
where an array may be defined as a fixed size aggregate data structure whose
elements may be changed or retrieved by reference to an index.

A two-dimensional array data structure can very easily be represented as a list of
lists (where the innermost lists represent the rows of the array). The function
definitions are fairly straightforward but rely upon the existence of some of the list
handling functions introduced in Chapter 3 and some of the higher order functions of
Chapter 4:

```
abstype 'a ARRAY = Array of (('a list) list)
with
  local

    (* "replace" applies a function "ff" to one of the
       elements of a list and returns a new list which is the
       same as the input list but with the element replaced
       by the result of the function application. *)

    exception Replace
    fun replace (pos :int) (ff :'a->'a)
                (anylist :'a list)
      = if (pos >length anylist) orelse (pos <= 0)
        then   raise Replace
        else   ((take (pos-1) anylist)
               @ [ff (get_nth pos anylist)]
               @ (drop pos anylist)) :'a list
  in

    (* "num_rows" and "num_cols" are useful for array bounds
       checking. *)

    fun num_rows ((Array array) :'a ARRAY)
        = length array :int

    fun num_cols ((Array nil) :'a ARRAY) = 0 :int
    |   num_cols (Array array) = length (hd array)

    (* init_array produces an initial array from (i) how many
       rows and columns the array should have and (ii) a
       starting value for all the elements. The function
       "repeat" is used to create a list of the right length
       to represent a row, and then again to construct an
       array of many such rows. *)

    exception Init_array
    fun init_array (nrows :int) (ncolumns :int)
                   (first_val :'a)
      = if ((nrows < 0) orelse (ncolumns < 0))
        then raise Init_array
        else Array (repeat nrows
                       (cons
                           (repeat ncolumns
                                   (cons first_val)
                                   nil))
                    nil) :'a ARRAY
```

```
(* change_item returns the input array with one of
   the items changed to a new value. The function
   "replace" is used twice; the outermost application
   selects the appropriate row and then the innermost
   application is applied to that row. The innermost
   application replaces the element in the "column"
   position with a new value and discards the old value
   — the combinator "K" is ideal for this purpose.
   Because the innermost occurrence of "replace" is a
   partial application, it doesn't get fully evaluated
   until after the appropriate row has been selected.*)

exception Change_item

fun change_item ((Array array) :'a ARRAY)
                (row :int)
                (column :int)
                (newvalue :'a)
  = if ((row <= 0) orelse (column <= 0) orelse
        (row > num_rows (Array array)) orelse
        (column > num_cols (Array array)))
    then raise Change_item
    else (Array (replace row
                  (replace column (K newvalue))
                  array)) :'a ARRAY

exception Get_item

fun get_item ((Array array) :'a ARRAY)
             (row :int)
             (column :int)
  = if ((row <= 0) orelse (column <= 0) orelse
        (row > num_rows (Array array)) orelse
        (column > num_cols (Array array)))
    then raise Get_item
    else (get_nth column (get_nth row array)) :'a
end

end
```

The ARRAY primitives can now be used directly in programs and also to build
more complex utilities:

```
(* "scan" is an extremely useful general-purpose function
    which effectively applies (accumulate ff state) to
    every initial segment of a list. It will be used in "get
    _row" and "get_col" in order to generate a list of
    increasing integers representing row numbers or column
    numbers — e.g. [1,2,3,4,5] *)

fun scan (ff :'a->'b->'a) (state :'a) (nil :'b list) =
    = [state] :'a list
|   scan ff state (front :: rest)
    = cons state ((scan ff) (ff state front) rest)

exception Get_col
fun get_col (data :'a ARRAY) (column :int)
    = let
        fun dummyrow x = repeat (num_rows x) (cons 1) []
        val rows = tl (scan plus 0 (dummyrow data))
    in
        if (column <= 0) orelse
           (column > num_cols data)
        then
            raise Get_col
        else
            (map (C (get_item data) column) rows):'a list
    end

exception Get_row
fun get_row (anarray :'a ARRAY) (row :int)
    = let
        fun dummycol x = repeat (num_cols x) (cons 1) []
        val cols = tl (scan plus 0 (dummycol anarray))
    in
        if (row <= 0) orelse (row > num_rows anarray)
        then   raise Get_row
        else   (map (get_item anarray row) cols) :'a list
    end
```

An array as a list of tuples

The first implementation of ARRAY can now be replaced with an implementation as a list of tuples, without changing the public interface functions and therefore without the need to change any other part of the program. As long as the names and the types of the interface functions do not change, SML guarantees abstraction; that is, because it is impossible for the **abstype** constructors to be used by any functions outside of the definition body, then it is guaranteed that the **abstype** body functions comprise the only functions which need to be changed if the underlying representation is changed. Sometimes the reason for a change in underlying representation is in order to extend the functionality of the type; the number of interface functions can always be safely increased (but cannot be safely decreased) without affecting parts of the program already written. However, in the following example the original functionality is retained:

```
abstype 'a ARRAY
       = Array of ( int * int * 'a *
                        ((int * int * 'a) list))
with

  local

    fun compare (row1 :int)(col1 :int)
              (row2 :int, col2 :int, _ :'a)
       = (row1 = row2) andalso (col1 = col2) :bool

    fun invalid (nrows :int) (ncols :int)
              (row :int) (col :int)
       = row > nrows orelse row <= 0 orelse
         col > ncols orelse col <= 0
  in

    (* The array is represented by its dimensions
       (nrows * ncols), the default value for all items
       in the array that have not been updated (def)
       together with a list of tuples representing the
       row and column position and new value of any updated
       item changes") *)

    fun num_rows
       ((Array (nrows, ncols, def, changes)) :'a ARRAY)
       = nrows :int

    fun num_cols
       ((Array (nrows, ncols, def, changes)) :'a ARRAY)
       = ncols :int

    exception Init_array
    fun init_array (nrows :int) (ncols :int) (default :'a)
       = if ((nrows < 0) orelse (ncols < 0))
         then raise Init_array
         else Array (nrows, ncols, default, []) :'a ARRAY

    (* Changing an item involves removing the entry from
       the changes list and appending the new entry. If
       the item has not been previously changed then the
       filter expression will leave changes unaltered.
       There is no check if the new value differs from
       the existing entry or the default value *)
```

```
exception Change_item
fun change_item
    ((Array (nrows,ncols,def,changes)) :'a ARRAY)
    (row :int) (col :int) (newvalue :'a)
    = let
        val checkdiff = not o (compare row col)
        val newchanges
            = (filter checkdiff changes)
              @ [(row,col,newvalue)]
      in
        if invalid nrows ncols row col
        then raise Change_item
        else
        (Array (nrows,ncols,
                def,newchanges)) :'a ARRAY
      end

(* Getting an item involves filtering it from the
   changes list; if there is no entry then the default
   entry will become the head of the items list
   otherwise it is the tail and ignored. *)

exception Get_item
fun get_item
    ((Array (nrows, ncols, def, changes)) :'a ARRAY)
    (row :int) (col :int)
    = let
        fun third (_ :int, _ :int, x :'a) = x :'a
        val items
            = (filter (compare row col) changes)
              @ [(row,col,default)]
      in
        if invalid nrows ncols row col
        then raise Get_item
        else (third o hd) items :'a
      end

end
end
```

The functions get_col and get_row defined using the first (list of lists) version of
ARRAY can now be substituted with the second (list of tuples) version *without
modification of the existing code;* all that is necessary is to recompile the program, to
ensure that the new representation is used throughout.

Exercise 6.11

A *queue* aggregate data structure (Aho *et al.*, 1983) can be defined as either being empty or as consisting of a queue followed by an element; operations include creating a new queue, inserting at the end of a queue and removing the first item in a queue. The following declares a set of primitives for a polymorphic **abstype** QUEUE:

```
val q_isempty    = fn :'a QUEUE -> bool
val q_remainder  = fn :'a QUEUE -> 'a QUEUE
val q_top        = fn :'a QUEUE -> 'a
val q_insert     = fn :'a QUEUE -> 'a -> 'a QUEUE
val q_create     = fn :unit -> 'a QUEUE
```

Provide an **abstype** representation.

6.5.4 *Guidelines for abstype primitive selection*

Apart from the criterion that an **abstype** must provide all the operations that are necessary and sufficient to manipulate the underlying **datatype**, there are no other rigid rules to determine which functions should be provided to make it easy to use. Two of the necessary primitives for all **abstype**s are *creation* and *inspection*. Many abstypes will also have *initialization* and *modification* primitives, the former sometimes being incorporated into the *creation* primitive (as with the ATREE definition). A useful set is an initialization primitive to create an 'empty' value, together with a modification primitive to change the underlying value and an inspection primitive to view that value – this works particularly well when the underlying type is recursive. Furthermore, it is often useful to provide the equivalents of map and reduce etc. for the abstract type. It is, however, unwise to provide too large a set of primitive functions, because this will tend to reinforce the current underlying representation and make it difficult to make future changes to this representation.

For example, the above ARRAY implementation provided primitives for creating a new array, together with those for inspecting and changing one element. It can be shown that these three are sufficient for array manipulation, but in practice an *equality* primitive and functions to extract the contents of a row or column would probably be provided. Indeed, for many **abstype**s it will often be the case that additional functions, which build on the basic primitives, should be offered by the implementor. The rationale for this is threefold:

1. To eliminate programmer effort and potential error, by writing these 'non-essential' primitives once only.

2. To provide efficient implementations based on a knowledge of the underlying **datatype** representation.

3.   There is sometimes a choice of which primitives comprise a necessary and sufficient set of operations. For example, an **abstype** for binary Boolean algebra could be represented by a unary **not** operator together with the dyadic **andalso** operator, or by **not** together with the dyadic **orelse** operator. In this case, it is obvious that both dyadic operators should be provided to reflect the programmer's view of the data.

Finally, there are many instances of general-purpose **datatype**s (such as COORDS) for which it is not possible to predict an adequate and easy to use set of primitives. For these **datatype**s it does not make sense to force them into an **abstype**.

6.6   *Summary*

The strong type system as presented in Chapter 1 provides a means of enforcing correct usage of SML's base, aggregate and function types. The strengths of such a type system are that it promotes good programming style and it detects many errors early in the software design cycle: the weakness of such a simple type system is that it imposes strict limitations on what may be expressed.

The first important step towards providing more expressive power was the ability to define functions with polymorphic types, as discussed in Chapter 2. In this chapter the type system was further expanded so that the programmer is no longer restricted to the basic SML types, but may build new types from the old ones and expect the type system to apply the same rigour to the new types as to the old.

The programmer can have direct control of the type-checking system in order to avoid errors; firstly, new **datatype**s may be defined in order to reflect the specialized use of an existing type or to build complex data structures that model the real world more closely; secondly, **abstype**s may be used to ensure that values of a certain type (a basic type or a new type) are only operated on by appropriately defined functions. Not only does this help to detect errors, it also serves to document the program and helps to keep the program structure clear. This principle is extended in Chapter 7 to enable the linking of definitions that are related by activity rather than type into program modules known as **structure**s.

7 · Modules

The SML features that have been described in the previous chapters are part of what is known as the SML Core language, which is mainly useful for small-scale programming tasks. An extension, based on a proposal presented by MacQueen (1984), known as the SML Modules language provides powerful facilities for larger program specification and construction, including:

1. **structure**s for module definition;
2. **signature**s for module specification;
3. **functor**s to enable module parameterization.

This chapter is divided into two parts. The first part is mainly concerned with the syntax and semantics of **structure**s and **signature**s, using small examples – though in practice these tools would normally be used with larger programs. The second part (from Section 7.4) introduces **functor**s and explores the pragmatics of using them for larger-scale software design and program development.

7.1 Structures

In addition to scope restriction (using **local** and **let**), SML permits sequences of definitions to be grouped together in what is known as a **structure**. This facility allows the creation of sub-program libraries for commonly used functions and type definitions. Although **structure**s are first discussed in isolation, they should normally be used in conjunction with **signature**s (discussed in Section 7.2).

Structure definition

The template for a **structure** definition is:

```
structure   struct_name =
struct
        some definitions
        can be anything legal within the Core Language
        or other structures
end
```

The following example shows how a **structure** may be used to form a library of commonly used utilities for list iteration:

```
structure LIST_SELECT_struct =
struct
  exception Drop and Take

  type 'a PREDICATE = 'a -> bool

  fun take (n :int) (alist :'a list)
  = let
      fun xtake _ nil = nil
      |   xtake 0 _    = nil
      |   xtake n (front :: rest)
          = front :: (xtake (n - 1) rest)
    in
      if n < 0 then raise Take
      else (xtake n alist) :'a list
    end

  fun drop (n :int) (alist :'a list)
  = let
      fun xdrop _ nil             = nil
      |   xdrop 0 alist           = alist
      |   xdrop n (front :: rest) = xdrop (n - 1) rest
    in
      if n < 0 then raise Drop
      else (xdrop n alist) :'a list
    end

  fun dropwhile (pred :'a PREDICATE) (nil :'a list)
      = nil :'a list
  |   dropwhile pred (front :: rest)
      = if pred front
        then dropwhile pred rest
        else (front :: rest)

  fun takewhile (pred :'a PREDICATE) (nil :'a list)
      = nil :'a list
  |   takewhile pred (front :: rest)
      = if pred front
        then front :: (takewhile pred rest)
        else nil
```

```
      fun filter (pred :'a PREDICATE) (nil :'a list)
          = nil :'a list
      |   filter pred (front :: rest)
          = if pred front
            then front :: filter pred rest
            else filter pred rest

      fun takeafter (pred :'a PREDICATE) (nil :'a list)
          = nil :'a list
      |   takeafter pred (front :: rest)
          = if pred front
            then rest
            else takeafter pred rest


   end
```

The SML system response has been omitted as it merely echoes the types of the defined functions.

Structure *access*

Accessing something defined within a **structure** can be achieved in two ways:

1. By using what is known as a *long identifier*, which is a name built from a **structure** name, followed by a dot and a name drawn from it:

    ```
    — LIST_SELECT_struct.take 3 ["and","one","more","list"];
    val it = ["and","one","more"] : string list

    — val singleton_list = LIST_SELECT_struct.take 1;
    val singleton_list = fn : 'a list -> 'a list

    — singleton_list ["yet","another","list","example"];
    val it = ["yet"] : string list
    ```

    It can be seen that LIST_SELECT_struct.take is to be considered a single name. Since . cannot appear as part of a legal **val** name no confusion can ever arise between **val** names and long identifiers.

2. By using the keyword **open** and then using the definitions as if they had been defined outside of a **structure**:

    ```
    open LIST_SELECT_struct

    val singleton_list = take 1
    ```

The Standard ML of New Jersey (version 0.66) response to **open**ing a **structure** is merely to echo the command; previous New Jersey versions, and other SML implementations, respond by echoing the types of the newly available names. In either case, the response is not interesting and so has been omitted.

The dangers of opening structures

The same rules of scope apply to **structures** as to any other SML sequence of definitions (at the top level or within a **local** or **let** clause). This means that there is some danger in **open**ing two **structures** that have the same internal names for different functions. The following example illustrates this point:

```
structure REAL_struct =
struct
     type NUMBER = real

     fun inc (n :NUMBER) = n + 1.0 :NUMBER
     fun dec (n :NUMBER) = n - 1.0 :NUMBER
end

structure INT_struct =
struct
     type NUMBER = int

     fun inc (n :NUMBER) = n + 1 :NUMBER
     fun dec (n :NUMBER) = n - 1 :NUMBER
end
```

Given the definitions of `REAL_struct` and `INT_struct,` then in the following SML session the opening of `INT_struct` causes `INT_struct.inc` to come into scope, hiding the original binding from `REAL_struct` where `inc` expected an argument of type `real`:

```
- open REAL_struct; (* must open one of the structures
                        first so that NUMBER is in scope *)
open REAL_struct;
...

- val (x :NUMBER) = 3.0;
val x = 3.0 : NUMBER

- inc x;
val it = 4.0 : NUMBER
```

```
— open INT_struct;
...

— inc x;
Error: operator and operand don't agree (tycon mismatch)
  operator domain: NUMBER
  operand:         REAL_struct.NUMBER
  in expression:   inc x
```

It is best to resist the temptation to open **structure**s at the top level of an SML program, unless they are of very general utility. Otherwise, the small gains in shorter names are outweighed by the increased possibility of errors and the loss in program documentation that is given by the use of long identifiers.[1]

7.1.1 *The properties of structures*

Structures have a number of properties which are worth highlighting, either to avoid possible syntax errors or because they are important to understand when using them in conjunction with **signature**s and **functor**s.

1. It is legal to define one **structure** within another; the main purpose of this will be shown in Section 7.3 in the discussion of **sharing**.

2. If a **structure** substr has been defined within another **structure** str then its components (for example, C1 and C2 etc.) can be accessed by an extension of the long identifier principle: for example, str.substr.C1.

3. A **structure** may be opened within another to achieve greater modularity. However, this may lead to name redefinition problems similar to those of opening a **structure** at the top level of a program. A solution is to use **functor**s, as presented in Section 7.4.

4. A **structure** definition can only be bound to another **structure**. Hence the following is legal:

    ```
    structure ANOTHER_INT_struct = INT_struct
    ```

    but attempting to give a **val** name to INT_struct would be illegal:

    ```
    — val WRONG_name = INT_struct;
    Error: unbound variable INT_struct
    ```

5. There is no equality defined over **structure**s. The reason is the same as for functions; it is not meaningful to check whether blocks of code are identical.

---

1. Furthermore, there is no facility to *close* a **structure** and thereby make its contents unavailable.

Exercise 7.1
Provide a **structure** definition to create a library of the combinators described in Chapter 4.

7.2   *Signatures*

The use of type expressions as a design tool and documentary aid has already been encouraged in previous chapters. Whilst it is not possible to declare the types of **val** names or functions independently of their definitions in the Core language, it is possible for entities contained within a **structure**. This is achieved by collecting together the type declarations for those bindings which are defined in a **structure**; they are then kept separate from it. The collection of type declarations is introduced by means of the keyword **signature**; the benefits include the separation of specifications from implementation decisions and the ability to provide programmers with different views of the same code.

This section firstly shows how a **signature** is defined and then gives details of what it can contain and how it may be used with a **structure** to ensure that the **structure** has definitions of the specified types.

Signature *definition*

The following presents a template for a **signature** definition:

> **signature** *sig_name* =
> **sig**
>   *exceptions,*
>   *type declarations and*
>   *name declarations*
> **end**

For example, the following declares that `OBJECT` is a type and that the other **val** names are functions of type `(OBJECT -> OBJECT)`; the type (which may be a type synonym, a **datatype** or an **abstype**) and the **val** names will be defined in a **structure** elsewhere:

```
signature OBJ_sig =
sig
        type OBJECT

        val grow :OBJECT -> OBJECT
        val shrink :OBJECT -> OBJECT
end
```

As with **structure** definitions the SML system response is not interesting since it merely echoes the **signature** declaration. However, the above syntax is new in two ways:

1. The type declaration is similar to defining a type synonym `type X = int` but it does not define the underlying type. This is because the actual definition of the type will be done subsequently in a **structure**.

2. A name declaration is similar to defining a **val** name `val X :int = 3` but it does not give a value. This syntax is used regardless of whether the name is subsequently given in the constrained **structure** as a **val** definition or a **fun** definition.

The above syntax enforces the intention that type information (in the **signature**) should be separated from implementation information (in the **structure**).

Once a **signature** has been defined, it can be associated with a **structure** in order to ensure that the latter meets a minimum specification. This process is known as *constraining* a **structure**. A template for this process is:

> **structure** *struct_name* :*sig_name* =
> **struct**
>   *some definitions*
> **end**

Thus `INT_struct` could have been defined in the following manner along with its constraining **signature**:[2]

```
— structure INT_struct :OBJ_sig =
  struct
        type OBJECT = int

        fun grow n = n + 1
        fun shrink n = n — 1
  end;

structure INT_struct :
    sig
        eqtype OBJECT

        val grow :OBJECT —> OBJECT
        val shrink :OBJECT —> OBJECT
    end
```

___

2. For an explanation of **eqtype** see Section 2.4.1 and the constraint rule 3 in Section 7.2.2.

7.2.1 *Signature components*

The purpose of a **signature** is to provide a high-level specification of the types of objects and functions within its constrained **structure**. To this end, the following expressions are permitted within a **signature**:

1. **exception**s.

2. **val** names with their type, for example:

```
signature SIG_sig =
sig
      type   OBJECT
      val thing :OBJECT
end
```

3. Functions, shown as **val** names, with their type expressions.

4. **type**s and **eqtype**s.

5. **datatype**s, with their constructors, for example:

```
signature SIG_sig =
sig
      type   OBJECT
      datatype ANOTHER_OBJECT
              = A_constructor of int
              I Another_constructor of OBJECT
end
```

6. **structure** names with their constraining **signatures**. For example, assuming the predefinition of `SMALL_sig`:

```
signature LARGE_sig =
sig
      structure SMALL_struct :SMALL_sig
          (* etc *)
end
```

7.2.2 *Signature constraint rules*

Four rules hold concerning the matching of identifiers declared in a **signature** and the definitions within its constrained **structure**. The first three rules ensure that the actual code meets the minimum specification. The fourth rule allows a **structure** to have both public and private code, by *hiding* any code that is not mentioned in the specification.

Rule 1 – name matching

Firstly, every type name and **val** name declared within a **signature** must have a corresponding definition in the constrained **structure** (as in the above example). If a definition is missing, an error arises:

```
— structure CHAR_struct :OBJ_sig =
  struct
        type OBJECT = string

        (* converts a lowercase character to Uppercase *)
        fun grow c
          = if (c >= "a") andalso (c <= "z")
              then chr ((ord c) + (ord "A") — (ord "a"))
              else c
  end;
Error: unmatched val spec: shrink
```

This rule has the clear advantage that it prevents a programmer from specifying something and then forgetting to code it!

Rule 2 – type matching

Secondly, any definition that appears within a constrained **structure** and that has a corresponding declaration in the **signature** must match the type declared in the latter. Hence, declaring grow to be of type real —> int will result in a type mismatch since the OBJ_sig has defined grow as a function whose source and target are of the same type:

```
— structure MISMATCH_struct :OBJ_sig =
  struct
        type OBJECT = real
        fun grow n = floor (n + 1.0)
        fun shrink n = floor (n — 1.0)
  end;

Error: value type in structure doesn't match signature spec
name: grow
spec:    OBJECT —> OBJECT
actual: real —> int

Error: value type in structure doesn't match signature spec
name: shrink
spec:    OBJECT —> OBJECT
actual: real —> int
```

In general, a definition will 'match' a **signature** declaration if it is not more specific than that declaration. Notice that in the following example MISLEADING will also be successfully constrained by the OBJ_sig:

```
structure MISLEADING :OBJ_sig =
struct
    type OBJECT = int

    fun grow (x :'a) = x :'a

    fun shrink (x :'a) = x :'a
end
```

However, an error will arise when attempting to apply MISLEADING.grow or MISLEADING.shrink to a value which is not of type int.

This rule reinforces the principle that programmers should consider the nature of the input and output types of their programs before worrying about the coding details.

Rule 3 – equality matching

In the definition of INT_struct the SML response[3] for the type OBJECT was to echo the keyword **eqtype** rather than **type**; this is because SML has detected that the underlying type for OBJECT is such that two values of type OBJECT can be tested for equality. In practice, it is possible to ensure that a type must be an **eqtype** by using this keyword, instead of the **type** keyword, in the **signature** definition:

```
signature EQ_sig =
sig
    eqtype OBJECT
    (* some more code *)
end
```

Any attempt to define OBJECT as a type that has not got equality defined upon it will now give rise to an error.[4] In brief, **eqtype**s include every type that does not contain a functional type or **abstype**.

---

3. Remember, as with all system responses given in this book, this is implementation dependent and is not defined in the standard language definition (Milner *et al.*, 1990).
4. Note that having a **signature** including the definition type THING does not preclude the actual type of THING from being an **eqtype**. This is analogous to the fact that the definition type ('a,'b) PAIR = ('a * 'b) does not preclude an instance of PAIR having components of the same type.

Rule 4 – privacy

Finally, any definition within a constrained **structure** that is not matched within its **signature** is private. Its existence is not echoed by the SML response to the **structure** definition, it cannot be referenced by a long identifier nor is it made available if the **structure** is opened:

```
— structure MORE_struct :OBJ_sig =
  struct
       type OBJECT = string

       fun last nil = ""
       |    last (front :: nil) = front
       |    last (_ :: rest) = last rest

       fun grow astring
           = astring ^ last (explode astring)

       val shrink = implode o rev o tl o rev o explode
                        (* rev is the built-in function for
                            reversing lists *)
    end;

structure MORE_struct:
sig
      eqtype OBJECT
      val grow: OBJECT —> OBJECT
      val shrink: OBJECT —> OBJECT
end

— MORE_struct.last;
Error: unbound variable or constructor in structure: last
```

A similar effect could have been obtained by defining last to be a **local** function within an unconstrained MORE_struct; however, the above approach provides flexibility in that the decision to make the function last visible or hidden is taken in the **signature**, not in the code of the **structure**.

Exercise 7.2
Provide a **signature** to match the **structure** defined in Exercise 7.1.

7.2.3 *Concealing type implementation details*

By using **signature**s it is possible to defer the decision whether an actual implementation will use a type synonym or a user-defined type. This can be done by using the keyword **type**, rather than the keyword **datatype**, in the **signature** body. This has the bonus of allowing the implementor a choice but has the consequence that a **datatype**'s constructors will become private to the **structure** (in a very similar manner to that of hiding an **abstype**'s constructors). If this option is taken then it is essential to provide primitives to make new instances of the **datatype** and to display its elements.

For example, if `NUM_struct`, constrained by `OBJ_sig`, were to use a **datatype** `OBJECT` then it would be necessary to extend both the **signature** and the **structure** to include primitives to create new values of `OBJECT`.[5]

```
signature OBJ_sig =
sig
        type OBJECT

        val grow :OBJECT -> OBJECT
        val shrink :OBJECT -> OBJECT
end

signature NUM_sig =
sig
        type OBJECT

        val grow :OBJECT -> OBJECT
        val shrink :OBJECT -> OBJECT
        val Int_to_OBJ :int -> OBJECT
        val Real_to_OBJ :real -> OBJECT
end

structure NUM_struct =
struct
     datatype OBJECT = Int of int
                     | Real of real
     val Int_to_OBJ = Int
     val Real_to_OBJ = Real

     fun grow (Int n) = Int (n + 1)
     |   grow (Real n) = Real (n + 1.0)

     fun shrink (Int n) = Int (n - 1)
     |   shrink (Real n) = Real (n - 1.0)
end
```

5. See Section 7.2.4 for details how this may be facilitated using the keyword **include**.

```
structure USEFUL_struct :NUM_sig = NUM_struct

structure USELESS_struct :OBJ_sig = NUM_struct
```

Given the above definitions, the following interaction might occur:

```
- val newOBJ = USELESS_struct.Int_to_OBJ 3;
Error: unbound variable or constructor name in
    structure: Int_to_OBJ

- val newOBJ = USEFUL_struct.Int_to_OBJ 3;
val newOBJ = Int 3 :NUM_struct.OBJECT
```

Exercise 7.3
Is there any effective difference between hiding a **datatype**'s constructors within a
structure and using an **abstype**?

7.2.4 *The properties of signatures*

The following list outlines some of the interesting properties of **signature**s:

1. There is no equality defined on them.

2. They are top-level objects, and cannot be defined within another object;
    furthermore (unlike **structure** definitions) they cannot be nested.

3. The keyword **include** can be used to save writing long **signature**s by
    incorporating the contents of existing **signature**s within a new definition:

    ```
    signature NUM_sig =
    sig
        include OBJ_sig

        val Int_to_OBJ :int -> OBJECT
        val Real_to_OBJ :real -> OBJECT
    end
    ```

4. It is not always necessary to define a **structure** and its constraining **signature**
    separately. One shorthand notation has the form:

    ```
    structure S : sig ...end =
    struct
      ...
    end
    ```

However, this format defeats the purpose of having distinct specifications and implementations.

Exercise 7.4
Given the **structure**:

```
structure QUESTION_struct =
struct
    abstype OBJECT = Obj of int
    with
        fun make_OBJ (x :int) = Obj x
    end
    val x = 3
    val y = 42.01
end
```

which of the following **signatures** will successfully constrain it?

```
signature SIG1_sig =
sig
end

signature SIG2_sig =
sig
    type OBJECT
    val x :OBJECT
end

signature SIG3_sig =
sig
    datatype OBJECT
    val x :OBJECT
end

signature SIG4_sig =
sig
    type OBJECT
    val make_OBJ :int -> OBJECT
    val x :int
    val y :real
end
```

7.3 Sharing

One of the major advantages of using **structures** is to allow for separate software development; a programmer can work on one part of a program independently of another part. This, however, sometimes leads to the problem of guaranteeing consistency when two or more **structures** are closely related and consequently need to have some definitions in common. Rather than make the programmer check manually that these common definitions are, in fact, the same at every stage of the program development, SML provides a **sharing** mechanism. This allows the programmer to specify that two **structures** share a mutual type or sub-structure; the consistency checking is then done by the SML system itself.

Sharing types

Section 6.5.2 has already discussed the issue of providing a common intermediate form (together with 'make' and 'show' functions) to allow conversion between two **abstypes**. A similar requirement arises for conversions between **structures** if they have internal **abstypes** or if their **signatures** hide the constructors of their internal **datatypes** (which is a good programming technique, since it provides better abstraction and modularity). Furthermore, in order to keep a program well structured, the conversion functions should themselves be packaged into a **structure**. The **sharing** keyword provides a general mechanism to achieve these aims.

For example, ARRAY_struct and TREE_struct might use **abstypes** internally. In order to allow for conversion, they should each also include a definition for an intermediate type COMMON together with functions to convert to and from the intermediate type. The following specifications of TREE_sig and ARRAY_sig will ensure that ARRAY_struct and TREE_struct provide the required type and functions:

```
signature TREE_sig =
sig
    type 'a COMMON
    type 'a TREE

    (* here would be a number of type declarations
       for the other functions in the TREE structure *)

    val TREE_to_COMMON :'a TREE -> 'a COMMON
    val COMMON_to_TREE :'a COMMON -> 'a TREE
end

signature ARRAY_sig =
sig
    type 'a COMMON
    type 'a ARRAY

    (* here would be a number of type declarations
       for the other functions in the ARRAY structure *)

    val ARRAY_to_COMMON :'a ARRAY -> 'a COMMON
    val COMMON_to_ARRAY :'a COMMON -> 'a ARRAY
end
```

By defining a new **structure** AT_struct and its corresponding **signature** AT_sig (which uses **sharing**), it is possible to instruct the SML system to check that TREE_struct and ARRAY_struct have the same underlying definition for the type COMMON and to package together the conversion functions between trees and arrays. In this manner, the array and tree implementations need not know about one another; for example, the array need not know whether the intermediate type it has provided will be used for conversion with a tree or with some other data type. The definitions of AT_struct and AT_sig are given below:

```
signature AT_sig =
sig
    structure T :TREE_sig
    structure A :ARRAY_sig

    sharing type T.COMMON = A.COMMON

    val ARRAY_to_TREE :'a A.ARRAY -> 'a T.TREE
    val TREE_to_ARRAY :'a T.TREE -> 'a A.ARRAY
end

structure AT_struct :AT_sig =
struct
    structure A = ARRAY_struct
    structure T = TREE_struct

    val ARRAY_to_TREE = T.COMMON_to_TREE o A.ARRAY_to_ COMMON
    val TREE_to_ARRAY = A.COMMON_to_ARRAY o T.TREE_to_ COMMON
end
```

Limits of type sharing

Any two non-contradictory types may be shared; it is even possible to share an **eqtype** with another specified type if the latter admits equality. Hence both of the following are legal:

```
signature MAYSHARE1sig =
sig
    type ('a,'b) Pair
    datatype ('a,'b) PairAssoc = Pcon of ('a * 'b) -> 'b
    sharing type Pair = PairAssoc
end
```

```
signature MAYSHARE2sig =
sig
    eqtype E
    datatype BOCHVAR = True | False | Meaningless

    sharing type E = BOCHVAR
end
```

Conversely, the following will fail because PairAssoc cannot have equality defined upon it:

```
signature CANTSHARE =
sig
    eqtype ('a,'b) Pair
    datatype ('a,'b) PairAssoc = Pcon of ('a * 'b) –> 'b

    sharing type Pair = PairAssoc
end
```

Sharing structures

In a similar manner, it is possible to specify that two **structures** share a common sub-structure of the same name. The syntax is identical to type **sharing** except that the keyword **type** is omitted from the specification. Thus given two **structures** S1 and S2 each with a sub-structure X, the following specification will guarantee that S1.X is the same as S2.X in all of its components' definitions:

```
signature COMMON_sig =
sig
        structure S1 :sig1
        structure S2 :sig2

        sharing S1.X = S2.X
end
```

7.4 Functors

The SML **functor** construct enables **structures** to be parameterized, in a similar manner to function parameterization and with similar benefits, but on a larger scale including the bonus of allowing the programmer to specify only those items that are needed when incorporating existing **structures**. The next section introduces the syntax of **functor**s and shows how they may be used by means of a simple example of incorporating an existing software library into a new program. Subsequent sections show further usage for software management and program customization.

7.4.1   Using a functor with a standard library

Simple **functor** definition

The **functor** construct is similar in format to that of the **structure** construct, except that it may be parameterized: the parameter may be any **structure** that satisfies the constraining **signature**. The template for a **functor** definition is:

> **functor**   *functor_name* (*param_struct :param_sig*) *:functor_sig* =
> **struct**
>
>> *some definitions*
>> *which can be anything legal within the Core language*
>> *or other structure definitions*
>
> **end**

As with all system responses, the response is implementation specific; for example, Standard ML of New Jersey will only echo those values that are declared in the target *functor-sig.*

Example – text justification

The example in the rest of this section discusses the design of a formatting program, *justify*, to perform text justification. The program will make use of a number of tried and tested list-handling functions that have already been collected into a **structure**. This will be the actual parameter to the formal parameter *param_struct* in the above template. An advantage of using a **functor** in this situation is that it is possible to constrain the number of list-handling function names that are visible inside the definition body and thereby reduce the possibility of a name clash.

Specification

The *justify* program will take a string of characters and a desired line width and transform it into a left and right justified text with lines of the desired line width. The last line will not be right justified. It is assumed that the selected line width is long enough to hold the longest word in the input string.

Target **signature** requirements

The first stage in the design of *justify* is to choose which objects will be shown to the outside world; that is, provide the program's **signature**:

```
signature JUSTIFY_sig =
sig
    val justify :int -> string -> string
end
```

This will take the place of *functor_sig* in the above template.

Program design overview

The program follows a divide and conquer principle. The input text is considered as an unformatted paragraph with possible multiple spaces, blank lines (two consecutive newline characters) and lines of different width than the desired line width. The final output will have a fixed line width and regular spacing between each word.

The first step is to compress the white-space characters (this has already been discussed in Section 5.2.2). Subsequently the text is split into lines, which are then split into words which are output with at least one space between them.

Extra spaces must be added if a word straddles a line divide. In this situation the word is shunted into the next line and the current line must be padded out with extra spaces to fill the gap. The program will evenly distribute extra spaces from the left, which is perhaps simplistic but the design makes a more elegant distribution quite easy to include later.

Functor *implementation*

The **functor** for the *justify* program is now presented. The code makes use of several functions to manipulate lists which are assumed to be contained within a general-purpose list-manipulation library. However, only those functions which are relevant to the program need be 'imported' into the program. This is achieved by constraining the parameter **structure** with a **signature** that declares those desired functions and none other. Thus, the *param_sig* part of the template has been replaced by TOOLS_sig, as defined below:

```
signature TOOLS_sig =
sig
    val drop :int -> 'a list -> 'a list
    val dropwhile :('a -> bool) -> 'a list -> 'a list
    val occurs :''a list -> ''a -> int
    val replicate :int -> 'a -> 'a list
    val take :int -> 'a list -> 'a list
    val takeafter :('a -> bool) -> 'a list -> 'a list
    val takewhile :('a -> bool) -> 'a list -> 'a list
end
```

Although the general-purpose library contains many functions, only those listed in the above **signature** will be visible inside the **functor** body and there is no need to worry about possible name clashes with other functions in the library. The name hiding still applies even if the library is **open**ed inside the **functor** body – this provides a way to allow the use of shorter identifiers (see, however, Section 7.4.3):

```
functor
    JUSTIFY_func (LIST_TOOLS_struct :TOOLS_sig)
                    :JUSTIFY_ sig =
struct

        (* beware: opening a structure here!
        in this instance there should be no danger of a
        name clash because this functor only has one
        parameter*)

    open LIST_TOOLS_struct

    type SLIST = string list

    fun isspace (c :string)
        =         (c = " ")
          orelse (c = "\t")
          orelse (c = "\n") :bool

    (* reduce multiple white space to a single space *)
    (* and delete all leading and trailing white space *)
     fun compress (line :SLIST)
         = let
             fun xcompress (nil :SLIST) = nil :SLIST
             |   xcompress (front :: rest)
                 = if isspace front
                   then
                     " " :: (xcompress
                                 (dropwhile isspace rest))
                   else
                       front :: (xcompress rest)
             val notrailing = rev o (dropwhile isspace) o rev
             val noleading = dropwhile isspace
         in
             (notrailing o xcompress o noleading) line :SLIST
         end

    (* split line and calculate extra spaces between
    words *)
    fun splitline (line :SLIST)
                  (gapcount :int)
                  (leftover :int)
```

```
    = let
        val word = takewhile (not o isspace) line
        val restofline = takeafter isspace line
        val extraspaces
            = (leftover div gapcount)
              + (if (leftover mod gapcount) = 0
                  then 0
                  else 1)
      in
        (word,
         extraspaces,
         restofline) :SLIST * int * SLIST
      end


(* split text and calculate number of left over spaces
   to pad out line *)
fun splittext (width :int) (text :SLIST)
    = let
        val revline = rev (take (width + 1) text)
        val leftover
            = length (takewhile (not o isspace) revline)
        val line = take (width - leftover) text
        val restoftext = drop (width - leftover + 1)
                              text
      in
        (line, leftover, restoftext)
        :SLIST * int * SLIST
      end


(* no extra padding needed if no more words
   or no more extra spaces - otherwise at least
   1 space between words *)
fun justifyline (line :SLIST) (_ :int) (0 :int)
            = line @ ["\n"] :SLIST
|   justifyline line 0 _
            = line @ ["\n"]
|   justifyline line gapcount leftover
            = let
                val (word, extraspaces, restofline)
                    = splitline line gapcount leftover
              in
              word
                @ replicate (extraspaces + 1) " "
                @ justifyline restofline
                            (gapcount - 1)
                            (leftover - extraspaces)
              end
```

```
(* splits text and justifies a line at a time passes
   number of gaps between words and number of
   leftover spaces *)

fun justifytext (width :int) (text :SLIST)
  = if length text <= width
                          (* last line in paragraph *)
      then text @ ["\n"] :SLIST
      else
          let
              val (line, leftover, restoftext)
                  = splittext width text
              val gapcount = occurs line " "
          in
              (justifyline line gapcount leftover)
              @ (justifytext width restoftext)
          end

fun justify (width :int) (text :string)
  = (implode (justifytext width
                  (compress (explode text))))
              :string

end
```

Applying a **functor**

The **functor** does not actually create a new **structure**. To create the *justify* program the **functor** must be applied to a **structure** as its actual parameter. This will instantiate a new **structure** with the definitions contained within its body and those contained within the actual parameter:

```
structure JUSTIFY_struct = JUSTIFY_func (LIST_TOOLS_ struct)
```

The structure LIST_TOOLS_struct would have been built from the LIST_ SELECTION_struct shown in Section 7.1 plus other functions for list iteration and list manipulation, as shown in Chapters 3 and 4. LIST_TOOLS_struct must, of course, contain the function replicate which, for completeness, is defined as follows:

```
exception Replicate

fun replicate (n :int) (item :'a)
  = if n < 1
    then raise Replicate
    else
```

```
let
    fun xrep (1 :int) = [item] :'a list
    |   xrep n        = item :: xrep (n - 1)
in
    xrep n :'a list
end
```

JUSTIFY_struct may now be used in exactly the same way as any other **structure**. It may, of course, also become the input parameter to another program that does more extensive text formatting.

7.4.2 Advantages of using functors

The advantages of the **functor** approach in the above example can be summarized as:

1. The advantage of modularity, just as with **structure**s. This not only allows the re-use of established software libraries (in the above case LIST_TOOLS_struct) but also makes it easy to incorporate any changes to them with minimum overheads.

2. Better documentation; because both the source and target **signature**s must be listed. This has the considerable bonus of *forcing* the programmer to consider type declarations as part of the program design.

3. A clean interface between the library and the program; only those definitions that are needed have been incorporated. LIST_TOOLS_struct may have contained a couple of dozen functions but only the eight that were needed have actually been made visible to the **functor** code. The **open**ing of this parameter is also safe because there can be no name redefinition conflict between its private names and those used within JUSTIFY_func itself.

4. Safer code: the encapsulation of the code within the **functor** body and its parameter reduces the temptation to use values that have been defined elsewhere. There is less likelihood of a programmer using **val** names which are defined outside of the **functor** and so the desired property of closure is encouraged.[6]

5. Separate software development: because the **functor** and its parameter are 'loosely coupled' it is possible to develop the code for each part separately. As will be shown in Section 7.6, there may also be the opportunity to re-use the code for closely related programs.

6. Separate compilation: if the **functor** exhibits closure then it may be possible to compile it separately from the rest of the program, as indicated in Appendix E.

---

6. Unfortunately, there is no guarantee of closure. For example, it is still possible to forget to incorporate a **structure** parameter and find that an unwanted version with the same name happens to be in scope.

7.4.3 The properties of functors

Functors are not functions

Functors could be considered as functions over **structure**s. This view is reinforced in that they also do not admit equality. However, they differ from functions in that it is not possible to pass them as parameters, nor to partially apply them nor to define them anywhere except at the top level of an SML session.

Functor parameters

Functors may take the null parameter (). It is also possible for them to take composite parameter lists which allows greater flexibility in program construction. A **functor** that allows more than one parameter can be defined in one of two ways. The first method requires the keyword **structure** to be used many times:

```
functor WP_func (structure S1 :S1_sig
                 structure S2 :S2_sig
                 structure S3 :S3_sig
                 ...
                 structure Sn :Sn_sig) :WP_sig =
struct
        (* etc *)
end
```

By contrast, the second method uses a simultaneous definition in order to avoid re-typing the **structure** keyword:

```
functor WP_func (structure S1 :S1_sig
                     and S2 :S2_sig
                     and S3 :S3_sig
                     and ...
                     and Sn :Sn_sig) :WP_sig =
struct
        (* etc *)
end
```

Similarly, there are two formats for applying a **functor** with more than one parameter to its actual parameters. Both of the following are legal:

```
structure WP_struct
= WP_func (structure S1 = Grep_struct
           structure S2 = JUSTIFY_struct
           ...
           structure Sn = ANOTHER_struct)
```

```
    structure WP_struct
    = WP_func (structure S1 = Grep_struct
                     and S2 = JUSTIFY_Struct
                     ...
                     and Sn = ANOTHER_struct)
```

Note that where a **functor** has more than one parameter there is a small risk of a name clash between the parameters' components. Rather than **open**ing them, it is better to employ long identifiers. For example:

```
functor EG_func (structure INTS : intsig
                 structure REALS : realsig) : EG_sig =
struct
      val times = INTS.times
      val realtimes = REALS.times
      ...
end
```

Exercise 7.5
Explain what is wrong with the following program:

```
signature N_sig =
sig
        type NUMBER
        val inc :NUMBER -> NUMBER
        val dec :NUMBER -> NUMBER
end

signature NTYPE_sig =
sig
        type NUMBER
        val i :NUMBER
end

functor NUMBERS_func (Ntype_struct :NTYPE_sig) :N_sig =
struct
        type NUMBER = Ntype_struct.NUMBER
        val i = Ntype_struct.i
        fun inc n = (n + i)
        fun dec n = (n - i)
end
```

7.5 Views

This section shows how **signature**s on their own are a useful tool for very high-level specification without worrying about coding details. In particular, they may be used to provide different views of the same code.

Consider a database that, amongst other requirements, must record the price of each component in stock. This database will be used by several application programs to implement data entry, to control sales, and to provide for its overall management. For example, the sales program may need to generate an invoice of the total cost of a product of several different quantities of various components. The underlying objects, with appropriate constraints, could include:

> *component:*
> > *which consists of:*
> > > *key:*   *which is a unique number*
> > > *description:*   *which is probably a character string*
> > > *price:*   *which cannot be a negative number*
>
> *quantity:*
> > *which cannot be a negative number*

From this brief description it can be seen that most of these objects have an underlying numeric domain. However, each object has a different meaning and not all the arithmetic operations are applicable to each of them. Thus, it is meaningless to attempt to add up keys or multiply prices. The required degree of control may be achieved by declaring the appropriate types and then declaring only those functions that are necessary to express the relationship between them.

```
signature COMP_sig =
sig
    type KEY
    type DESCRIPTION
    type PRICE
    datatype COMPONENT
            = Component of (KEY * DESCRIPTION * PRICE)
    val make_component :(int * string * real)
                            -> COMPONENT

       (* some more declarations*)

    type QUANTITY
    val cost :KEY -> QUANTITY -> PRICE
end
```

Notice that COMPONENT has been explicitly declared as a **datatype** rather than the more general type declaration given for KEY and PRICE. The purpose of using an explicit **datatype** (with visible constructors) is that it is thereby possible to express the relationship between KEY, DESCRIPTION, PRICE and COMPONENT in the **signature** alone (without recourse to the **structure** code).

For the system designer, it would be necessary to have an overview of the entire set of objects within a component, although such knowledge is not necessary for every applications programmer. For example, a programmer responsible for a data-entry suite need not worry about the function cost. Similarly, a programmer concerned with sales need not worry about make_component. There are considerable benefits if each programmer or programming team can be confident that their coding efforts are not inadvertently going to interfere with other programmers and that other programs are not inadvertently going to affect their implementation details. These controls are simply achieved by the appropriate use of constraining **signature**s to give different *views* of a common library of type definitions and function definitions.

The common library will be constrained by the signature COMP_sig given above. Its code will be contained in COMMON_struct:

```
structure COMMON_struct :COMP_sig =
struct
        (* some code *)
end
```

The systems designer needs access to everything that COMP_sig makes visible and will therefore either employ the above COMMON_struct, or for future program development it can become the parameter to a **functor** with an appropriate OVERVIEW_sig **signature**:

```
functor OVERVIEW_func (COMMON: COMP_sig) :OVERVIEW_sig =
struct
        (* some code *)
end

structure OVERVIEW_struct
        = OVERVIEW_func (COMMON_ struct)
```

However, the data-entry and sales applications programmers only require a limited view of the database and will therefore have instances constrained by appropriately limited **signature**s. Since these two views are so similar, coding effort can be spared by use of the **include** feature:

```
signature BOTH_sig =
sig
    type KEY
    type DESCRIPTION
    type PRICE
```

```
datatype COMPONENT
            = Component of (KEY * DESCRIPTION * PRICE)

        (* some more declarations *)

end

signature DATA_ENTRY_sig =
sig
    include BOTH_sig
    val make_component :(int * string * real)
                            -> COMPONENT
end

signature SALES_sig =
sig
    include BOTH_sig
    type QUANTITY
    val cost :KEY -> QUANTITY -> PRICE
end
```

These **signatures** will each be used with their own **functor**, which can be parameterized with the latest version of `COMMON_struct`. Thus, for the programmer concerned with sales applications:

```
functor SALES_APP_func (COMMON :SALES_sig) :SALES_ APP_sig =
struct

        (* some code *)
end

structure SALES_APP_struct = SALES_APP_func (COMMON_ struct)
```

The above approach is quite similar to that employed in constructing the *justify* program; in this case the `COMMON_struct` is treated as a library.

An alternative strategy is to use a nullary **functor** and constrain the target **structure**s. In this approach, the nullary **functor** will actually contain the full database code (as defined in the previous approach by `COMMON_struct`) and be constrained by `COMP_sig`. The views can be created as followed:

```
structure OVERVIEW_struct :OVERVIEW_sig = COMMON_ func()
structure DATA_ENTRY_struct :DATA_ENTRY_sig
                        = COMMON_func()
structure SALES_struct :SALES_sig = COMMON_func()
```

Exercise 7.6
Explain what would happen given the following command sequence:

```
signature N_sig = sig end;
functor N_func() = struct val x = 1 end;

structure A_struct :N_sig = N_func();
structure B_struct = N_func();
structure C_struct = N_func() :N_sig;
```

7.6   Re-usable software – grep revisited

The *grep* utility presented throughout the text is now extended as another example of program construction using **functors**. The sublist activities are separated from the lex part of the program and parameterized on them. In addition to giving the program greater modularity it also has the advantage of making the sublist code *re-usable*. It is now possible to have different representations of the meta-characters (for example to deal with the UNIX Bourne Shell[7] file generation codes), and also different implementations of the 'lexical analyser'.

The rest of this section continues the design shown in Chapter 3 to incorporate the other *grep* meta-characters. The inclusion of 'range' meta-characters leads to a slight revision in the way that regular expressions are represented and how any particular regular expression element is compared against its corresponding searched line character. However, the original search strategy remains essentially unaltered.

7.6.1   Incorporating 'end of line' and 'start of line' meta-characters

As shown in Section 3.9.2, the regular expression can be expressed as a list of pairs; the first component representing the type of match (zero or more, or one only) and the second component the actual value to be matched. This principle can be extended to cater for the meta-characters to anchor a search to the start of a line (ˆ) or to the end of a line ($). To anchor a match from the start of the line means that the sublist function is only applied once (that is, it does not recurse). Matching the end of the line can only succeed if the searched line is empty when the end of line meta-character is encountered (as the last element) in the regular expression list. These considerations give rise to an extended MTYPE **datatype**, with SOL for start of line and EOL for end of line:

```
datatype MTYPE = ZERO_MORE I ONCE I SOL I EOL
```

---

7. This is a job control language which provides an interface between the user and the UNIX Operating System: see Bourne (1982).

The existing *grep* program must be changed in three places:

1. lex: to recognize the new meta-characters.

2. sublist: to anchor the regular expression match to the start of the search line.

3. startswith: to succeed in a match, if the search line is empty when EOL is met in the regular expression.

The actual code is presented in Section 7.6.3, after discussion of the other meta-characters.

7.6.2 Incorporating 'any' and 'range' meta-characters

The final stage of the initial design is to incorporate the . and [...] meta-characters for *any character* and for a *range* of characters respectively.[8] A case analysis in Table 7.1. shows all the possible combinations. Such an inspection reveals that the matching requirements of the new meta-characters are in fact quite similar to that of matching a single character.

Table 7.1. Case analysis for *any* and *range* meta-characters

Number of occurrences	Object affected
One Only	A given single character
Zero or More	A given single character
One Only	Any single character
Zero or More	Any single character
One Only	Any single character from the range [...]
Zero or More	Any single character from the range [...]
One Only	Any single character not in the range [...]
Zero or More	Any single character not in the range [...]

Ranges

One method of treating a ranged regular expression element is to expand it into a single character string list and then check whether the current line position matches any of the characters in the list by using the function member (introduced in Section 3.6.1). For example, the range "[b-e]" can be expanded into the range list ["b","c","d","e"] and "[a-d_1-3]" can be expanded to ["a","b","c", "d","_","1","2","3"].

  With this approach a single actual value can be treated as a single item range, for example "a" can be converted to the range list ["a"].

---

8. Notice that 'Zero or More of any single character in a range' does not constrain the pattern to be a number of occurrences of the *same* character from the range – rather, for each new occurrence a different character may be chosen from the range.

Negative ranges

Negative ranged regular expression elements such as "[^a-d]" (which imply that a single character should be chosen which may be any character *except* those in the range) can be treated in one of two ways:

1. A range list could be generated with all the values that are not in the range "[a-d]", that is ["e","f", ...], and member can be used as a test for equality.

2. The range "[a-d]" could be expanded to ["a","b","c","d"] and the truth value returned by member subsequently inverted.

Both options are equally valid. The first option probably requires extra initial work to construct the range list. The latter requires either additional match types NOT_ONCE and NOT_ZERO_MORE or an additional component to the regular expression tuple that indicates what to do with the result of member. The design followed here is the second option (using an additional tuple element) for reasons now discussed.

Any

On inspection it can be seen that the . meta-character is really a convenient shorthand for the range "[\0-\127]" which could be expanded accordingly. An alternative approach is to consider it in terms of *not matching nothing*, that is given member returns false for the empty list nil then . is really not (member(nil, _)).

Type requirements

The latter method using member implies that a consistent treatment of all the wild cards and actual values can be achieved by representing a regular expression element as a triple:

```
(MTYPE * EQFUN * RANGE)
```

with the predefinitions:

```
datatype MTYPE = ZERO_MORE | ONCE | SOL | EOL
type RANGE = string list
```

The equality functional type EQFUN will either be same or notsame based on a version of member that translates a string and a RANGE to a Boolean value:

```
datatype EQFUN = Eqfun of (string * RANGE) -> bool

val (same :EQFUN)    = Eqfun member
val (notsame :EQFUN) = Eqfun (not o member)
```

Signature *requirements*

The *grep* program need only show the outside world the fact that it takes a string representing the raw regular expression and a list of strings to be searched and returns a list of strings that have been matched. Hence its **signature** is simply:

```
signature GREP_sig =
sig
     val grep :string -> string list -> string list
end
```

Its requirements from the lexical analyser are:

1. A `lex` function to convert the string to a regular expression list (and so it must know the format of a regular expression list).

2. Details of the `MTYPE` enumerations to enable meta-character pattern matching.

3. Details of the `EQFUN` **datatype** to deconstruct the embedded membership function.

Hence the parameter to the *grep* **functor** (which will be called `GREP_func`) must be constrained by the following **signature**:

```
signature LEX_sig =
sig
     datatype MTYPE = SOL I EOL I ONCE I ZERO_MORE
     type RANGE
     datatype EQFUN = Eqfun of (string * RANGE) -> bool
     val lex :string list -> (MTYPE * EQFUN * RANGE) list
end
```

The underlying type of `RANGE` is irrelevant to the `sublist` functions because it is only used by the membership functions, and so it need only be declared a **type** within `LEX_sig`.

Notice that `LEX_sig` does not declare `SLIST` and `REGLIST`. This is because the `GREP_func` functions which use them must know about their underlying types. Hence, if `LEX_sig` included the declarations:

```
type SLIST
type REGLIST
val lex : SLIST -> REGLIST
```

then the expression `lex (explode regexp)` in the definition of `grep_pred` (see below) would cause a type clash between the result type of `explode` which is `string list` and the source type of `lex` which is the hidden type `SLIST`. Since

functors must be defined before they can be applied to their parameters, there is no way that SML can know that SLIST is intended to be a type synonym for string list unless it is explicitly stated within the **functor** body.

7.6.3 Implementation of GREP_func

The new version of startswith is now presented in a **functor** to facilitate different lexical analysers. The actual code is remarkably similar to the previous version (shown in Chapter 3) because the basic search strategy has not been altered:

```
functor GREP_func (LEX_struct :LEX_sig) :GREP_sig =
struct
    (* Beware! opening a structure here. In this instance
       there should be no danger of name clashes because this
       functor only has one parameter *)

    open LEX_struct

    (* also notice that this functor assumes a certain
       specification for the function lex - For example, it
       is assumed that lex only generates SOL and EOL tokens
       at the start and end of lines respectively. *)

    type REGEXP  = (MTYPE * EQFUN * RANGE)
    type REGLIST = REGEXP list
    type SLIST   = string list

    fun startswith (nil :REGLIST) (_ :SLIST) = true :bool

    |   startswith ((ZERO_MORE, _ , _ ) :: regrest) nil
        = startswith regrest nil

    |   startswith [(EOL, _ , _ )] line = (line = nil)

    |   startswith _ nil = false

    |   startswith ((ZERO_MORE, (Eqfun ismatch), range)
                    :: regrest)
                   (lfront :: lrest)
        = startswith regrest (lfront :: lrest)
               orelse
            (ismatch (lfront, range)
                   andalso
            startswith ((ZERO_MORE, (Eqfun ismatch), range)
                    :: regrest)
                   lrest
        )
```

```
|   startswith ((_, (Eqfun ismatch), range) :: regrest)
                 (lfront :: lrest)
    = ismatch (lfront, range)
              andalso
      startswith regrest lrest

fun sublist  (((SOL, _, _ ) :: regexp) :REGLIST)
             (line :SLIST)
   = (startswith regexp line) :bool


|   sublist regexp line
    = (startswith regexp line)
              orelse
      let
        fun xsublist nil = false
        |   xsublist ( _ :: lrest)
            = (startswith regexp lrest)
              orelse
              (xsublist lrest)
      in
        xsublist line
      end

fun grep_pred (regexp :string) (line :string)
    = sublist (lex (explode regexp)) (explode line) :bool

fun filter (pred :'a -> bool) (nil :'a list)
    = nil :'a list
|   filter pred (front :: rest)
    = if  (pred front)
      then front :: (filter pred rest)
      else filter pred rest

fun grep (regexp :string) (lines :SLIST)
    = filter (grep_pred regexp) lines :SLIST
end
```

Extending the lexical analyser

The code for the extended lexical analyser is a straightforward matter of listing which patterns have special meanings for *grep* and converting them to the appropriate format for the matching algorithms to manipulate. In problems of this of this nature the technique of case analysis (discussed in Chapter 3) is of particular importance:

```
structure LEX_struct :LEX_sig =
struct

    type RANGE = string list
    datatype MTYPE = ONCE | ZERO_MORE  | SOL | EOL
    datatype EQFUN = Eqfun of (string * RANGE) -> bool

    type REGEXP  = (MTYPE * EQFUN * RANGE)
    type REGLIST = REGEXP list
    type SLIST   = string list

    fun member ((_, nil) :''a * ''a list) = false :bool
    |   member (item, front :: rest)
        = (item = front) orelse member (item, rest)

    val same    = Eqfun member
    val notsame = Eqfun (not o member)

    exception Lex_range

    fun lex (("  ^  " :: rest) :SLIST)
        = ((SOL, same, nil) :: xlex rest) :REGLIST

    |   lex p = xlex p

    and
        xlex (nil :SLIST) = nil :REGLIST

    |   xlex ("\\" :: ch :: "*" :: rest)
        = (ZERO_MORE, same, [ch]) :: xlex rest

    |   xlex ("\\" :: ch :: rest)
        = (ONCE, same, [ch]) :: xlex rest

    |   xlex ("\\" :: nil)
        = [(ONCE, same, ["\\"])]

    |   xlex ("." :: "*" :: rest)
        = (ZERO_MORE, notsame, nil) :: xlex rest

    |   xlex ("[" :: " ^ " :: rest)
        = let
            val (range_part, exp_rest)
                = lexrange (notsame, nil) rest
          in
            range_part :: (xlex exp_rest)
          end
```

```
|   xlex ("[" :: rest)
    = let
        val (range_part, exp_rest)
          = lexrange (same, nil) rest
      in
        range_part :: (xlex exp_rest)
      end

|   xlex ("." :: rest)
    = (ONCE, notsame, nil) :: xlex rest

|   xlex (ch :: "*" :: rest)
    = (ZERO_MORE, same, [ch]) :: xlex rest

|   xlex ("$" :: nil)
    = [(EOL, same, nil)]

|   xlex (ch :: rest)
    = (ONCE, same, [ch]) :: xlex rest
and
    lexrange ((_,_) :EQFUN * RANGE) (nil :SLIST)
    = raise Lex_range

|   lexrange (mtype, range) ("\\" :: ch :: rest)
    = lexrange (mtype, ch :: range) rest :REGEXP * SLIST

|   lexrange (_, nil) ("]" :: _)
    = raise Lex_range            (* empty range *)

|   lexrange (mtype, range) ("]" :: "*" :: rest)
    = ((ZERO_MORE, mtype, range), rest)

|   lexrange (mtype, range) ("]" :: rest)
    = ((ONCE, mtype, range), rest)

|   lexrange (mtype, range) (start :: "-" :: stop :: rest)
    = if (start > stop)
      then raise Lex_range
      else
        lexrange (mtype, (expand range start stop)) rest
|   lexrange (mtype, range) (ch :: rest)
    = lexrange (mtype, ch :: range) rest
and
    expand (range :RANGE) (start :string) (stop :string)
    = if (start = stop)
      then stop :: range
      else expand (stop :: range)
                  start
                  (chr ((ord stop) - 1)) :RANGE
end
```

Notice that the above code was presented in a top-down manner using the keyword **and**. Although this makes all the **and**-ed functions visible at the same level, it is safe in this case because `LEX_sig` ensures that only the `lex` function will be visible to `GREP_func`. Furthermore, the auxiliary functions are not polymorphic (so there is no problem with **and** restricting their use to a single type).

Applying `GREP_func`

A new instance of *grep* can now be created and the resulting **structure** employed:

```
structure GREP_struct = GREP_func (LEX_struct)

- GREP_struct.grep "^[^a−z]ML" ["XML","sML","^SML"];
val it = ["XML"] : string list
```

7.6.4   Using a different lexical analyser

The UNIX Bourne Shell has a number of meta-characters for file name expansion that are similar but not identical to the *grep* meta-characters. Table 7.2 can be compared to Table 3.1 for their differences. For example, it can be seen that the wild card for a single character is different and there is no point in looking for a file name anchored at the start of a line. Otherwise the `ZERO_MORE,` `ONCE` and `RANGE` requirements are semantically the same, and so the `sublist` and `startswith` functions can work equally well for a **structure** that meets the Bourne Shell parsing requirments as for the *grep* requirements.

Table 7.2.   Meta-characters for Bourne Shell parsing

Character	Meaning
c	Any non-special character *c* matches itself
c	Turn off any special meaning of character *c*
?	Any single character
[...]	Any one of characters in ...
	(e.g. 1–9 covers all ASCII values between 1 and 9)
[!...]	Any one of characters not in ...
*	Matches any string (including the empty string)
A new line is not matched by anything.	

The meta-characters shown in Table 7.2 can be simply emulated by changing the Lex functions as follows:

```
structure BOURNE_LEX_struct :LEX_sig =
struct

   (* type definitions and membership functions
      as for grep LEX_struct *)

   (* lexrange and expand functions as for grep
      LEX_struct *)

   (* lex and xlex need to be rewritten *)

end
```

The `BOURNE_LEX_struct` can now be used as a parameter to `GREP_func` in exactly the same manner as for `LEX_struct`:

```
structure BOURNE_EXPAND_struct
         = GREP_func (BOURNE_LEX_struct)

— BOURNE_EXPAND_struct.grep "^[^a−z]ML"
                            ["XML","sML","^SML"];
val it = ["sML","^SML"] : string list
```

Exercise 7.7
Give the definition of the Lex function within BOURNE_LEX_struct.

7.7 Summary

This concluding chapter has introduced the SML Modules extension, which provides powerful facilities for the specification and construction of large programs. Large-scale programming benefits enormously from the rigorous application of the concepts of closure, modularity, encapsulation and self-documentation, as described and recommended throughout this book. With the addition of the Modules extension, SML provides a rich variety of tools for abstraction and control at many levels, from **local**s through to **abstype**s, **structure**s and **functor**s

Appendix A
File Handling

This appendix discusses the SML file handling definitions, including provisions for files to be opened for input or output as a stream of characters. The input–output library is based on the philosophy that only essential facilities need be built in and that the programmer then has the freedom to develop more sophisticated routines to fit individual requirements. However, a number of extensions to the input–output primitives have been proposed; the reader is referred to their site manual for particulars.

The discussion in this appendix highlights the fact that SML standard input–output lacks referential transparency and may sometimes require a different style of programming to that displayed in the main text.

A.1 File input and output

A.1.1 File input

Opening a file for input

A file may be opened for reading by using the function `open_in` with the name of the file as its string parameter. A successful open will return a file pointer (of type `instream`) which can subsequently be used to reference that file:[1]

```
val infp = open_in "rawdata"
```

The system response may give details about the file, but this is implementation dependent.

Reading from files

The input file may now be read by using the function `input` with the file pointer and number of characters to be read as its two parameters. A string is returned:

---

1. Note that it is possible to have more than one pointer open to a given input file. This enables different functions to process the same file at different rates.

```
val newstring = input (infp, SIZE)
(* where SIZE is the number of characters to be read *)
```

The second parameter to input enables a programmer to read a fixed amount of data. If the amount of input left to be read from the file has a length which is less than SIZE then input will return a string of that length.

Looking ahead

The end of file may be detected by checking whether the built-in predicate end_of_stream returns true when applied to the file pointer:

```
if end_of_stream ifp

then (* nothing left to read *)

    ...

else (* something left to read *)
    ...
```

The next character on the input stream may be inspected, but not actually 'consumed', using the function lookahead. For example:

```
if (lookahead ifp) = "\n"
then (* the next character is a new line *)
    ...
else (* the next character is some other value *)
    ...
```

A.1.2   File output

Opening a file for output

A file may be created for writing by using the function open_out. If the parameter to open_out is the name of an existing file its contents will be erased:[2]

```
— val outfp = open_out "results";
val outfp = — : outstream
```

---

2. The standard language definition has no built-in function to open a file to append to it. This can be achieved either by copying its contents to another file and then continuing to write to that file, or by using one of the site dependent extensions, such as openAppend.

Writing to files

The built-in function `output` takes a file pointer together with a string, and writes the latter to the file to which the former refers. The value `()` is returned:

```
- output (outfp, "a string");
val it = () : unit;
```

A.1.3 Input–output exceptions

The exception `Io` will be raised automatically if files cannot be opened by `open_in` or `open_out` or if an attempt is made by `output` or `input` to access an unopened file.

A.1.4 Special streams

There are two 'special' file streams, `std_in` and `std_out`, which respectively indicate the standard input (normally the keyboard) and standard output (normally the screen). These streams are automatically opened at the start of an SML session and provide convenient communication with the terminal. One of their uses is to prototype file processing routines; this is because the programmer can directly see the consequences of any file input or output. Once the program works as intended the special streams can be replaced by other file parameters.

A.1.5 File closing

Input and output files may be closed using `close_in` and `close_out` respectively, both taking file pointers as their parameters and returning `()`. In practice, explicit file closing is often not necessary, as all streams are normally closed on exit from the SML system. Nevertheless, there are three kinds of situation where it is necessary:

1. Where it is required to read from and write to the same file within a single program.
2. Where the number of files open exceeds the operating system limits.
3. Where it is required to flush the output to the file, to ensure all data items have been written.

A.2 Formatted input and output

SML does not define the operations for formatted input and output, hence it is the duty of the programmer to design these functions. Fortunately, this is normally quite easy.

A.2.1 *Formatted output*

The overloaded operator `makestring`[3] will convert integers, real numbers and Booleans to strings, which can be output directly. For example:

```
fun writeint (ofp :outstream) (n :int)
    = output (ofp, makestring n) :unit
```

If `makestring` did not exist it would be necessary to write separate conversion functions, such as `int_to_string` shown in Section 2.10. It should be noted that `makestring`, if available, is only overloaded for the base types – it is therefore necessary to write formatting functions for all other types that will be output.

A.2.2 *Formatted input*

The following function `readwhile` serves as a general-purpose routine to read from a named input stream until a given condition fails to be satisfied. The subsequent functions show how it could be used to form the basis of a formatted input library. However, notice that these functions are, in general, *not* referentially transparent, because the `input` function is not referentially transparent; this problem is explored further at the end of this appendix.

```
fun readwhile (pred :string -> bool) (ifp :instream)
    = if end_of_stream ifp
          orelse
        (not o pred) (lookahead ifp)
      then ""
      else input (ifp, 1) ^ readwhile pred ifp :string

(* will read an integer *)
fun readint (ifp :instream)
    = let
        fun isdigit x = (x >= "0") andalso (x <= "9")
      in
        string_to_int (readwhile isdigit ifp) :int
        (* string_to_int has been defined in Chapter 4 *)
      end

(* will consume entire input *)
fun readstring (ifp :instream)
    = readwhile (K true) ifp :string
      (* where K has been defined in Chapter 4 *)
```

---

3. Note that **makestring** is not part of the initial SML environment, as defined in Milner *et al.* (1990), although it is available in many implementations of SML, including Standard ML of New Jersey.

```
(* will consume one word *)
fun readword (ifp :instream)
    = let
        fun not_space x
            = (x <> " ") andalso (x <> "\t") andalso (x <> "\n")
      in
        readwhile not_space ifp :string
      end

(* will consume a Boolean value or raise an exception *)
fun readbool (ifp :instream)
    = let
        exception Readbool
        fun check "true" = true
        |   check "false" = false
        |   check _ = raise Readbool
      in
        check (readword ifp) :bool
      end
```

The next example `readline` actually requires the end of line character to be read, which means that attempting to re-use `readwhile` is inappropriate:

```
fun readline (ifp :instream)
    = if end_of_stream ifp
      then ""
      else if (lookahead ifp) = "\n"
            then input (ifp, 1)
            else input (ifp, 1) ^ readline ifp :string
```

Finally, the function `readN` will read up to N characters from a specified input stream and return a tuple containing a count of the number of characters actually read together with those characters. This is useful for manipulating 'blocks' of data:

```
fun readN (n :int) (ifp :instream)
    = let
        fun xreadN (0 :int) ((count, outstring) :int * string)
            = (count, outstring) :int * string
        |   xreadN n (count, outstring)
            = if end_of_stream ifp
              then (count, outstring)
              else xreadN (n − 1)
                        (count + 1,
                         outstring ^ input (ifp,1))
      in
        xreadN n (0, "") :int * string
      end
```

A.3 Using input and output

A.3.1 Using input – grep revisited

In general, using input is straightforward. For example, the *grep* program developed throughout the main text can be adapted to work for file input:

```
type SLIST = string list

fun in_grep (regexp :string) (filename :string)
    = let
        fun xsplitlines ("" :string) (acc :string)
            = [acc] :SLIST
              (* if the file ends with a newline character,
                 xsplitlines will return an empty string as
                 the last line of the file *)
        |   xsplitlines ("\n" :: rest) acc
            = acc :: xsplitlines rest ""
        |   xsplitlines (x :: rest) acc
            = xsplitlines rest (acc ^ x)

        fun splitlines text
            = xsplitlines text "" :SLIST

        val file_to_lines
            = (splitlines o readstring o open_in) :SLIST
      in
        grep regexp (file_to_lines filename) :SLIST
      end
```

However, this approach may fail if the input file is very big and the system cannot hold all of the string in memory. The following code solves this problem by processing just one input line at a time:

```
fun grep_in_lines (regexp :string) (filename :string)
    = let
        val ifp = open_in filename

        fun xgrep "" = [] :string list
        |   xgrep astring
            = (grep regexp [astring]) @ xgrep (readline ifp)
      in
        xgrep (readline ifp) :string list
      end
```

For other programs (such as *justify*) the readN function may be more suitable.

A.3.2 *Example: file copying*

The following example discusses the design of a function to copy the contents of a named input file to a named output file, discarding all white-space characters. One approach is to read the entire input file, compress it and then write the compressed version to the output file. This, however, means that the entire input file must be held in a string – with the same problem as discussed with the previous *grep* example.

An alternative approach is to read the file in portions, saving only a portion at a time, compressing it and writing the result to the output file. The memory used for saving a portion can be re-used for the next portion, thereby allowing much larger files to be copied. The extreme example of this alternative approach is to read the input file a character at a time; if the character is not a white-space character, then it is immediately written to the output file and otherwise is discarded. This is a reasonable strategy but the following implementation highlights the fact that file-handling sometimes forces the programmer into contrived solutions:

```
fun compresscopy (infile :string) (outfile :string)
    = let
        val ifp = open_in infile
        val ofp = open_out outfile

        fun xcopy ()
        = if end_of_stream ifp
          then ()
          else if  lookahead ifp = " "
                   orelse lookahead ifp = "\t"
                   orelse lookahead ifp = "\n"
               then xcopy (K () (input (ifp,1)))
               else xcopy (output (ofp, input (ifp,1)))
      in
        xcopy () :unit
      end
```

In order to understand the above code, it is necessary to consider what should be done for non-white-space characters and what should be done for white-space characters. For non-white-space characters the code should do two things:

1. Output the character.

2. Recurse to process the next character.

The above requirement is met in the expression:

```
xcopy (output (ofp, input (ifp,1)))
```

which writes what it has just read, resulting in () and then re-applies xcopy to ()
which is ignored as a 'dummy' parameter. This leaves the treatment of white-space
characters. If the built-in lookahead function detects that the next input value is a
white-space character then it is read but discarded and replaced with () by means of
the K combinator (as defined in Chapter 4):

```
xcopy (K () input(ifp,1))
```

Though this approach may seem a little contrived there does not appear to be a
more elegant solution for character-by-character copying. However, the concept of a
function compresscopy which returns no value except () is not in keeping with
the functional approach, since it encourages a style of 'programming by side-effect'
rather than programming with values. A 'side-effect' is an action which is caused by
the evaluation of a function but which does not contribute to the value returned by
the function; the use of side-effects destroys the desirable property of referential
transparency, as will be shown in the next subsection.

A.3.3   Input is not referentially transparent

It is important to be aware that the function input is not referentially transparent.
This fact is shown in that the following function f can produce different values than
the function g:

```
fun f (infp :instream)
    = let
       val x = input(infp,1)
    in
       x ^ x :string
    end

fun g (infp :instream)
       = input(infp,1) ^ input(infp,1) :string
```

The function f will read from the input file just once, whilst the function g will read it
twice. Hence, if the file pointed to by infp contained the string "AB" then the
application f infp will yield the result "AA"; however, the application g infp will
yield the result "AB". If the function input were referentially transparent (that is, if it
always returned the same result when given the same arguments) then the same
result would occur for both functions.

By contrast, the function readstring is referentially transparent, since it will
always return the same result for the same value of ifp (assuming the file has not
been written to during the course of the program). The moral is that referentially

transparent input is achievable in SML as long as the system has sufficient memory to hold all of the input file as a single data structure. If this is not possible, then the programmer should attempt to localize the use of side-effects so that the rest of the program is not affected.

A.3.4 Output is not referentially transparent

Just as input is not referentially transparent, neither is the function output. This fact is shown in the following code, where p, q and r all have the same value [(), ()] but each causes a different effect on the output file. p will cause no output to the file, q will cause a single hello to be output to the file and r will cause two hellos to be output to the file:

```
val x = ()
val opf = open_out "myfile"
val y = output (opf, "hello")

val p = x :: x :: []

val q = y :: y :: []

val r = output(opf, "hello")
        :: (output(opf, "hello") :: [])
```

A touchstone for referential transparency is that it should always be possible to substitute names of equal value anywhere in the program without changing the meaning of the program – in the above example this is clearly not possible since substituting p for r has a significant effect on what is written to the output file. It is difficult to achieve output in a manner which is referentially transparent; some other functional languages use a technique whereby the output of the program is redirected so that it is written to the output file (coupled with a mechanism to determine which file should receive the next portion of output), which has the benefit of ensuring that output is achieved 'by value' rather than 'by side-effect'. However, SML has no such provision.

In conclusion, referentially transparent output is generally not achievable in SML and so the programmer should attempt to localize the use of output side-effects so that the rest of the program is not affected.

Appendix B
Additional Features
of SML

This appendix introduces all the other non-imperative features of SML which are not covered in the main text. The first section presents some facilities for shortening expressions, including rules for tuple naming and manipulation. The second section shows how functions may be made **infix** or **nonfix** and given user-defined precedences. The final section introduces anonymous functions and discusses the equivalence of functions and **val** definitions.

B.1   Convenient abbreviations

B.1.1   The case statement

SML offers a shorthand notation to save repeating an expression when there are several patterns to be matched. Its general syntax is:

> **case** *arg*
> **of** *pattern1* => *body1*
> | *pattern2* => *body2*
> . . .
> | *patternN* => *bodyN*

where *arg* could be a single value or a compound expression. As with all pattern matching, the patterns within a **case** construct are tested sequentially until a successful match is found. Similarly, the SML system will give a warning if all possible cases are not considered.

The following example is similar to the standard UNIX facility *wc*, which counts the total number of characters, words and lines in the given files. The *wc* program takes input from one file using the SML input facilities `open_in` and `input` to form a string of characters. The end of file marker is detected using the `end_of_stream` function. The string is then converted into a list of characters by means of `explode` which acts as input to `xwc`:

```
signature WC_sig =
sig
        val wc : string -> (int * int * int)
end
```

```
structure WORDCOUNT_struct : WC_sig =
struct
  type SLIST = string list

  fun xwc (text :SLIST) (nlines :int)
          (nwords :int) (nchars :int)
    = case text
      of nil                      => (nlines, nwords, nchars)
                                     :int * int * int
       | (" " :: rest)            => xwc rest nlines
                                     nwords (nchars + 1)
       | ("\t" :: rest)           => xwc rest nlines
                                     nwords (nchars + 1)
       | ("\n" :: rest)           => xwc rest (nlines + 1)
                                     nwords (nchars + 1)
       | (_ :: nil)               => (nlines, nwords + 1, nchars + 1)
       | (_ :: " " :: rest)       => xwc rest nlines
                                     (nwords + 1) (nchars + 2)
       | (_ :: "\t" :: rest)      => xwc rest nlines
                                     (nwords + 1) (nchars + 2)
       | (_ :: "\n" :: rest)      => xwc rest (nlines + 1)
                                     (nwords + 1) (nchars + 2)
       | (_ :: second :: rest)    => xwc (second :: rest) nlines
                                     nwords (nchars + 1)

  fun wc infile = xwc ((explode o readstring o open_in) infile) 0 0 0
end
```

B.1.2 Layered patterns – as

The keyword **as** allows an aggregate value to be used both as a single entity and also deconstructed into its component parts. For example:

```
fun insert (item :int) (nil :int list)
        = [item] :int list

 | insert item (anylist as (front :: rest))
        = if item < front
            then item :: anylist
            else front :: insert item rest
```

Here, the second parameter will be matched as the single value anylist or as the constructed list (front :: rest).

B.1.3 *Type abbreviations – withtype*

The keyword **withtype** allows a **datatype** or **abstype** to contain a reference to a **type** synonym. The following example from Milner (1987) illustrates its use:

```
datatype ('a,'b) TREE = Tip of 'a
                      | Node of 'b * ('a,'b) FOREST
withtype
          ('a,'b) FOREST = ('a,'b) TREE list
```

After using **withtype** both the **datatype** and the **type** are in scope. Perhaps contrary to expectations, this does *not* make one definition private to the other. Its major purpose is to make definitions more readable; however, the above could have been replaced by the two sequential definitions shown below (this substitution may be more difficult to achieve where the **type** synonym and the **datatype** are mutually recursive):

```
datatype ('a,'b) TREE = Tip of 'a
                      | Node of 'b * ('a,'b) TREE list
type    ('a,'b) FOREST = ('a,'b) TREE list
```

Notice that the type bound by **withtype** is not recursively interpreted but will refer to any prior binding. The following is legal, but dependent upon a former definition of basetype being in scope:

```
datatype NEW = Ncon of basetype
withtype basetype = (basetype * int).
```

B.1.4 *Records*

For program self-documentation purposes the programmer has been encouraged to give names to tuple types (for example type ''a EQUALITY_PAIR = (''a * ''a)). It is also possible to achieve the effect of giving a name to each component of a tuple by means of SML's *record* definition facility, which uses the following template:

> **type** *RECORD_NAME* = {
>   *name1* : *type1*,
>   *name2* : *type2*,
>   ...
>   *nameN* : *typeN*
>   }

The SML system response is to echo the record name and its components, though not necessarily in the same sequence as they are entered. This indicates that SML recognizes the components by their name, rather than by any position in the description.[1]

The following example defines a record type called COMPONENT with three attributes:

```
— type COMPONENT = {
                    key          : int,
                    description  : string,
                    price        : real
                    };
type COMPONENT = {key:int,
                  description:string,
                  price:real}
```

Initialization and use of a value of a COMPONENT is demonstrated below:

```
— val part1 = {key          = 3,
               description = "grommet",
               price        = 102.10
               } :COMPONENT;
val part1 = {description="grommet",
             key=3,price=102.1} : COMPONENT
— part1 = {description="false",
           key=1, price=111.1};
val it = false : bool
```

Additionally, individual attributes may be accessed directly using the built-in prefix operator #. The following shows how to obtain the key attribute from a given COMPONENT instance:

```
— #key part1;
val it = 3 : int
```

The # operator is overloaded to work for all records and so it is necessary to have the definition of a record's type in scope in order to select attributes from it. The above example succeeds because part1 is an instance of a known record type. The following fails because the type of anyrec has not been specified:

```
fun wrongselectprice anyrec = #price anyrec
```

---

1. Actually the formal definition of the language considers an N-tuple to be a *derived form* with its equivalent form an anonymous record of the shape: {1 = value1, 2 = value2, ..., N = valueN}.

Rules for records

1. Unique name rule:

   Attribute names within a record must be unique but their ordering is irrelevant.

2. Pattern matching rule:

   Records can be pattern matched in a similar way to tuple matching, as shown in the definition for the function `cheap`:

   ```
   fun cheap {key, description, price}
       = price < 100.0

   - cheap part1;
   val it = false : bool
   ```

   Records can also be pattern matched in a similar manner to their initialization, for example:

   ```
   fun special_offer {key,
                      description = "grommet",
                      price}
       = price / 2.0

   |   special_offer {key,
                      description,
                      price} = price
   ```

Wild cards for records

A 'wild card' token is also available; this is indicated by a sequence of three fullstops `...` which appear once at the end of the pattern to be matched. If the wild card is used then the record type must always be indicated, to cater for the fact that two record types can have an attribute of the same name. The following is a correct pattern match using a wild card:

```
fun costly ({price, ... } :COMPONENT)
    = price > 100.0
```

However, the following two attempts at abbreviating the record type `COMPONENT` fail: the first because the wild card appears more than once and not at the end of the pattern; the second because the name of the record type has been omitted.

```
fun wrong_costly ({ ..., ..., price} :COMPONENT)
   = price > 100.0

fun wrong_costly {price, ... }
   = price > 100.0
```

B.2   Function notation

The following section describes SML directives for manipulating function formats to allow for infix functions, right associativity, different precedences and conversion of infix functions to prefix functions. This facility is not strictly necessary but may sometimes make programs more readable and also allows 'customized' notation, giving the effect of a different language. It should however be treated with some caution as programs may also become more difficult to debug.

Functions as operators – infix

By means of the keyword **infix**, it is possible to declare dyadic SML functions to be used as operators, that is, for the function name to appear between its operands. The simplest way of achieving this effect is presented in the following example which defines >> to be an infix function[2] that corresponds to logical *implication*. Firstly, the declaration infix >> indicates that an infix operator called >> will be defined. The subsequent definition places the operator name in infix position, which confirms its infix status:

```
infix >>
fun true >> false = false
|    _    >> _     = true

- false >> false;
val it = true : bool
```

Right associative functions – infixr

The default associativity of any infix function is from the left. Hence the expression:

```
false >> false >> false
```

will be parsed as:

```
(false >> false) >> false
```

and so evaluates to false.

2. See Appendix D for the use of symbols in function names.

This default can be changed by the keyword **infixr**. Whatever the prior associativity, the SML system will make **infixr**'s parameter right associative:

```
infixr >>
```

The expression `false >> false >> false` now parses as:

```
false >> (false >> false)
```

and will evaluate to `true`.

Operators as functions – **nonfix**

Finally, all infix functions can be converted to uncurried prefix functions by means of the **nonfix** keyword, which will take effect from the point in the SML program where first used. Alternatively, the keyword **op** can be used for localized effect, as shown in Chapter 4:

```
nonfix >>

- >> (true, false);
val it = false : bool
```

Precedence

The default precedence for user-defined **infix** and **infixr** functions is 0; i.e. any other operator in an expression will be evaluated before they are. Assuming P, Q and R to be arbitrary Boolean expressions, then

```
P >> Q <> R
```

will parse as:

```
P >> (Q <> R)
```

and the instance:

```
false >> true <> true
```

will evaluate to `true`.

However, this evaluation order can be changed by assigning a precedence number (a high number indicates a high precedence) alongside the **infix** or **infixr** keyword. Thus assigning `>>` to be of precedence level 7 will mean that it will be evaluated before any of the built-in logical operators:

```
infix 7 >>
```

Now the above expression will parse as:

```
(P >> Q) <> R
```

and the above instance will evaluate to `false`.

The main guideline with the precedence of operators is to avoid relying upon the built-in order of evaluation and use brackets for safety and for documentation purposes. (See also Appendix D, Table D.2.)

Changing built-in operators

The above directives for fixity and precedence also apply to the built-in operators such as `+`. In fact, a particularly perverse programmer could change the obvious definition of `+` so that it became a right-associative operator for exponentiation with a precedence higher than any other operator. The utmost care should be exercised in changing the meaning of built-in operators.

B.3   fn notation and anonymous functions

This section introduces an alternative notation for function definitions and shows how anonymous functions may be used.

B.3.1   fn notation

When a function definition is entered using **fun** the system responds with an indication that the function has an unprintable value, represented by the keyword **fn**:

```
— fun twice x = 2 * x;
val twice = fn : int —> int
```

The keyword **fn** may also be used as part of an alternative form of function definition, as is now demonstrated:

```
— val twice = fn x => 2 * x;
val twice = fn : int —> int
```

The use of this notation also highlights the difference between curried and non-curried functions, as is shown in the two following function definitions:

```
— val uncurried_plus
    = fn ((x,y) :int * int) => x + y;
val uncurried_plus = fn : int * int —> int

— val curried_plus
    = fn (x :int) => fn (y :int) => x + y;
val curried_plus = fn : int —> int —> int
```

Notice that this notation cannot be used for recursive definitions without additionally using the keyword **rec**, as shown at the end of this appendix.

B.3.2 *Anonymous functions*

In the above examples, using **fn** involves more work for the programmer. However, this syntactic form can be used to generate *anonymous functions* and hence save the bother of inventing new names for expressions that are only used once. In the following example, the function body of twice has been taken as the function argument to map:

```
— map (fn x => 2 * x) [1,2,3];
val it = [2,4,6] : int list
```

This removes any need to define twice at all. In a similar manner, the function length could be presented as:

```
val length = reduce (fn x => fn y => 1 + y) 0
```

In practice, anonymous functions can use alternative patterns, as shown in the following definition of hd, and any other feature that a named function might use – though often at the expense of the clarity gained by a sensible naming policy:

```
exception Hd

val hd = fn (front :: rest) => front
         |  nil            => raise Hd
```

B.3.3 *Recursive value definitions*

The use of **val** with **fn** can only be used for non-recursive function definitions. In order to create recursive functions it is necessary to use either **fun** or its equivalent form, **val rec**.[3] This is demonstrated in the following recursive definition:

3. Actually the SML formal definition (Milner *et al.*, 1990) considers **fun** to be a *derived form* of **val rec**.

```
val rec length
    = fn alist => if alist = nil
                  then    0
                  else    1 + length (tl alist)
```

Although **fun** and **val rec** are equivalent, in practice defining functions using **fun** is always clearer.

Appendix C
Procedural Language
Features of SML

SML provides a number of procedural language features. Just like the file-handling facilities presented in Appendix A, these features are non-functional and may compromise the referential transparency of a program. They should therefore be treated with care.

C.1 Variables

SML allows any value to be declared a ref (meaning 'reference') variable and then allows, as the name implies, this value to change. This is *not* the same as re-binding a name. Reference variables can be used in the same manner as **val** names.

Defining a ref value

The syntax for defining a reference variable is straightforward. The built-in type constructor ref precedes the actual value being defined:

```
- val x = ref 3;
val x = ref 3 : int ref
```

Using a ref value

A reference variable can be altered using the *assignment* operator := as follows:

```
- x := 4;
val it = () : unit
```

Here, the assignment operator changes the value of x but does not make the new value available. This is done by the dereferencing operator !:

```
- !x;
val it = 4 : int
```

Notice that, although `ref` is a polymorphic constructor, once a variable is given an actual type then the variable is a monotype. Hence, given the above definition of x the following is illegal: `x := 3.0`.

C.2 Iteration and sequencing

SML provides a built-in imperative language style **while . . do** loop, together with a means of *sequencing* expressions. Any group of expressions enclosed in round brackets and separated by semicolons is evaluated; the result of the entire sequence is the result of the last expression – the intermediate results are discarded. This discarding of results only makes sense if non-functional expressions occur in the sequence and use side-effects, for example to write to a file.

The following is the famous factorial function written in imperative SML code:

```
fun factorial (n :int)
    = let
          val tot = ref 1          (* default total *)
          val i = ref n            (* loop variable *)
      in
          while !i > 1 do          (* factorial < 2 is 1 *)
          (                        (* begin sequence *)
              tot := !tot * !i;    (* continue sequence *)
              i := !i - 1
          );                       (* end sequence *)
          !tot :int                (* dereference result *)
      end
```

Using sequencing – file copy

The following example shows the use of *sequencing* without reference variables, in a reworking of the `compresscopy` function (discussed in Appendix A). Here, the first action is to discard a white-space character or write any other character to the output file and the next action is to re-apply `xcopy` – without the need for the 'dummy' parameter of type `unit` used in Appendix A:

```
fun compresscopy (infile :string) (outfile :string)
    = let
          fun xcopy (ifp :instream) (ofp :outstream)
              = if end_of_stream ifp
                then ()
                else
                    if (lookahead ifp) = " "
                        orelse
                        (lookahead ifp) = "\t"
```

```
then
    (
    input (ifp,1);
    xcopy ifp ofp
    )
else
    (
    output (ofp, input (ifp,1));
    xcopy ifp ofp
    )
in
    xcopy (open_in infile) (open_out outfile) :unit
end
```

Using side-effects — the print function

The print function[1] writes its parameter to the screen, as a side effect, before the SML system prompt, and then returns the value (). Hence print may appear on its own or as the right-hand side of an expression or as part of an SML sequence, as is demonstrated in the following SML session:

```
- print "hallo world\n";
hallo world
val it = () : unit

- val result = print "goodbye world\n";
goodbye world
val result = () : unit

- result;
val it = () : unit

- val message = (print "once\n"; "again");
once
val message = "again" : string
```

The final bracketed example is another instance of SML sequencing to allow input or output to be bypassed. This feature could enable a function to be traced by careful placing of print sequences within a recursive function application. However, it must be stressed that a well-specified and organized program should never need debugging in this manner. The use of the type system, sensible control of environments and closed structures should normally render this use redundant.

1. Note that print is not part of the initial SML environment, as defined in Milner et al., 990). It is, however, available in many implementations.

C.3 *Handling exceptions*

The SML **exception** mechanism allows for the programmer to do more than just
raise an **exception** and halt further evaluation. It is also possible to 'trap' particular
error conditions or special cases and give more meaningful error messages or indeed
to continue evaluation with special values; the extended facility is best demonstrated
by a simple example.

If the function xsquarestring is evoked then the exception ZERO or NEG would
be raised when n is 0 or less than 0 respectively:

```
exception ZERO
exception NEG of int

fun xsquarestring (n :int)
    = if n = 0
        then raise ZERO
        else if n < 0
                then raise NEG n
                else (n * n) :int
```

However, if the following function squarestring is applied to 0 then the message
"cannot process zero values" is output and if applied to a negative integer
the message "cannot process negative" is output followed by the value of that
negative integer:

```
fun squarestring (x :int)
    = makestring (xsquarestring x) :string
    handle ZERO        => "cannot process zero values"
    |      NEG param => "cannot process negative "
                          ^ (makestring param)
```

The following points are worth highlighting:

1. If one of the patterns in a **handle** expression has a parameter then its type must
    be indicated when the corresponding **exception** is declared.

2. The **handle** expression can take **exception**s with values of differing types and/or
    with no associated value.

3. The wild card _ can appear as a universal exception pattern. In addition, any
    name which is not an exception name will be treated as a wild card.

4. The body of each alternative pattern in a **handle** expression can be any
    expression but must be of the same type as the target type of the function itself.

5. An **exception** can also be raised again from its handler.

Appendix D
The Initial SML
Environment

This appendix provides lists of reserved and predefined names and symbols that should be available at the start of all SML sessions. It is mainly an adapted selection from Appendix C and D of *The Definition of Standard ML* (Milner *et al.*, 1990) and the *Standard ML of New Jersey Online Reference Manual* (Appel and MacQueen). It should be noted that not all SML systems exactly correspond and many will provide a richer initial set-up.

D.1   *Reserved names*

Reserved names and symbols *cannot* be re-bound and it is good practice to *avoid* re-binding any name or symbol that is predefined.

D.1.1   *Core and module language reserved names and symbols*

abstype and andalso as case do datatype else end exception fn fun handle if in infix infixr let local nonfix of op open orelse raise rec then type val with withtype while[1]

() [] {} , : ; ... _ | = => -> #

eqtype functor include sharing sig signature struct structure

Comments

Comments are started by the two character sequence **(*** and terminated by the two character sequence ***)**. They may be nested.

---

1. Additionally Standard ML of New Jersey reserves the names: **abstraction** and **overload**.

D.1.2 *Legal identifiers*

An identifier is either:

1. *Alphanumeric*: including any sequence of letters (A–Z, a–z), digits (0–9), underscores (_) or single quotes (') but *starting with a letter or a single quote*.

2. *Symbolic*: any uninterrupted sequence of the symbols

    ! % & $ # + — / : < = > ? @ \ ~ ' ^ | *

Reserved words, identifiers with spaces and a mixture of symbols and alphanumeric characters are not legal identifiers. For example, the three character sequence +++ is a legal identifier, whilst the three character sequences a+b, _++ and + + are not.

Note that polytypes can be indicated by preceding a legal identifier with a single quote, for example 'mypolytype. Single quotes cannot be used to start **val** names or functions.

Special attention should also be paid to the full stop character ., which cannot be used as part of a name, since it is used to distinguish structure components.

D.2 *Predefined names*

This section lists the minimum set of functions, operators, types, constructors, exception names and input–output features that should be available in an SML system. They are not reserved – care must be taken not to redefine them. Table D.1 lists the predefined functions. Table D.2 lists all the predefined infix operators; when used in prefix form with **op** they are treated as uncurried, dyadic functions.

D.2.1 *Predefined exceptions, types and constructors*

Predefined exceptions

```
Abs Diff Div Mod Neg Prod Quot Sum
Exp Floor Ln Sqrt Ord Chr
Interrupt Io Bind Match
```

Match and Bind are raised upon pattern matching failure and Interrupt is raised by external intervention (for example, by typing *<control>-C* on a UNIX system).

Predefined types

```
unit bool int real string list ref exn
```

Predefined constructors

```
true false nil :: ref
```

Notice that the name 'ref' appears as a predefined function, as a constructor and as a type name. This is also true of some other names, but their meaning is always clear from the context in which they are used.

The name i t

The name i t is bound to the result of the last evaluated expression. It should *never* be explicitly rebound by the programmer.

Table D.1. Predefined functions

Name	Type
abs	*num* –> *num*
~	*num* –> *num*
floor	real –> int
real	int –> real
sqrt	real –> real
sin	real –> real
cos	real –> real
arctan	real –> real
exp	real –> real
ln	real –> real
not	bool –> bool
size	string –> int
ord	string –> int
chr	int –> string
explode	string –> string list
implode	string list –> string
map	('a –> 'b) –> 'a list –> 'b list
rev	'a list –> 'a list
ref	'_a –> '_a ref
!	'a ref –> 'a

Note: *num* indicates that the operator will take either i n t, or r e a l (but not a mixture).

Table D.2. Predefined operators

Name	Type	Precedence	Associativity	Commutative	Associative
/	real * real -> real	7	left	no	no
div	int * int -> int	7	left	no	no
mod	int * int -> int	7	left	no	no
*	num * num -> num	7	left	yes	yes
+	num * num -> num	6	left	yes	yes
-	num * num -> num	6	left	no	no
^	string * string -> string	6	left	no	yes
::	'a * 'a list -> 'a list	5	right	no	no
@	'a list * 'a list -> 'a list	5	left	no	yes
=	''a * ''a -> bool	4	left	yes	no
<>	''a * ''a -> bool	4	left	yes	no
<	NorS * NorS -> bool	4	left	no	no
>	NorS * NorS -> bool	4	left	no	no
<=	NorS * NorS -> bool	4	left	no	no
>=	NorS * NorS -> bool	4	left	no	no
:=	'a ref * 'a -> unit	3	right	no	no
o	('b -> 'c) * ('a -> 'b) -> 'a -> 'c	3	left	no	no

Note: The token *NorS* indicates integer, real number or string (but not a mixture). This is specific to the New Jersey implementation — relational operations on strings are not part of the standard language definition.

D.2.2 *Predefined input and output functions*

Table D.3 gives predefined input and output functions; the two types instream and outstream denote input and output streams respectively. In addition, the following standard input–output channels are predefined: std_in (of type instream) and std_out (of type outstream).

Table D.3. Predefined input and output functions

Name	Type
open_in	string -> instream
open_out	string -> outstream
close_in	instream -> unit
close_out	outstream -> unit
input	instream * int -> string
output	outstream * string -> unit
lookahead	instream -> string
end_of_stream	instream -> bool

Appendix E
SML Interfaces

This appendix outlines a number of features that enhance an SML system in the context of a wider host programming environment. Details and availability of these and other features may vary from implementation to implementation and it is best to check the user manual before attempting to employ them.

E.1   Host system interface

Facilities include:

1. *Saving the environment.* It may be possible to save the definitions generated by the current SML session and then re-employ this environment in a subsequent SML session, as if all the definitions had been entered interactively. Similarly, it may be possible to separately compile closed **functor** and **signature** code and incorporate it into an SML session. This is useful for large-scale program development since it encourages referential transparency in the **functor** design. There may also be the added bonus that the development is quicker since compilation only takes place once rather than every time a file is used.

2. *Editor interface.* Often an editor can be invoked and new code can be edited and used during an SML session. This can be achieved either by using a system command or by running SML within a programming support environment such as the *emacs* editor or the *Poplog* environment. This is useful for system prototyping but production programs should be constructed and loaded in an ordered manner.

3. *Operating system commands.* Commands offered by the host operating system may be executed by invoking an appropriate system interfacing function. This will allow anything from printing the time of day to running other system or user programs.

E.2   The Edinburgh SML library

In addition to that code which is provided by each implementation (such as the provision of `makestring` or `hd` and `tl`), but is not part of the initial environment as defined in Milner *et al.*, (1990), there is an extensive, portable 'standard library' of useful **structure**s. This is directly available from Edinburgh University (Berry, 1991) and provides new types, such as: Vectors, Pairs, List Pairs, Stream Pairs and Bytes; additional operations on Bools, Ints, Reals, Strings and Lists; simple combinator functions; improved input and output operations, together with functions that interact with the host file system and the user. It also supports a UNIX-style *make* facility, which allows the programmer some flexibility in configuration control.

Appendix F
Delaying Evaluation

This appendix shows how SML can delay the evaluation of expressions to achieve something similar to the *lazy evaluation* mechanism[1] found in some functional programming languages.

F.1 *Simulating conditional expressions*

With the exception of **if .. then .. else** and the Boolean special forms, **andalso** and **orelse**, SML is *eager* in its evaluation of its function parameter(s); they are evaluated before the function itself is invoked. The consequences are that some 'natural' definitions of functions will produce unnatural results. For example the following 'obvious' attempt to define **if .. then .. else** as a prefix function will fail under certain circumstances, as SML will evaluate all three of the parameters to cond before executing its function body:

```
— fun cond (test :bool) (thence :'a) (otherwise :'a)
    = if test
      then thence
      else otherwise :'a

val x = 1
val y = 0;
...
— cond (y <> 0) (x div y) 0;
uncaught exception Div
```

In this instance (y <> x), (x div y) and 0 are all evaluated before cond has a chance to impose its selection control structure; unfortunately (x div y) results in a system error.

To bypass this 'problem', whilst the first parameter to cond must always be evaluated (and so needs no modification), the second and third parameters must

---

1. The term 'lazy evaluation' normally refers to a combination of call-by-name evaluation of function parameters, and sharing the results of evaluating parameters, so that parameters are evaluated *at most once.*

somehow have their evaluation suspended. One way to achieve this is to make use of higher order functions. The `thence` and `otherwise` parameters are now treated as anonymous functions themselves (see Appendix B), each of which take `unit` as their parameter. On applying `cond` the functions are not actually executed until the body of `cond` is executed. This gives rise to the somewhat obscure definition:

```
— fun cond (test :bool) (thence :unit —> 'a)
                        (otherwise :unit —> 'a)
            = if test
              then thence ()
              else otherwise ();

val cond = fn : bool —> (unit —> 'a) —> (unit —> 'a) —> 'a
```

The example function application of `cond` will now give the expected results if rewritten as:

```
cond (y <> 0) (fn () => x div y) (fn() => 0)
```

Though this style of programming is not clear, nor is it generally desirable in SML, there are other functional programming languages which are not eager in their evaluation approach. Such languages include Miranda (see Holyer, 1991) and Haskell (see Fasel, 1992); these languages do not require the unwieldy syntax of the above example to achieve the same semantics.

F.2 Delayed data structures

The principle of delaying evaluation can be combined with that of functional **datatype**s to create recursive functional data structures (see Reade, 1989). In the following example, `STREAM` is either empty or consists of a function which will generate a tuple consisting of an individual element together with another instance of that **datatype**:

```
datatype 'a STREAM = Empty
                   | Stream of unit —> ('a * 'a STREAM)
```

Using this definition it is easy to mimic the behaviour of the standard list functions. For example, the built-in constructor `cons` could be written as:

```
fun cons (item :'a) (astream :'a STREAM)
    = let
          fun f () = (item, astream)
      in
        Stream f
      end
```

It is clearly not very sensible to use this new type as a working definition for the list type; however, it can be usefully employed to create a possibly infinite sequence, or *stream* of related elements. For example, a generator for a sequence of dots could be defined as:

```
- val dotlist
    = let
        fun dots () = (".", Stream dots)
      in
        Stream dots
      end;
val dotlist = Stream fn : string STREAM
```

Similarly, a generator for a sequence of natural numbers could be defined as:

```
val nats
    = let
        fun from n
            = let
                fun f () = (n, from (n + 1))
              in
                Stream f
              end
      in
        from 1
      end
```

To extract elements of the sequence it is necessary to generate the actual sequence of values. The following function `generate` will create a tuple consisting of a list of the first n items in the sequence, followed by the remainder of the sequence. Unlike storing values in a list, which is evaluated eagerly and therefore requires a large amount of memory to be assigned in one lump, the above sequence is evaluated in a piecemeal, or 'lazy', fashion by the function embedded in the **datatype**. This means that there is a greater opportunity for the system to re-use memory and that it is possible for the program to manipulate possibly infinite sequences of values:

```
exception Generate
fun generate (0 :int) (astream :'a STREAM)
    = (nil :'a list, astream :'a STREAM)
  | generate n Empty = raise Generate
  | generate n (Stream f)
    = let
        val (front, astream) = f()
        val (rest, streamrest) = generate (n - 1) astream
      in
        (front :: rest, streamrest)
      end
```

To extract a list of actual values is straightforward:

```
fun takeStream (n :int) (astream :'a STREAM)
    = fst (generate n astream) :'a list

fun printdots (n :int)
    = implode (takeStream n dotlist) :string

— printdots 3;
val it = "..." : string
```

Similarly, the first n actual values can be ignored – to give a new sequence, starting at the next value:

```
fun dropStream (n :int) (astream :'a STREAM)
    = snd (generate n astream) :'a STREAM

— dropStream 10 nats
val it = Stream fn : int STREAM

— takeStream 5 (dropStream 500 nats)
val it = [501,502,503,504,505] : int list
```

Solutions to Exercises

Solutions for Chapter 2

Exercise 2.1 (page 34)

Provide a function to check if a character is alphanumeric, that is, lower case, upper case or numeric.

One solution is to follow the same approach as in the function `isupper` for each of the three possibilities and link them with the special operator `orelse`:

```
fun isalpha c
    = (c >= "A" andalso c <= "Z")
      orelse
      (c >= "a" andalso c <= "z")
      orelse
      (c >= "0" andalso c <= "9")
```

An alternative approach is to define the functions `isupper`, `islower` and `isdigit` and combine them:

```
fun isalpha c
    = (isupper c) orelse (islower c) orelse (isdigit c)
```

This approach shows the advantage of re-using existing simple functions to build more complex functions.

Exercise 2.2 (page 41)

What happens in the following application and why?

```
fst (3, (4 div 0))
```

A divide by zero error is raised by the system. This is because the arguments to `fst` are evaluated before it is applied.

Exercise 2.3 (page 41)

Define a function `dup` which takes a single element of any type and returns a tuple with the element duplicated.

The answer is just a direct translation of the specification into SML:

```
fun dup (x : 'a) = (x, x)
```

Exercise 2.4 (page 42)
Evaluate the application (all_equal (1, 1, 1.0)).

A type mismatch arises because the restricted polymorphic operator = only works for the same type of operands; it is not defined to work for the type (int * real).

Exercise 2.5 (page 44)
Modify both versions of the function SolomonGrundy so that Thursday and Friday may be treated with special significance.

The pattern matching version is easily modified; all that is needed is to insert the extra cases somewhere before the default pattern:

```
fun SolomonGrundy "Monday"   = "Born"
  | SolomonGrundy "Thursday" = "Ill"
  | SolomonGrundy "Friday"   = "Worse"
  | SolomonGrundy "Sunday"   = "Buried"
  | SolomonGrundy anyday      = "Did something else"
```

By contrast, the conditional version is rather messy:

```
fun SolomonGrundy day
    = if day = "Monday"
      then "Born"
      else if day = "Thursday"
              then "Ill"
              else if day = "Friday"
                      then "Worse"
                      else if day = "Sunday"
                              then "Buried"
                              else "Did something else"
```

Exercise 2.6 (page 50)
Define a function intmax which takes an integer pair and returns the greater of its two components.

This requires the type of at least one of x or y to be indicated:

```
fun intmax ((x, y) :int * int)
    if x > y
    then x
    else y :int
```

For clarity, the result type is also given.

Exercise 2.7 (page 54)
Define a recursive function to add up all the integers from 1 to a given upper limit.

A recursive solution to this problem is:

```
fun addints (1 :int) = 1 :int
  | addints n         = n + addints (n - 1)
```

The terminating condition is the first pattern (the integer 1) and the parameter of recursion is n, which converges towards 1 by repeated subtraction. Note that addints fails if it is applied to a number less than 1. See also Section 2.9.

Exercise 2.8 (page 55)
Write printdots in an accumulative recursive style. This will require more than one function – remember that functions must be defined before they can be applied.

The accumulator will hold the growing sequence of dots; since the number n cannot be used for this purpose another parameter is needed. This involves the definition of an auxiliary function to incorporate the accumulator:

```
fun xprintdots ((0, dotstring) :int * string)
      = dotstring :string
  | xprintdots (n, dotstring)
      = xprintdots (n - 1, dotstring ^ ".")

fun printdots (n :int) = xprintdots (n, "") :string
```

Notice that the function printdots initializes the accumulator dotstring with an empty string.

Exercise 2.9 (page 55)
Write the function plus in a stack recursive style.

The parameter of recursion is y and the terminating condition is when y is 0. In this version, x no longer serves as an accumulator, but as the second operand to the final addition:

```
fun plus ((x, 0) :int * int) = x :int
  | plus (x, y)              = 1 + plus (x, y - 1)
```

Exercise 2.10 (page 55)
Write the function integer_divide without using the SML divide operators.

The division is straightforward; what requires some thought is the handling of positive and negative values of the operands. Not every problem has an elegant pattern matching solution!

```
exception Divide
fun posdiv ((n, m) :int * int)
      = if n < m
        then 0
        else 1 + posdiv (n - m, m) :int
```

```
fun integer_divide ((n, 0) :int * int)
    = raise Divide
  | integer_divide (n, m)
    = if (n < 0) andalso (m < 0)
      then posdiv (~n, ~m)
      else if (m < 0)
            then ~(posdiv (n, ~m))
            else if (n < 0)
                  then ~(posdiv (~n, m))
                  else posdiv (n, m) :int
```

Notice that the function applications ~(posdiv (n, ~m)) and ~(posdiv (~n, m)) must be bracketed to evaluate to an integer result for the unary negation function ~. If the brackets were omitted then SML would attempt to apply ~ to the function posdiv rather than to its result.

Solutions for Chapter 3

Exercise 3.1 (page 68)
Give the two possible correct versions of wrong_y.

Either the first operand should be an integer or the second operand should be a list of integer lists:

```
val correct_y1 = 1 :: [2,3]
val correct_y2 = [1] :: [[2,3]]
```

Exercise 3.2 (page 69)
Which of the following are legal list constructions?

```
val list1 = 1 :: []
val list2 = 1 :: [] :: []
val list3 = 1 :: [1]
val list4 = [] :: [1]
val list5 = [1] :: [1] :: []
```

The correct constructions are list1, list3 and list5.

The construction list2 fails because :: is right-associative. Thus, list2 is defined to be (1 :: ([] :: [])), which is the same as (1 :: [[]]), which in turn is a type error because it attempts to join an integer to a list of lists. The construction list4 fails because it attempts to add a list (in this case the empty list) to a list of integers, which causes a type error.

Exercise 3.3 (page 71)
SML adopts the view that it is meaningless to attempt to extract something from nothing: generating an error seems a reasonable treatment for such an attempt. What would be the consequences if hd and tl were to evaluate to nil when applied to an empty list?

The consequence would be that the following equality would no longer hold for all values of anylist:

```
anylist = hd anylist :: tl anylist
```

The equality would not hold when anylist was nil, since the right-hand side would evaluate to [nil]. Furthermore, such definitions for hd and tl would be totally incompatible with the SML type system: for example, any function which applied hd to a list of integers could not be sure whether the value returned was going to be an integer or a list!

Exercise 3.4 (page 73)
Is ^ a constructor?

It is not a constructor for the same reason that @ is not a constructor. For example, in the expression:

```
"SML" = s2 ^ s3
```

the identifiers s2 and s3 each have at least four possible values.

Exercise 3.5 (page 73)
At first sight it would also appear that makestring can be bypassed by defining a function that quotes its numeric parameter:

```
fun NtoS (n :int) = "n" :string
```

Explain what the above function *actually* does.

All it does is produce the string "n". The quotation marks are *not* constructors, unlike the square brackets which denote the list aggregate format.

Exercise 3.6 (page 74)
Explain why (implode (explode Astring)) always evaluates to Astring but (explode (implode Alist)) is not always the equivalent of Alist.

Because implode is a many-to-one function, whereas explode is one-to-one. For example, implode ["S", "M", "L"] and implode ["SM", " L"] both give the same answer ("SML"): by contrast, explode "SML" will produce the result ["S", "M", "L"] but can never produce the result ["SM", "L"]. Hence:

```
implode (explode "SML")
== implode ["S", "M", "L"]
== "SML"

explode (implode ["SM", "L"])
== explode "SML"
== ["S", "M", "L"]
```

Exercise 3.7 (page 76)
Write a stack recursive function to add all numbers less than 3 which appear in a list of integers.

```
type ILIST = int list

fun addlessthanthree (nil :ILIST)
    = 0 :int
|   addlessthanthree (front :: rest)
    = (if (front < 3)
        then front
        else 0) + (addlessthanthree rest)
```

Exercise 3.8 (page 77)
The following function listmax is accumulative recursive. Rather than using an explicit accumulator it uses the front of the list to hold the current maximum value.

```
type ILIST = int list

exception Listmax

fun listmax nil = raise Listmax

|   listmax ((front :: nil) :ILIST)
    = front :int

|   listmax (front :: next :: rest)
    = listmax ( if front > next
                    then (front :: rest)
                    else (next :: rest))
```

Rewrite listmax so that it uses an auxiliary function and an explicit accumulator to store the current largest item in the list.

The explicit accumulator is initialized with the front of a non-empty list; the rest of the code is remarkably similar:

```
type ILIST = int list

exception Listmax

fun xlistmax ((nil, maxvalue) :ILIST * int)
    = maxvalue :int

|   xlistmax (front :: rest, maxvalue)
    = xlistmax (rest, if front > maxvalue
                        then front
                        else maxvalue)
fun listmax nil = raise Listmax
|   listmax ((front :: rest) :ILIST)
    = xlistmax (rest, front) :int
```

Exercise 3.9 (page 79)
What happens if a negative value of n is supplied to the first version of d r o p?

Eventually (f r o n t : : r e s t) will converge to n i l and an **exception** will be raised.

Exercise 3.10 (page 79)
Write the function s h o r t e r t h a n used by the final version of d r o p.

The approach taken is similar to that in defining the function s t a r t s w i t h in Section 3.7.2. Both the number and the list converge towards terminating conditions, respectively by the integer one and by one element at a time. Hence, zero indicates that there may still be items in the list, in which case the list cannot be shorter than the specified number. Conversely, n i l indicates that the list is shorter than the number of items to be discarded.

```
fun  shorterthan  ((0,  _)  :int  *  'a  list)
        =  false  :bool
  |    shorterthan  (_,  nil)  =  true
  |    shorterthan  (n,  front  ::  rest)
        =  shorterthan  (n  —  1,  rest)
```

Exercise 3.11 (page 79)
Write the function c o n c a t which is the equivalent of the built-in ˆ operator.

One method is to combine the two input strings into a string list and convert that list into a single string. The first step can be done by employing the list aggregate notation, the second step is achieved using i m p l o d e:

```
fun  concat  ((s1,  s2)  :string  *  string)
        =  implode  [s1,  s2]  :string
```

Exercise 3.12 (page 86)
Use structural induction to design the function t a k e, which works similarly to d r o p but takes the first n items in a list and discards the rest.

The type of the function is:

```
int  *  'a  list  —>  'a  list
```

The general case is:

```
take  (n,  front  ::  rest)  =  ???
```

There are two parameters of recursion; the inductive hypothesis must therefore assume that t a k e (n — 1, r e s t) evaluates to an appropriate list. The inductive step is to construct a list of the f r o n t value (which must be retained) with that list:

```
take  (n,  front  ::  rest)
=  front  ::  take  (n  —  1,  rest)
```

The terminating cases are:

1. Taking no elements, this must just give an empty list:

```
take (0, _) = nil
```

2. Attempting to take some items from an empty list, which is an error:

```
take (_, nil) = raise Take
```

Notice that asking for zero items from an empty list is covered by `take (0, _)` and therefore this pattern must appear first.

The final code is:

```
exception Take

fun take ((0, _) :int * 'a list)
      = nil :'a list

|    take (_, nil) = raise Take

|    take (n, front :: rest)
      = front :: take (n - 1, rest)
```

This approach deals with negative numbers in the same manner as the first definition of `drop`.

Exercise 3.13 (page 87)

Write a function `fromto` which takes a list and two integers and which outputs all the elements in the list starting from the position indicated by the first integer up to the position indicated by the second integer. For example:

```
- fromto (3, 5, ["a","b","c","d","e","f"]);
val it = ["c","d","e"]
```

To meet this specification it is necessary to assume that it is possible to extract the first n elements from a list and that it is also possible to drop the first m elements from a list. It is feasible to attempt to write this function from first principles but a lot easier to re-use existing code:

```
fun fromto ((m, n, alist) :int * int * 'a list)
      = drop (m - 1, take (n,alist)) :'a list
```

Exercise 3.14 (page 93)

Modify the `skipcomments` program to cater for nested comments.

```
type SLIST = string list

fun incomments (("*" :: ")" :: rest) :SLIST)
      = rest :SLIST
```

```
|    incomments ("(" :: "*" :: rest)
     = incomments (incomments rest)

|    incomments (front :: rest)
     = incomments rest

fun skipcomments (nil :SLIST)
     = nil :SLIST

|    skipcomments ("(" :: "*" :: rest)
     = skipcomments (incomments rest)

|    skipcomments (front :: rest)
     = front :: skipcomments rest
```

Notice the adjustment is minor; the nesting of comments is a recursive requirement and its treatment is recursively achieved by matching the start of a nested comment within incomments, which itself ignores comments.

An alternative, though not recommended, solution would have been to use mutual recursion within skipcomments, without changing the original definition of incomments:

```
fun notrecommended_skipcomments (nil :SLIST)
     = nil :SLIST

|    notrecommended_skipcomments ("(" :: "*" :: rest)
     = incomments (notrecommended_skipcomments rest)

|    notrecommended_skipcomments (front :: rest)
     = front :: notrecommended_skipcomments rest
```

As with mutually defined functions, it is quite difficult to reason how and why this function succeeds.

Exercise 3.15 (page 97)
It would appear that sublist now no longer needs its first function pattern because this is checked as the first pattern in startswith. Explain why this is incorrect, and also whether the second pattern of sublist can safely be removed.

It is not safe to remove the first pattern because matching the empty regular expression with an empty line to be searched would now be met by the second pattern and incorrectly evaluate to false. The second pattern cannot be removed because it serves as the terminating condition for recursion along the line to be searched.

Exercise 3.16 (page 97)
An incorrect attempt to optimize the startswith program would combine startswith and sublist in one function:

```
type SLIST = string list
fun sublist ((nil, _) :SLIST * SLIST) = true :bool
  |   sublist (_, nil) = false
  |   sublist ((regfront :: regrest), (lfront :: lrest))
      = ( (regfront = lfront)
            andalso
            sublist (regrest, lrest)
        )
        orelse
        sublist ((regfront :: regrest), lrest)
```

This follows the general inductive case that the result is true if the front two items of the lists are equal and the result of a sublist search of the rest of the two lists is also true. Alternatively the entire regular expression matches the rest of the search line.
Show why this approach is wrong.

The above does not exclude applications such as:

```
sublist (explode "abc", explode "ab_this_will_be_ignored_c")
```

which returns the result **true**.

Exercise 3.17 (page 104)
Explain the presence of the final pattern in the function startswith, even though it should never be encountered.

The type **REGTYPE** could have any number of possible strings, rather than just the strings "ONCE" and "ZERO_MORE"; the final pattern is intended to suppress the system warning message. A safer solution is presented in Section 6.2.

Exercise 3.18 (page 104)
What would happen if the second and third pattern in startswith were swapped?

The function would still produce the same results; the two patterns are mutually exclusive and it does not matter which appears first.

Exercise 3.19 (page 104)
Alter the sublist function so that "A∗" matches the empty string.

The naive solution is to introduce an extra pattern as the new first pattern:

```
fun sublist ([("ZERO_MORE", _)], nil) = true
...
```

However, this does not cater for regular expressions of the form "A∗B∗". An easy solution is to ensure that startswith is always applied at least once; this solution is presented in Chapter 7.

Solutions for Chapter 4

Exercise 4.1 (page 109)
Write the function make_uncurried which will allow a curried, dyadic function to accept a tuple as its argument.

This is the mirror of make_curried:

```
fun make_uncurried ff (x,y) = ff x y
```

Its type is:

```
('a -> 'b -> 'c) -> 'a * 'b -> 'c
```

Exercise 4.2 (page 114)
Give the types of the following compositions:

```
tl o (op @)
abs o fst
chr o chr
```

The first composition has the type:

```
'a list * 'a list -> 'a list
```

which shows that it is legitimate to compose functions which have tupled sources. However, the second expression is invalid because abs is overloaded and SML cannot resolve the overloading (unless fst is explicitly defined to work on either integers or real numbers). The final composition is invalid because the target type of chr is different from its source type.

Exercise 4.3 (page 116)
Explain why repeat is non-robust and provide a robust version.

The function should check that n is not a negative integer; the best way to achieve this is to separate the validation from the processing:

```
exception Repeat

fun repeat (n :int) (ff :'a -> 'a) (result :'a)
    = if n < 0
        then raise Repeat
        else xrepeat n ff result :'a
```

where the auxiliary function xrepeat is the same as the original version of repeat. Chapter 5 shows how the auxiliary function can be tightly coupled to the new version of repeat.

Exercise 4.4 (page 116)
Define a function to achieve a result similar to an imperative programming language 'while' loop. Do not name the function 'while' because this is a reserved word (as shown in Appendix C).

The function has the same shape as `repeat`.

```
fun whiletrue (pred :'a ->bool) (ff :'a -> 'a) (state: 'a)
    = if pred state
      then whiletrue pred ff (ff state)
      else state :'a
```

Another noteworthy point is that there is no guarantee that the condition (`pred state`) will ever be satisfied. This is a general problem of computing, known as the *halting problem* (see Rayward-Smith, 1986). Stated briefly, it is impossible to write a program that will infallibly determine whether an arbitrary function (given some arbitrary input) will terminate or loop forever. One consequence is that there is no point in attempting excessive and unnecessary validation of such general-purpose iterative structures as `whiletrue`.

Exercise 4.5 (page 119)
In the definition of `map_two` source lists of unequal length have been treated as an error. It is an equally valid design decision to truncate the longer list; amend the definition to meet this revised specification.

This is a trivial task; the last error-handling pattern can be converted to have an action that returns the empty list. This pattern also caters for the case of both lists being empty:

```
fun map_two (ff :'a ->'b -> 'c)
            ((front1 :: rest1) :'a list)
            ((front2 :: rest2) :'b list)
    = (ff front1 front2)
      :: map_two ff rest1 rest2 :'c list

|   map_two _ _ _ = nil
```

Exercise 4.6 (page 120)
Explain why the following definitions are equivalent:

```
fun f1 x alist = map (plus x) alist
fun f2 x = map (plus x)
val f3 = (map o plus)
```

The definition of `f2` is that of a partially applied function; SML can infer that it requires an extra list parameter from the type of `map`. The definition of `f3` makes use of the following equivalence:

```
(f o g) x = f (g x)
```

In this case `f` is `map` and `g` is `plus` and the `x` can be discarded for the same reason as in the definition of `f2`.

To a certain extent it is a matter of taste which function should be used; `f1` has the advantage that *all* of its arguments are visible at the function definition, whilst conversely `f3` has the advantage of brevity and perhaps the fact that the programmer can concentrate on what the function does rather than what it does it to. There are no absolute guidelines here but it is important to be able to read all three kinds of definitions. Finally, it should be noted that the type of each function is the same, that is:

```
int -> int list -> int list
```

Exercise 4.7 (page 126)
Some functions cannot be generalized over lists as they have no obvious default value for the empty list; for example it does not make sense to take the maximum value of an empty list. Write the function reduce1 to cater for functions that require at least one list item.

From the specification it is clear that an empty list must be considered an error, otherwise the first item in the list can be used as the default value to reduce. This is a good example of re-using code:

```
exception Reduce1

fun reduce1 ff nil = raise Reduce1
|   reduce1 (ff :'a -> 'a -> 'a)
            ((front :: rest) :'a list)
      = reduce ff front rest :'a
```

Exercise 4.8 (page 126)
Write two curried versions of member (as specified in Section 3.6.1), using reduce and accumulate respectively and discuss their types and differences.

The reduce version is straightforward and uses the prefix, curried functions defined in Section 4.1.3:

```
fun reduce_member (anylist :'' a list) (item :''a)
      = reduce (either o (equal item))
               false
               anylist :bool
```

A hand evaluation of (reduce_member [1,2,3] 1) shows:

```
reduce_member [1,2,3] 1
== reduce (either o (equal 1)) false [1,2,3]
== ((either o (equal 1)) 1)
      (reduce (either o (equal 1)) false [2,3])
== (either (equal 1 1))
      (reduce (either o (equal 1)) false [2,3])
== either true (reduce (either o (equal 1)) false [2,3])
== true orelse (reduce (either o (equal 1)) false [2,3])
== true
```

The accumulate version is less straightforward; this is not an example where accumulate can be safely substituted for reduce. An attempt to define member as:

```
fun accumulate_member anylist item
    = accumulate (either o equal item) false anylist
```

will only work if **item** and the elements of **anylist** are of type **bool**. This is easily verified by checking the type of the above function:

```
val accumulate_member = fn : bool list -> bool -> bool
```

For example, a hand evaluation of **accumulate_member** to a list **[a,b,c]** (where the list elements are of arbitrary type) shows:

```
accumulate_member [a,b,c] item
== accumulate (either o equal item) false [a,b,c]
== accumulate (either o equal item)
             ((either o equal item) false a) [b,c]
== accumulate (either o equal item)
             (either (equal item false) a) [b,c]
```

= = ? This must either be an error or item must be of type bool, since equal expects both its arguments to be of the same type

In order to make the function more general, the default value **false** must become the second of the parameters to the functional argument. This is easily achieved using the **C** combinator :

```
fun accumulate_member (anylist :''a list) (item :''a)
    = accumulate (C (either o (equal item)))
                 false
                 anylist :bool
```

A hand evaluation of **(accumulate_member [1,2,3] 1)** now shows:

```
accumulate_member [1,2,3] item
== accumulate (C (either o (equal 1))) false [1,2,3]
== accumulate (C (either o (equal 1)))
             (C (either o (equal 1)) false 1) [2,3]
== accumulate (C (either o (equal 1)))
             ((either o (equal 1)) 1 false) [2,3]
== accumulate (C (either o (equal 1)))
             (either (equal 1 1) false) [2,3]
== accumulate (C (either o (equal 1)))
             (true orelse false) [2,3]
== accumulate (C (either o (equal 1))) true [2,3]
== ...
```

Exercise 4.9 (page 128)
Define the function **dropwhile** which takes a list and a predicate as arguments and returns the list without the initial sublist of members which satisfy the predicate.

This has a similar form to **takewhile**:

```
fun dropwhile (pred :'a -> bool) (nil :'a list)
    = nil :'a list
```

```
|   dropwhile pred (front :: rest)
    = if pred front
        then dropwhile pred rest
        else (front :: rest)
```

Exercise 4.10 (page 128)

The set data structure may be considered as an unordered list of unique items. Assuming the existence of the function member (as defined in Section 3.6.1) then the following function will yield a list of all the items common to two sets:

```
fun intersection (aset ''a list) (bset :''a list)
    = filter ((make_curried member) aset) bset :''a list
```

Write a function union to create a set of all the items in two sets.

The union of two sets can be considered as all the members of the first set that are *not* in the second set, together with that second set. The answer makes use of the design for intersection, but inverts the truth value of the predicate to filter in order to exclude common members (by means of the composition of not with member):

```
val cmember = make_curried member

fun union (aset :''a list) (bset :''a list)
    = aset @ filter (not o (cmember aset)) bset :''a list
```

An alternative specification is to remove the duplicates from the result of appending the two sets.

Exercise 4.11 (page 130)

An equivalent version of stringsort using accumulate would require that the arguments to insert str_lessthan be reversed. Why is this the case?

For the same reasons as discussed with the accumulative version of member. The default value nil becomes the first argument to the insert str_lessthan and an attempt would be made to compare it with an actual value. This will only work if that value is also an empty list.

Exercise 4.12 (page 131)

A function foldiftrue which reduces only those elements of a list which satisfy a given predicate could be defined as:

```
fun foldiftrue (pred :'a -> bool)
               (ff :'a -> 'b -> 'b)
               (default :'b)
               (nil :'a list)
    = default :'b

|   foldiftrue pred ff default (front :: rest)
    = if pred front
        then (ff front (foldiftrue pred ff default rest))
        else foldiftrue pred ff default rest
```

Write this function in terms of a composition of reduce and filter.

```
fun foldiftrue (pred :'a -> bool)
               (ff :'a -> 'b -> 'b)
               (default :'b)
  = (reduce ff default) o (filter pred) :'a list -> 'b
```

The composed style is probably easier to read; the explicit recursion may appear algorithmically more efficient but this really depends upon the underlying implementation – which might automatically convert function compositions to their equivalent explicit recursive form (Darlington *et al.*, 1982).

Solutions for Chapter 5

Exercise 5.1 (page 141)
Write a function, using **local** definitions, to return the string that appears before a given sublist in a string. For example: beforestring ("and", "Standard ML") will return the string "St".

This is yet another example where it makes sense to re-use existing code, in this case the startswith function designed in Chapter 3:

```
local
    type SLIST = string list
    type SLIST_PAIR = SLIST * SLIST

    fun startswith ((nil, _) :SLIST_PAIR)
        = true :bool
    |   startswith (_, nil) = false
    |   startswith (front1 :: rest1, front2 :: rest2)
        = (front1 = front2)
          andalso
          startswith (rest1, rest2);

    exception Beforestring

    fun xbefore (_ :SLIST) (nil :SLIST)
        = raise Beforestring
    |   xbefore blist (front :: rest)
        = if startswith (blist, front :: rest)
          then nil
          else front :: xbefore blist rest :SLIST
in
    fun beforestring (bstring :string) (astring :string)
        = implode (xbefore (explode bstring)
                           (explode astring)) :string
end
```

Note that it is also acceptable to incorporate **type** and **exception** declarations within a local clause.

Exercise 5.2 (page 144)
As Exercise 5.1 but use **let** expressions instead of **local** declarations.

The answer is a simple reworking of the answer to Exercise 5.1:

```
fun beforestring (bstring :string) (astring :string)
    = let
         type SLIST = string list
         type SLIST_PAIR = SLIST * SLIST

         fun startswith ((nil, _) :SLIST_PAIR)
             = true :bool
         |   startswith (_, nil) = false
         |   startswith (front1 :: rest1, front2 :: rest2)
             = (front1 = front2)
                 andalso
                 startswith (rest1, rest2);

         exception Beforestring

         fun xbefore (_ :SLIST) (nil :SLIST)
             = raise Beforestring
         |   xbefore blist (front :: rest)
             = if startswith (blist, front :: rest)
                 then nil
                 else front :: xbefore blist rest :SLIST

         val blist = explode bstring
         val alist = explode astring
      in
         implode (xbefore blist alist) :string
      end
```

Exercise 5.3 (page 146)
Explain the scope of the various values of and evaluate the application of s i l l y to the argument "silly":

```
fun silly (silly :string) =
let
        val silly = silly ^ silly
        val silly = silly ^ silly
in
        silly ^ silly :string
end
```

The following rewrites the function with a suffix indicating which occurrence of silly is within scope. For example val silly3 = silly2 ^ silly2 should be read as silly3 takes its value from silly2, and will be in scope from that point to the end of the function definition or until a new version of silly comes into scope (which it does on the next line).

```
fun silly1 (silly2 :string)
    = let
        val silly3 = silly2 ^ silly2
        val silly4 = silly3 ^ silly3
      in
        silly4 ^ silly4
      end
```

A hand evaluation shows that silly2 has the value "silly", silly3 has the value "silly silly", silly4 has the value "silly silly silly silly", and the function application evaluates to "silly silly silly silly silly silly silly silly". The moral of this exercise is to have a clear naming policy.

Exercise 5.4 (page 149)
Explain the system response to the following:

```
fun x _ = 3
and
val y = x
```

This will give rise to an error since the kind of definition after an **and** must be that same as that which preceded it. SML expects to find a function name and instead discovers the reserved word **val**.

Solutions for Chapter 6

Exercise 6.1 (page 157)
Write a function to calculate the distance between a pair of COORDS.

The hardest part of this solution is to remember the geometry:

```
datatype COORDS = Coords of real * real * real

fun distance ((Coords (x1,y1,z1)) :COORDS)
             ((Coords (x2,y2,z2)) :COORDS)

    = let
          fun square (n :real) = (n * n) :real
      in
          sqrt (square (x2 — x1) +
                square (y2 — y1) +
                square (z2 — z1)) :real
      end
```

Exercise 6.2 (page 164)
Given the **datatype**

```
datatype ACTION = Stop | No_change | Start
                | Slow_down | Prepare_to_start
```

write a function to take the appropriate action at each possible change in state for the data type TRAFFIC_LIGHT.

```
exception BrokenLights

fun drive (Green :TRAFFIC_LIGHT) (Amber :TRAFFIC_LIGHT)
    = Slow_down :ACTION
|   drive Amber Red        = Stop
|   drive Red Red_amber    = Prepare_to_start
|   drive Red_amber Green  = Start
|   drive x y
    = if (x = y)
      then No_change
      else raise BrokenLights
```

Exercise 6.3 (page 164)
A Bochvar three-state logic has constants to indicate whether an expression is true, false or meaningless. Provide a **datatype** definition for this logic together with functions to perform the equivalent three-state versions of **andalso**, **orelse** and logical *implication*. Note that if any part of an expression is meaningless then the entire expression should be considered meaningless.

```
datatype BOCHVAR = True | False | Meaningless

fun andB (True :BOCHVAR) (True :BOCHVAR) = True :BOCHVAR
|   andB Meaningless _ = Meaningless
|   andB _ Meaningless = Meaningless
|   andB _ _ = False

fun orB (False :BOCHVAR) (False :BOCHVAR) = False :BOCHVAR
|   orB Meaningless _ = Meaningless
|   orB _ Meaningless = Meaningless
|   orB _ _ = True

fun impB (True :BOCHVAR) (False :BOCHVAR) = False :BOCHVAR
|   impB Meaningless _ = Meaningless
|   impB _ Meaningless = Meaningless
|   impB _ _ = True
```

Exercise 6.4 (page 171)
Explain why it is not sensible to attempt to mirror the tree data structure using nested lists.

It is necessary to know the depth of the tree before the correct level of list nesting can be determined; this is because SML does not allow lists to contain elements of mixed types and, for example, a double-nested list is of a different type than a triple-nested list. If the depth of the tree is known then each nested list can have the same depth – but this defeats the purpose of the tree data structure, which is designed to be of arbitrary depth.

Exercise 6.5 (page 171)
A number of useful tree manipulation functions follow naturally from the specification of a binary tree. Write functions to parallel the list manipulation functions m a p and l e n g t h (in terms of how many nodes exist in the tree).

The equivalent of **map** just traverses the tree, applying the parameter function to each non-empty node:

```
fun maptree (ff :'a -> 'b) (Tnil :'a TREE)
    = Tnil :'b TREE
  |  maptree ff (Tree (ltree, node, rtree))
    = Tree (maptree ff ltree, ff node, maptree ff rtree)
```

The equivalent of **length** could be written by traversing the tree and adding 1 for each non-empty node, although an easier method is to re-use some existing code:

```
val nodecount = length o tree_to_list
```

Exercise 6.6 (page 172)
What would have been the consequence of writing the function l i s t _ t o _ t r e e as:

```
fun list_to_tree order
    = reduce (insertleaf order) Tnil
```

This will fail because **reduce** expects its first argument to be a function of the form:

```
'a -> 'b -> 'b
```

whereas (**insertleaf order**) has the type:

```
'a TREE -> 'a -> 'a TREE
```

which has the general form:

```
'a -> 'b -> 'a
```

It is always worth looking at a function's types for program design and debugging purposes.

Exercise 6.7 (page 172)
Write a function to remove an element from a sorted tree and return a tree that is still sorted.

The base cases are: deleting terminal nodes (e.g. node 0 and node 7), which leaves the rest of the tree unaltered, and attempting to delete a node from an empty tree, which is an error.

 The general case is that of deleting non-terminal nodes. Here, only the sub-tree below the deleted node needs to be re-sorted. One method is to replace the deleted value with the highest value in the left sub-tree below the deleted node. Thus, given the following sample tree, deleting node 8 will require the value 8 to be replaced with the value 7. The node which contained the replacement value must now be deleted; this may cause yet another re-sorting of the tree.

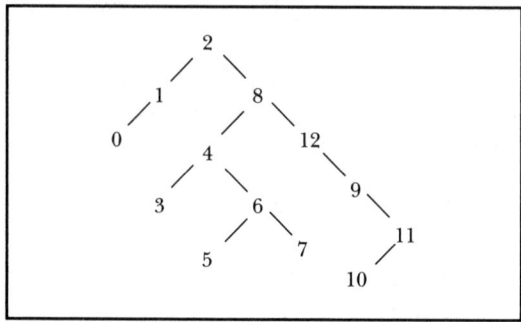

Figure A.1. A Sample Tree

For example, to delete node 12 will require the value 11 to take the place of 12; this means that node 11 must next be deleted from its original position, thus causing the value 10 to take its place; this means that node 10 must next be deleted from its original position, which can be achieved with a simple deletion and with no need to consider further sub-trees.

Following the above informal specification:

```
type ''a ORDER = ''a -> ''a -> bool

exception Delnode

fun delnode (_ :''a ORDER) (_ :''a) (Tnil :''a TREE)
     = raise Delnode
        (* item to be deleted not in tree *)
 |   delnode order item (Tree(ltree, node, rtree))
     = if item = node
       then
          if ltree = Tnil
          then rtree
               (* 'promote' right sub-tree *)
          else
               (* replace deleted node with new root and
               delete new root from left sub-tree *)
               let
                  fun findhighest (Tree (_, node, Tnil))
                      = node
                  |   findhighest (Tree (_, _, rtree))
                      = findhighest rtree

                  val newroot = findhighest ltree
               in
                  Tree (delnode order newroot ltree,
                          newroot, rtree)
               end
       else
          (* look for item in rest of tree *)
          if order item node
          then Tree (delnode order item ltree,
                  node, rtree)
          else Tree (ltree, node,
                  delnode order item rtree) :''a TREE
```

Note that when the condition item = node is true the method proceeds by chosing a new root from the left sub-tree; hence there is no need to check if the right sub-tree is empty.

There is a simpler approach which merely flattens the tree, then deletes the item from the resultant list, and then turns the list back into a tree using list_to_tree. However, this approach immediately leads to a pathologically unbalanced tree, because the list argument to list_to_tree is totally sorted and therefore all tree nodes will have only one branch.

Exercise 6.8 (page 175)
Provide function definitions for the NAT primitives if a recursive underlying data representation is used as follows: abstype NAT = Zero | Succ of NAT.

The solution to this exercise shows that the natural numbers can be modelled using only constructors (Succ and Zero); there is no need for any underlying built-in type. The **abstype** body provides a sample of the arithmetic and relational operators, as well as makeNat and showNat interfaces:

```
abstype NAT = Zero | Succ of NAT
with
    exception Naterror

    fun makeNat (x :int)
        = if x < 0
          then raise Naterror
          else let
                   fun xmakeNat 0 = Zero
                   |   xmakeNat x = Succ (xmakeNat (x - 1))
               in
                   xmakeNat x :NAT
          end

    fun plusNat (x :NAT) (Zero :NAT) = x :NAT
    |   plusNat x (Succ y) = plusNat (Succ x) y

    fun minusNat (x :NAT) (Zero :NAT) = x :NAT
    |   minusNat Zero _ = raise Naterror
    |   minusNat (Succ x) (Succ y) = minusNat x y

    fun timesNat (x :NAT) (Zero :NAT) = Zero :NAT
    |   timesNat x (Succ Zero) = x
    |   timesNat x (Succ y) = plusNat x (timesNat x y)

    fun lessthanNat (Zero :NAT) (_ :NAT) = false :bool
    |   lessthanNat _ Zero = true
    |   lessthanNat (Succ x) (Succ y) = lessthanNat x y

    fun equalNat (x :NAT) (y :NAT) = (x = y) :bool

    fun showNat (Zero :NAT) = 0 :int
    |   showNat (Succ x) = 1 + showNat x
end
```

Note that the definition of plusNat is remarkably similar to the accumulative recursive definition of plus shown in Chapter 2.

Exercise 6.9 (page 178)
What is the difference between:

```
abstype PAIR = Pair of (int * int)
with
    fun makepair x y = Pair (x,y)
    fun swap (Pair (x,y)) = Pair (y,x)
    ...
end


makepair 3 4 = makepair 5 6
```

and

```
local
    datatype PAIR = Pair of (int * int)
in
    type PAIR = PAIR
    fun makepair x y = Pair (x, y)
    fun swap (Pair (x,y)) = Pair (y,x)
    ...
end


makepair 3 4 = makepair 5 6
```

The **abstype** representation does not allow a test for equality on any instance of a **PAIR**, whereas the **datatype** representation does allow such a test.

Exercise 6.10 (page 180)
An alternative representation of the ATREE could be to drop the TREE constructors and have the abstype constructors:

```
abstype 'a OTHER_TREE
    = Anil of ('a -> ('a -> bool))
    | ATree of (('a -> 'a -> bool)
                * 'a OTHER_TREE * 'a * 'a OTHER_TREE)
with

    (* implementation *)

end
```

What would be the consequences for the abstype implementation?

The ordering function would be contained at each node in **OTHER_TREE** rather than just once at the highest root in the tree.

Exercise 6.11 (page 186)

A *queue* aggregate data structure can be defined as either being empty or as consisting of a queue (Aho *et al.*, 1983) followed by an element; operations include creating a new queue, inserting at the end of a queue and removing the first item in a queue. The following declares a set of primitives for a polymorphic **abstype** QUEUE:

```
val q_isempty   = fn :'a QUEUE -> bool
val q_remainder = fn :'a QUEUE -> 'a QUEUE
val q_top       = fn :'a QUEUE -> 'a
val q_insert    = fn :'a QUEUE -> 'a -> 'a QUEUE
val q_create    = fn :unit -> 'a QUEUE
```

Provide an **abstype** representation.

Just as with the **ARRAY** example in Section 6.5.3, there are a number of different possible underlying implementations for this **abstype**, and as far as the meaning of a program is concerned, it should not matter which implementation is chosen. The reason for choosing one implementation rather than another is often one of algorithmic complexity, based on an assumption about the pattern of accesses and updates; however, this subject is beyond the scope of this book.

For this **abstype**, it would be possible to use a simple list as the underlying type. However, the following construction shows an equally valid alternative:

```
abstype 'a QUEUE = Qnil | Queue of 'a QUEUE * 'a
with
        exception Q_top and Q_remainder

        fun q_create (() :unit) = Qnil :'a QUEUE

        fun q_insert (queue: 'a QUEUE) (item :'a)
            = Queue (queue, item) :'a QUEUE

        fun q_top Qnil
            = raise Q_top
        |   q_top (Queue (Qnil, qfirst) :'a QUEUE)
            = qfirst :'a
        |   q_top (Queue (qrest, qfirst))
            = q_top qrest

        fun q_remainder Qnil
            = raise Q_remainder
        |   q_remainder (Queue (Qnil, qfirst) :'a QUEUE)
            = Qnil :'a QUEUE
        |   q_remainder (Queue (qrest, qfirst))
            = Queue (q_remainder qrest, qfirst)

        fun q_isempty (Qnil :'a QUEUE) = true :bool
        |   q_isempty _ = false
    end
```

Solutions for Chapter 7

Exercise 7.1 (page 193)
Provide a **structure** definition to create a library of the combinators described in Chapter 4.

The following definition shows that it is a simple matter to collect individual functions and incorporate them into a structure.

```
structure COMBINATORS =
struct

    (* prefix composition *)
    fun B (ff :'b -> 'c) (gg :'a -> 'b) (x :'a)
        = ff (gg x) :'c

    (* swap arguments *)
    fun C (ff :'a -> 'b -> 'c) (x :'b) (y :'a)
        = ff y x :'c

    (* cancel second argument *)
    fun K (x :'a) (y :'b)
        = x :'a

    fun make_curried (f :'a * 'b -> 'c) (x :'a) (y :'b)
        = f(x,y) :'c
    fun make_uncurried (f :'a -> 'b -> 'c) ((x, y) :'a * 'b)
        = f x y :'c

    (* Identity *)
    fun I (x :'a) = x :'a

    (* a more general version of B *)
    fun S (ff :'a -> 'b -> 'c) (gg :'a -> 'b) (x :'a)
        = ff x (gg x) :'c

    (* duplicate arguments *)
    fun W (f :'a -> 'a -> 'b) (x :'a)
        = f x x :'b

end
```

Note that the above includes some combinators not mentioned in Chapter 4.

Exercise 7.2 (page 198)
Provide a signature to match the **structure** defined in Exercise 7.1.

It is also a simple matter to collect individual type expressions and collect them into a **signature**:

```
signature COMBINATOR_sig =
sig
    val B : ('a -> 'b) -> ('c -> 'a) -> 'c -> 'b
    val C : ('a -> 'b -> 'c) -> 'b -> 'a -> 'c
    val I : 'a -> 'a
    val K : 'a -> 'b -> 'a
    val S : ('a -> 'b -> 'c) -> ('a -> 'b) -> 'a -> 'c
    val W : ('a -> 'a -> 'b) -> 'a -> 'b
    val make_curried : ('a * 'b -> 'c) -> 'a -> 'b -> 'c
    val make_uncurried : ('a -> 'b -> 'c) -> 'a * 'b -> 'c
end
```

Exercise 7.3 (page 200)
Is there any effective difference between hiding a **datatype**'s constructors within a **structure** and using an **abstype**?

There are two major differences. The first is that there is no equality defined on instances of **abstype**s but there is on instances of **datatype**s, even if they are hidden within a **structure**. The second is that the important separation of **signature** and **structure** allows the implementation decision to be deferred.

Exercise 7.4 (page 201)
Given the **structure**:

```
structure QUESTION_struct =
struct
    abstype OBJECT = Obj of int
    with
        fun make_OBJ (x :int) = Obj x
    end
    val x = 3
    val y = 42.01
end
```

which of the following **signature**s will successfully constrain it?

```
signature SIG1_sig =
sig
end

signature SIG2_sig =
sig
    type OBJECT
    val x :OBJECT
end

signature SIG3_sig =
sig
    datatype OBJECT
    val x :OBJECT
end
```

```
signature SIG4_sig =
sig
    type OBJECT
    val make_OBJ :int -> OBJECT
    val x :int
    val y :real
end
```

The first **signature** is successful because the minimal SIG1_sig matches anything. The second **signature** SIG2_sig will fail because x is not of type OBJECT in QUES-TION_struct. The third **signature** SIG3_sig is not legal; the **datatype** declaration requires at least one constructor. Furthermore, it declares a **datatype** instead of an **abstype**. Finally, SIG4_sig will successfully match the actual **abstype** and its function with the declared type OBJECT and the function make_OBJ.

Exercise 7.5 (page 212)
Explain what is wrong with the following program:

```
signature N_sig =
sig
        type NUMBER
        val inc :NUMBER -> NUMBER
        val dec :NUMBER -> NUMBER
end

signature NTYPE_sig =
sig
        type NUMBER
        val i :NUMBER
end

functor NUMBERS_func (Ntype :NTYPE_sig) :N_sig =
struct
        typeNUMBER = Ntype.NUMBER
        val i = Ntype.i
        fun inc n = (n + i)
        fun dec n = (n - i)
end
```

Quite simply, SML cannot resolve the overloaded addition and subtraction operators when NUMBERS_func is defined. It does not matter that the parameter will contain enough information when the **functor** is applied.

Exercise 7.6 (page 216)
Explain what would happen given the following command sequence:

```
signature N_sig = sig end;
functor N_func() = struct val x = 1 end;
```

```
structure A_struct :N_sig = N_func();
structure B_struct = N_func();
structure C_struct = N_func() :N_sig;
```

A_struct would be initialized, though nothing would be visible to the outside world, because of the minimal N_sig. B_struct would be initialized and the value x would be visible, because N_func has not got a constraining **signature**. Attempting to initialize C_struct would fail because it is not possible to constrain **functor**s when applying them.

Exercise 7.7 (page 225)
Give the definition of the lex function within BOURNE_LEX_struct.

The major difference is in the treatment of the * meta-character, which must be interpreted as one or more rather than zero or more matches:

```
(* see Chapter 7 for type synonyms,
   datatypes and subsidiary functions
   used in this code *)

fun lex (nil :SLIST) = nil :REGLIST
|   lex ("\\" :: ch :: "*" :: rest)
    = (ONCE, same, [ch])
      :: (ZERO_MORE, same, [ch])
      :: lex rest
|   lex ("\\" :: ch :: rest)
    = (ONCE, same, [ch]) :: lex rest
|   lex ("\\" :: rest)
    = lex rest
|   lex ("?" :: "*" :: rest)
    = (ZERO_MORE, notsame, nil) :: lex rest
|   lex ("[" :: "!" :: rest)
    = let
        val (range_part, exp_rest)
            = lexrange (notsame, nil) rest
      in
        range_part :: (lex exp_rest)
      end
|   lex ("[" :: rest)
    = let
        val (range_part, exp_rest)
            = lexrange (same, nil) rest
      in
        range_part :: (lex exp_rest)
      end
|   lex ("?" :: rest)
    = (ONCE, notsame, nil) :: lex rest
|   lex (ch :: "*" :: rest)
    = (ONCE, same, [ch])
      :: (ZERO_MORE, same, [ch])
      :: lex rest
|   lex (ch :: rest)
    = (ONCE, same, [ch]) :: lex rest
```

Bibliography

Annotated bibliography

SML background

Gordon M., Milner A. and Wadsworth C. *Edinburgh LCF*

The first book to describe ML, which was the precursor to SML. It introduces the Edinburgh Logic for Computable Functions (LCF) for studying the properties of recursively defined functions. It also contains a small bibliography highlighting the LCF, logical and proof methodology backgrounds, together with the older functional languages and the polymorphic type discipline which influenced the design of ML.

SML definition

Milner R., Tofte M. and Harper R. *The Definition of Standard ML*

Milner R. and Tofte M. *Commentary on Standard ML*

These references provide a formal description of both the grammar and meaning of SML. They should be of interest to anyone who needs to understand the full semantics of SML and also to people studying program language design and semantics in general. The first reference also contains a brief appendix describing the development of SML.

Appel A. and MacQueen D. *Standard ML of New Jersey Online Reference Manual*

Online documentation – available with the New Jersey implementation; this contains details of the additional New Jersey features and built-in library functions.

Berry D. *The Edinburgh SML Library*

This describes the portable SML library structures which can be added to the initial environment provided by each implementation.

SML programming

Harper R. *Introduction to SML*

Tofte M. *Four Lectures on SML*

The first of these brief pamphlets gives a summary of SML, suitable for an experienced functional programmer. The latter concentrates on using the Modules system to build an interpreter for a subset of SML.

Paulson L. *ML for the Working Programmer*

An advanced textbook with an emphasis on efficiency. Though mainly a practical book for the experienced programmer, there is also some theoretical background. Of particular interest are the examples of a lambda-calculus interpreter and a tactical theorem prover. This book also contains syntax charts for SML.

Reade C. *Elements of Functional Programming*

A relatively advanced textbook; it uses a language that is recognizable as SML but has the purpose of covering functional programming in general and so introduces other notations as necessary. Chapters 4 and 6 give some extended examples of functional software. The book also introduces more theoretical issues, including; denotational semantics, type systems, lambda calculus and combinators and a discussion of implementation considerations.

Sokolowski S. *Applicative High Order Programming*

Concentrates on the use of higher order functions and the nature of polymorphism in SML.

Wikstrom A. *Functional Programming using Standard ML*

An introductory book suitable for completely novice programmers; it provides a gentle explanation of the SML Core language.

History and future of functional programming

Backus J. *Can programming be liberated from the von Neumann style.*

A seminal paper which discusses the problems of basing programming languages on the Turing computational model; it then outlines a functional style of programming language (now known as FP).

Landin P. *The next 700 programming languages*

Apart from having a great title, this paper is important for highlighting the relation between a language's written representation and its meaning. The proposed language ISWIM (*If you See What I Mean*) deals with expressions rather than procedural statements. As such it probably shares with LISP the genesis of modern functional programming languages.

Hudak P. *Conception, Evolution and Application of Functional Programming Languages*

This excellent reference has a self-explanatory title!

Functional programming in general

Bird R. and Wadler P. *Introduction to Functional Programming*

This book is loosely based on a lazy functional language known as Miranda; its emphasis is on mathematical examples and the algebraic manipulation of functions. It is suitable for a range of abilities from the mathematically oriented beginner to the more advanced programmer.

Burge W. *Recursive programming techniques*

Probably the first book to discuss the functional style of programming, and still relevant. It also has several very useful parsing and sorting algorithms which demonstrate the functional programming style.

Darlington J., Henderson P. and Turner D. *Functional programming and its applications*

Contains a number of interesting articles from theoretical background to practical applications

Eisenbach S. (ed.) *Functional Programming, Languages, tools and architectures*

A collection of introductory articles covering other functional programming languages (HOPE and FP), practice, theory and implementation. Chapter 4 is of particular interest in that it shows that the functional style of programming can be used to good effect with a procedural language.

Field A. and Harrison P. *Functional Programming*

An intermediate to advanced level book which uses Hope as the base functional language. It has a modern approach and covers a lot of ground, from an introduction to functional programming through to implementation techniques.

Glaser H., Hankin C. and Till D. *Principles of Functional Programming*

One of the first general textbooks in this area; it also gives a gentle introduction to the lambda-calculus and some related topics. The first chapter gives a language-independent example of functional program development.

Henson M. *Elements of Functional Languages*

A general-purpose text with a treatment of program transformation.

MacLennan B. *Functional Programming Theory and Practice*

This book introduces the practice and theory of functional language by using mathematical notation in preference to a particular Functional programming language. Discusses performance and implementation issues.

Functional programming and formal methods

Burstall R. *Inductively Defined Functions in Programming Languages*

Rydeheard D. and Burstall R. *Computational Category Theory*

Sannella D. *Formal Specification of ML Programs*

Thompson S. *Type Theory and Functional Programming*

Turner D. *Functional Programs as Executable Specifications*

The above give a small sample of the relationship between functional programming and formal methods in computing.

Implementation of functional languages

Diller A. *Compiling Functional Languages*

An advanced book, providing an overview of a wide range of techniques used in Functional language compilers. Uses Lispkit LISP as the base language.

Henderson P. *Functional Programming, Application and Implementation*

One of the first books dealing with functional programming. It has some good examples of programming using higher order functions based on a purely functional subset of LISP (called Lispkit). The book discusses how Lispkit might be isolated from LISP. Since LISP is still widely used in the world of artificial intelligence the use of a good functional style of programming in LISP is to be encouraged.

Peyton Jones S. L. *The Implementation of Functional Programming Languages*

Apart from dealing with the implemention of functional programming languages, this book also gives an overview of the lambda-calculus and some other theoretical issues required for an understanding of implementations.

Lambda calculus

Barendregt H. *The Lambda Calculus: Its Syntax and Semantics*

Michaelson G. *Functional Programming through Lambda Calculus*

Revesz G. *Lambda-Calculus, Combinators and Functional Programming*

The lambda-calculus is a small but important mathematical language which forms the basis of understanding many of the theoretical issues of functional programming languages and of programming language theory in general.

The first of these books is the standard reference book for the lambda-calculus; it is more of a mathematical interest rather than being essential for a computer programmer. The second text is a gentle guide, whilst the third takes a more rigorous approach which leads to techniques for functional programming implementation.

References

Aho, A., Hopcroft, J. and Ullman, J. (1974), *The Design and Analysis of Computer Algorithms*, Addison-Wesley.

Aho, A., Hopcroft, J. and Ullman, J. (1983), *Data Structures and Algorithms*, Addison-Wesley.

Aho, A., Sethi, R. and Ullman, J. (1984), *Compilers*, Addison-Wesley.

Appel, A. and MacQueen, D., *Standard ML of New Jersey Online Reference Manual*.

Backus, J. (1978), 'Can programming be liberated from the von Neumann style?', *Communications of the ACM*, vol. 21, no. 8, pp. 613–41.

Barendregt, H. (1984), *The Lambda Calculus: Its syntax and semantics*, North-Holland.

Berry, D. (1991), *The Edinburgh SML Library*, ECS–LFCS–91–148, Laboratory for Foundations of Computer Science, Edinburgh University.

Bird, R. and Wadler, P. (1988), *Introduction to Functional Programming*, Prentice Hall.

Brooks, F. P. (1975), *The Mythical Man-month*, Addison-Wesley.

Burge, W. (1975), *Recursive Programming Techniques*, Addison-Wesley.

Burstall, R. (1987), *Inductively Defined Functions in Functional Programming Languages*, Report ECS–LFCS–87–25, Laboratory for Foundations of Computer Science, Edinburgh University.

Darlington, J., Henderson, P. and Turner, D. (1982), *Functional Programming and its Applications*, Cambridge University Press.

Diller, A. (1988), *Compiling Functional Languages*, Wiley.

Eisenbach, S. (ed.) (1987), *Functional Programming Languages: Tools and architectures*, Ellis Horwood.

Fasel, J., Maduk, P., Peyton-Jones, S. and Wadler, P. (1992), *Haskell Special Issue*, ACM SIGPLAN Notices, vol. 27, no. 5.

Field, A. and Harrison, P. (1988), *Functional Programming*, Addison-Wesley.

Glaser, H., Hankin, C. and Till, D. (1984), *Principles of Functional Programming*, Prentice Hall.

Gordon, M. (1979), *The Denotational Description of Programming Languages*, Springer.

Gordon, M., Milner, A. and Wadsworth, C. (1979), *Edinburgh LCF*, Lecture Notes in Computer Science 78, Springer.

Harper, R. (1986), *Introduction to SML*, Report ECS–LFCS–86–14, Laboratory for Foundations of Computer Science, Edinburgh University: (revised edn 1989 by Rothwell, N. and Mitchell, K.).

Harper, R., MacQueen, D. and Milner, R. (1986), *Standard ML*, Report ECS–LFCS–86–2, Laboratory for Foundations of Computer Science, Edinburgh University.

Henderson, P. (1980), *Functional Programming: Application and Implementation*, Prentice Hall.

Henson, M. (1987), *Elements of Functional Languages*, Blackwell Scientific Publications.

Holyer, I. (1991), *Functional Programming with Miranda*, Pitman.

Hudak, P. (1989), 'Conception, evolution and application of functional programming languages', *ACM Computing Surveys*, vol. 21, no. 3, pp. 359–411.

Kernighan B. and Pike R., (1984), *The UNIX Programming Environment*, Prentice-Hall.

Landin, P. (1966), 'The next 700 programming languages', *Communications of the ACM*, vol. 9, no. 3, pp. 157–64.

MacLennan, B. (1990), *Functional Programming Theory and Practice*, Addison-Wesley.

MacQueen, D. (1984), 'Modules for Standard ML', in *Proceedings of the 1984 Symposium on LISP and Functional Programming*, ACM.

Matthews, D. (1991), *A Distributed Concurrent Implementation of Standard ML*, Report ECS–LFCS–91–174, Laboratory for Foundations of Computer Science, Edinburgh University.

Michaelson, G. (1989), *Functional Programming through Lambda Calculus*, Addison-Wesley.

Milner, R. (1987), *Changes to the Standard ML Core Language*, Report ECS–LFCS–87–33, Laboratory for Foundations of Computer Science, Edinburgh University.

Milner, R. and Tofte, M. (1991), *Commentary on Standard ML*, MIT Press.

Milner, R., Tofte, M. and Harper, R. (1990), *The Definition of Standard ML*, MIT Press.

Paulson, L. (1991), *ML for the Working Programmer*, Cambridge University Press.

Peyton Jones, S. L. (1987), *The Implementation of Functional Programming Languages*, Prentice Hall.

Rayward-Smith, V. (1986), *A First Course in Computability*, Blackwell Scientific Publications.

Reade, C. (1989), *Elements of Functional Programming*, Addison-Wesley.

Revesz, G. (1988), *Lambda-Calculus, Combinators and Functional Programming*, Cambridge University Press.

Rydeheard, D. and Burstall, R. (1988), *Computational Category Theory*, Prentice Hall.

Salmon, R. and Slater, M. (1987), *Computer Graphics: Systems and Concepts*, Addison-Wesley.

Sannella, D. (1986), *Formal Specification of ML Programs*, Report ECS–LFCS–86–15, Laboratory for Foundations of Computer Science, Edinburgh University.

Sokolowski, S. (1991), *Applicative High Order Programming*, Chapman and Hall.

Standish, T. (1980), *Data Structure Techniques*, Addison-Wesley.

Thompson, S. (1991), *Type Theory and Functional Programming*, Addison-Wesley.

Tofte, M. (1989), *Four Lectures on SML*, Report ECS–LFCS–89–73, Laboratory for Foundations of Computer Science, Edinburgh University.

Turner, D. (1985), 'Functional programs as executable specifications' in Hoare, C. and Shepherdson, J. (eds) *Mathematical Logic and Programming Languages*, Prentice Hall.

Wikstrom, A. (1987), *Functional Programming using Standard ML*, Prentice Hall.

Index